Video Interaction Analysis

Ulrike Tikvah Kissmann (ed.)

Video Interaction Analysis
Methods and Methodology

Frankfurt am Main · Berlin · Bern · Bruxelles · New York · Oxford · Wien

Bibliographic Information published by the Deutsche Nationalbibliothek
The Deutsche Nationalbibliothek lists this publication in the Deutsche Nationalbibliografie; detailed bibliographic data is available in the internet at <http://www.d-nb.de>.

Cover illustration:
The use of X-ray images in
doctor-patient consultations.
© Ulrike Tikvah Kissmann

ISBN 978-3-631-57473-7

© Peter Lang GmbH
Internationaler Verlag der Wissenschaften
Frankfurt am Main 2009
All rights reserved.

All parts of this publication are protected by copyright. Any utilisation outside the strict limits of the copyright law, without the permission of the publisher, is forbidden and liable to prosecution. This applies in particular to reproductions, translations, microfilming, and storage and processing in electronic retrieval systems.

Printed in Germany 1 2 3 4 5   7

www.peterlang.de

Contents

Introduction

Ulrike Tikvah Kissmann
Video interaction analysis: Methodological perspectives on
an emerging field 9

Linguistic Anthropology and Conversation Analysis

Charles Goodwin
Video and the analysis of embodied human interaction 21

Marjorie Harness Goodwin
Constructing inequality as situated practice 41

Antonia L. Krummheuer
Conversation analysis, video recordings, and human-computer
interchanges 59

Sociological Hermeneutics

Ulrike Tikvah Kissmann
How medical forms are used: The study of doctor-patient
consultations from a sociological hermeneutic approach 87

Roger Haeussling
Video analysis with a four-level interaction concept:
A network-based concept of human-robot interaction 107

Ethnography and Phenomenology

Larissa Schindler
The production of «vis-ability»: An ethnographic video analysis
of a martial arts class   135

Lars Frers
Video research in the open – Encounters involving
the researcher-camera   155

Focussed Ethnography

Hubert Knoblauch
Social constructivism and the three levels of video analysis   181

Cornelius Schubert
Videographic elicitation interviews: Exploring technologies,
practices and narratives in organisations   199

About the contributors   223

Introduction

Ulrike Tikvah Kissmann

Video interaction analysis: Methodological perspectives on an emerging field

Looking through the kaleidoscope

This book presents a collection of approaches to the emerging field of video analysis in the social sciences. Firstly, by using the image of a kaleidoscope it refers to the growing importance of visuality in qualitative research such as, for example, Goodwin and Goodwin (1997), Knoblauch et al. (2006), Raab (2007), Mondada (2007a), Friebertshäuser et al. (2007). The great amount of publications reflects the raising significance of gazes and gestures for the reconstruction of social order (cf. Bourdieu 1998; for an earlier study see Simmel 1923). It generally responds to the growing importance of interaction for the study of society. This is demonstrated in Emanuel Schegloff's work (1992) on intersubjectivity or in Charles Goodwin's work (1981), one of the first studies on videotaped interactions. Secondly, the use of the metaphor of the kaleidoscope aims at showing that there is not a single method or methodology in the field of video analysis. The social sciences rather dispose of a collection of «splinters» like in a kaleidoscope. Although the importance of visual qualitative methods has grown, video analysis cannot draw upon an empirical as well as a sociological account of action and the broad acceptance of «microanalysis» as a tool for the study of society (cf. Schegloff 1996). Much of the sociological discussion still has to be carried out. This book has the role of a kaleidoscope and, therefore, will structure the diverse approaches in order to identify their traditions. By this means, it assembles studies from linguistic anthropology as well as conversation analysis, sociological hermeneutics, ethnography, phenomenology and finally focused ethnography. As it will be shown, the presented traditions can overlap and sometimes draw on the same authors. For example Alfred Schütz's work (1962) on social reality was decisive for Garfinkel's study on trust (1963) as well as for interpretative social science in general. The reference to the former author can be found in many articles in this volume.

Single gazes and gestures were analyzed by means of video as early as in the 1970s (cf. Luckmann/Gross 1977). However, in-depth video analysis has only recently become the subject of sociological reflections. The practices of video recording and analysis are nowadays embedded in a larger discussion on the practices of seeing and producing visual data, a procedure that is discussed, for example, in Knoblauch/Schnettler (2007). The researcher draws upon such practices when he or she positions the camera in a certain angle or chooses a certain object for shooting. As this book arose from the international workshop

«Video Interaction Analysis – and how to do it» in May 2007 at Humboldt-University in Berlin it aims at tackling practical issues in the process of inquiry and analysis. In this introduction I will firstly elaborate on the practices of shooting. By that means, I will answer my first question of the workshop in 2007 on how we choose the interactions that we film. Secondly, the issue of segmentation of video data will be portrayed. It corresponds to my second question during the workshop. There I asked how we select the excerpt of the film that has to be analyzed. Thirdly, the problem of analytical unit will be dealt with. Drawing on conversation analysis, I will raise the issue whether units of interaction are discrete and pre-determined or subject to contingency. This section aims at portraying the underlaying concept of action. Finally, the structure of this volume will be described and the articles summarized.

Practices of video recording

In the course of the conference the presenters responded to my first question by suggesting that a thorough participant observation has to precede the beginning of shooting. Marjorie Harness Goodwin, for example, watched the playground three years before she began the shooting. This issue is referred to as, for example, the «praxeology of seeing» (cf. Mondada 2006a) or the «professional vision» (cf. Goodwin 1994). By getting acquainted with the field the researcher develops his or her professional vision and the necessary knowledge as, for instance, where the camera is best set up before the action. In this sense, shooting can be considered an embodied practice that assembles visible social fields and by that means constitutes the research field. Additionally, in Cornelius Schubert's study on the practices of anesthesiologists the author also conducted interviews in order to gain information about the field. Interviews therefore can add to the professional vision of the research field.

Almost all authors in this volume collected natural data for video analysis (the exception is Roger Haeussling). «Natural» means that the recordings were made in situations affected as little as possible by the researcher. Lars Frers deals with this issue in his article. He describes the interactions between participants and the researcher-camera and asks how the fact of being filmed affects the situation that is being filmed. The way the video data is produced has to be part of a methodological reflection because video recording is an embodied practice and as such constitutive of the production of visibility. To put it differently, camera movements and other technical choices are embedded in talk-in-interaction: they are an integral part of stream of speech, bodily conduct, gestures, gazes and the material environment which mutually elaborate each other. In this volume, Charles Goodwin develops an approach to the analysis of action that takes into account the simultaneous use of these multiple resources by participants. As he demonstrates, actions are assembled and understood through semiotic fields. The later notion describes a range of structurally different kinds of sign phenomena instantiated in diverse media as, for instance, the camera movement and other technical choices in the above case.

Segmentation of video data

My second question during the workshop aimed at tackling the question on how we select the excerpt of the film that has to be analyzed. How do we know when the relevant interaction starts and ends? Lorenza Mondada distinguishes in her work on segmentation (2008) the exogenous and the endogenous mode of structuring video data. The exogenous way of segmentation draws on the researcher's formal criterions whereas the endogenous type is a practical problem of the participants themselves. Finally, Mondada enumerates a third type which strikes a balance between the two former modes. In the third type, the analyst takes the participants' view seriously and defines segmentation less as a formal problem in its own right. Rather the researcher reconstructs *how* the participants achieve phases and transitions during action. The last view corresponds to a concept of segmentation that is not a *result* of a methodology. Rather, it is a methodical *practice* in the sense Garfinkel (1967) uses the term. The identification of segments in video data therefore aims at the reconstruction of how the participants accomplish structures through talk, gazes, gestures, body movements and artefacts in the interaction. An answer to the question of segmentation is also presented in this volume in Larissa Schindler's article on apprenticeship in a martial art class. There, the instructor teaches the beginnings and endings of fighting movements. The participant himself refers to the relevant interactions. However, as Schindler points out, the sociological audience that watches the video, does not see easily what is being displayed. In order to understand the instructor's demonstrations, the sociological audience needs ethnographic knowledge in addition, such as, background knowledge from participant observation. Therefore, the acquisition of professional vision is necessary for the practices of shooting as well as for the video analysis.

In Ulrike Kissmann's article the misunderstandings that occurred in doctor-patient consultations are selected and subjected to a step-by-step interpretation. The author chose segments of 5 seconds for the latter. However, it would have been possible to select excerpts of, for example, 4 or 6 seconds. This way of structuring video data is fundamental to the methodology of sociological hermeneutics. It aims at establishing the «parenthesis of context» (cf. Raab/Tänzler 2006) where the researcher frees him- or herself from common sense as well as standardized explanations. Thereby, the step-by-step technique creates a distance to the researcher's own subjective meanings and enables him or her to reconstruct the context in which the video data gain meaning. This type of segmentation is neither exogenous nor endogenous. Rather, it strikes the balance between the two and aims at reconstructing how the participants achieve meaning in and through interaction.

Sociological hermeneutics draws on a different understanding of data interpretation than, for instance, conversation analysis. As Thomas Luckmann (1981) argues, the subjective meaning of action can be reconstructed by reference to its objective meaning, and the objective meaning can be inferred by its subjective meaning. Hermeneutic video analysis therefore starts with the subjective meaning that the interpreters attribute to the video taped interaction of the participants. However, data interpretation aims at reconstructing the participants' subjective meanings. Because the actors' and observers' subjective systems of relevance may diverge significantly, sociological hermeneutics establishes the above mentioned parenthesis of context. The observers elaborate on the possible context in which the interaction of the actors gains meaning and, in doing so, on the way through which meaning is achieved from the intersubjective perspective (cf. Soeffner 1989, 2004). Thus, the subjective meaning of the participants can be reconstructed by reference to its objectified meaning obtained during collective analysis. Such objectified meanings consist, for instance, of social, cultural or institutional categories that are applicable to that interaction and that are intelligible from the intersubjective standpoint.

Action revisited: contingency versus predetermination

Analytical units have been discussed at length in linguistics. Whereas the sentence is considered the basic unit in written language, the question remains open with regard to spoken language (cf. Gülich 1999). Since talk is achieved in interaction its units are more difficult to define. In conversation analysis the basic analytical unit of talk, the «turn-constructional unit», was introduced by Harvey Sacks, Emanuel Schegloff and Gail Jefferson (1974). It can constitute turns in themselves or be the building block of turns. A key feature of turn taking is the «precision timing» of turn beginnings and endings, respectively (cf. Jefferson 1973; Mondada 2007b). The precise timing of turn transition refers to the circumstance that speakers collaboratively achieve a state in which the next speaker begins in overlap with the current speaker, starts at the end of turn or uses a break of silence between turns. Current publications at the intersection of linguistics and conversation analysis elaborate on «precision timing» and its inherent «projectability» (cf. Ford 2004; Mondada 2006b). Because participants collaboratively achieve turn transitions, these publications start from the fact that language is composed of projectable units as shared resources for participants. Cecilia E. Ford argues in her article (2004) that the attempt to define units can also present an obstacle to understanding units in talk. An account of language which affords only discrete units, whose boundaries are rigid and fixed, constitutes a problem rather than a solution to the contingent real-time interaction. To this end, Ford demonstrates that the unitary nature of the unit is compromised and the arrival at possible completion of turn is open to participants' negotiations.

The underlying concept of action is characterized by contingency and situatedness. Cecilia Ford compares her own challenge of taking into account contingency to Lucy Suchman's work (1987) on situated actions. The latter criticizes cognitive scientists for conceiving of action as pre-determined plans. Using Suchman's example, Ford draws parallels between the quest to define discrete units in interaction and the attempt of cognitive scientists to implement prepackaged plans in human-machine interaction. Both reveal the shortcomings of such a pre-determined notion of action. The other side of this issue is discussed in Hubert Knoblauch's article in this volume. Drawing on social constructivism, Knoblauch argues that the meaning of action cannot be reduced to situative contexts. According to him the most distinctive feature in contrast to the ethnomethodological approach is that social constructivism maintains that meanings can be habitualized, routinized and institutionalized socially in various forms. They become fixed patterns that also shape action. Therefore, as Knoblauch puts it, it is not sufficient to elaborate on the situated and contingent character of interactions only.

In this volume, Antonia L. Krummheuer and Roger Haeussling study human-computer and human-robot interchanges, respectively. From an ethnomethodological and conversation analytical view Antonia Krummheuer asks if the participants distinguish between whether their co-partner is a human or a technical artifact. Her analysis shows the situated and hybrid character of the interchange. In contrast to this, Roger Haeussling adapts a network-based concept of interaction that goes beyond human-robot cooperation as situated activity and identifies the dependencies to superior contexts such as the influence of social networks.

Structure of this volume

As a kaleidoscope, this book will structure the diverse approaches in order to identify their traditions. Therefore, the first section assembles the articles that refer to conversation analysis as well as linguistic anthropology. Charles Goodwin's, Marjorie Harness Goodwin's and Antonia L. Krummheuer's articles are located in that first part. The second chapter collects the articles that draw on sociological hermeneutics, such as, Ulrike Kissmann's and Roger Haeussling's contributions. The third section assembles an ethnographic and a phenomenological approach: Larissa Schindler's and Lars Frers' papers. The fourth chapter represents focused ethnography with Hubert Knoblauch's and Cornelius Schubert's articles.

CHARLES GOODWIN analyses the interaction of two girls, Carla and Diana, who are playing hopscotch. He shows that Carla takes into account the patterns of orientation visibly displayed by Diana's gaze and posture by changing her own actions in response to them. With his data Charles Goodwin focuses on socially organized, interactively sustained configurations of multiple participants who use the public visibility of the actions being performed by each others' bodies, the unfolding sequential organization of their talk, and the semiotic structure in the settings they inhabit to organize courses of action in concert with each other.

As a linguistic anthropologist MARJORIE HARNESS GOODWIN is interested in documenting how talk is used to build social organization within face-to-face interaction. Traditional studies of girls' groups have focused on orientations towards an ethic of care, empathy, collaboration, and wanting to form connections with others. In contrast to this, Marjorie Harness Goodwin shows that a pervasive feature of girls' social organization on the playground is open attack on one another's face and construction of inequality. She discusses how girls construct Angela, an African American working-class girl, as socially different from other girls and how they control the local social order. The author demonstrates that the girls replicate in situ the class differences and ethnic inequalities that organize their larger society.

ANTONIA L. KRUMMHEUER shows how conversation analysis can be adopted for the interpretation of video recordings of human-computer interchanges. She analyses video data of the interaction between an embodied conversational agent and the visitors of a public event where the virtual agent was presented. This personified software program is supposed to be able to «interact» in a human-like fashion and visitors of the event were able to «talk» with it. Krummheuer's article aims at understanding the specific character of human-agent interchange, and it questions whether the sociological term «interaction» can be used to describe it.

Drawing on sociological hermeneutics ULRIKE KISSMANN analyses misunderstandings in doctor-patient consultations. She describes the interpretations of medical forms that doctors use in the preoperative admission of patients to a hospital. Two ways of record keeping are portrayed in her article: the «administrative duty» and the «signpost» mode. The latter case is compared to the doctor's biographical interview. It reveals that he associates the medical profession with the positive experiences he had with doctors during his escape from the GDR in summer of 1989. It is argued that the interpretative achievement that was found during the video analysis draws on these biographical experiences.

ROGER HAEUSSLING illustrates his relationalistic-hermeneutical position and perspective which he developed and which relies on Harrison C. White's network theory. He presents how his method can be adopted for human-robot cooperations. In Haeussling's approach actors are explained through relational and positional constellations. Thereby, questions of the ability to act or of who acts are defused and human and machine do not have to be treated in a radically symmetrical way as in the actor-network-theory. Moreover, the author develops a multi-level categorization system that serves as an evaluation scheme for all human-robot interactions.

LARISSA SCHINDLER studies the transfer of knowledge in a martial arts class from an ethnographic approach. She focuses on «vis-ability», the ability to see what is being displayed, be it the members of the martial arts class or the sociological data session of a video recording of the martial arts class. Firstly, she argues that during the training the production of the vis-ability of fighting movements consists of two instantaneously occurring interactions. One of them is the interaction of the instructor and the martial arts audience and the other is the interaction of the instructor and his partner. Secondly, she argues that it does not suffice to show the video data during the data session in order to transfer the ethnographic knowledge to the sociological audience. Rather, it is crucial to bridge the sociological view of the audience with the background knowledge that results from participant observation.

LARS FRERS studies encounters of everyday life on railway and ferry terminals. Drawing both on Merleau-Ponty's phenomenology of the body and on work published in the field of science and technology studies the author describes himself as a hybrid of man and machine: a camera-researcher. He argues that the presence of the camera-researcher establishes a hierarchy of gaze in the public space that is being studied. The hierarchy of gaze puts the camera-researcher in an advantaged position compared to people passing through his or her area of observation. Frers investigates on how the encounters – verbal and nonvocal – change with, for instance, according to the camera-researcher's clothes and postures. The author concludes that the hierarchy of gaze is highly influential. However it does not determine what is happening.

HUBERT KNOBLAUCH presents his concept of three levels of video analysis and the ensuing methodology of focused ethnography. He argues that interaction as the very subject matter of video analysis is of utter importance to any social constructivist analysis. The fact that actors are not explicitly aware of the meaning of minute details of action although they understand their meanings hints at the importance of «practice» as habitual forms of actions built into the ongoing process of interaction. These objectified meanings are not easily accessed by visual data only. As Knoblauch puts it, it is here where ethnography comes in, the method by which the typical meanings of specific social fields are recovered. Ethnography accounts for the socially constructed «objectivity» of the social world as pre-existing.

CORNELIUS SCHUBERT portrays a particular elicitation technique, namely the videographic elicitation interview. He demonstrates that it is a promising way to generate accounts of «invisible» phenomena, such as, work routines and practices that are not visible on video data. In Schubert's study, the interview technique aims at generating anecdotes in which knowledge of relevant safety issues of machine work are presented. For that purpose, short video sequences are shown to the interviewees as a «focus» for discussion. Schubert's emphasis lies on the explorative character of videographic elicitation interviews and how they help to create narratives as accounts of technologies and as accounts of organizational order. The presented videographic elicitation interviews were conducted as a part of a focused ethnographic study of the work of anesthesiologists in surgical operation rooms.

Acknowledgements

I would like to thank Siegrid Steinhauer for formatting the text of this volume and Adrian de Silva for proofreading it. I also gratefully acknowledge the support of Lorenza Mondada when I was a visiting scholar at her department at the University of Lyon. Finally, I wish to thank the German Research Foundation (Deutsche Forschungsgemeinschaft) for funding my actual research project «The effect of computerized knowledge in the operating room from a gender perspective» and for supporting the international workshop «Video Interaction Analysis – and how to do it» at Humboldt-University in Berlin in May 2007.

References

Bourdieu, Pierre, 1998: *La domination masculine*. Paris: Seuil.
Ford, Cecilia E., 2004: Contingency and units in interactions. In: *Discourse Studies*, 6, 1, 27-52.
Friebertshäuser, Barbara/Heide von Felden/Burkhard Schäffer (eds.), 2007: *Bild und Text – Methoden und Methodologien visueller Sozialforschung in der Erziehungswissenschaft*. Opladen & Farmington Hills: Barbara Budrich.
Garfinkel, Harold, 1963: A concept of, and experiments with, «trust» as a condition of stable concerted actions. In: O.J. Harvey (ed.), *Motivation and social interaction*. New York: Ronald Press, 187-238.
Garfinkel, Harold, 1967: *Studies in ethnomethodology*. Oxford et al.: Polity Press.
Goodwin, Charles, 1981: *Conversational organization. Interaction between speakers and hearers*. New York et al. Academic Press.
Goodwin, Charles, 1994: Professional vision. In: *American Anthropologist*, 93, 3, 606-633.
Goodwin, Charles/Marjorie Harness Goodwin, 1997: Seeing as situated activity. Formulating planes. In: Yrjö Engeström/David Middleton (eds.), *Cognition and communication at work*. Cambridge: Cambridge University Press, 61-95.
Gülich, Elisabeth, 1999: Les activités de structuration dans l'interaction verbale. In: Jeanne-Marie Barbéris (ed.), *Le français parlé. Variétés et discours*. Montpellier: Praxiling, 21-47.
Jefferson, Gail, 1973: A case of precision timing in ordinary conversation: overlapped tag-positioned address terms in closing sequences. In: *Semiotica*, 9, 47-96.
Knoblauch, Hubert/Bernt Schnettler (eds.), 2007: *Powerpoint-Präsentationen. Neue Formen der gesellschaftlichen Kommunikation von Wissen*. Konstanz: UVK.

Knoblauch, Hubert/Bernt Schnettler/Jürgen Raab/Hans-Georg Soeffner (eds.), 2006: *Video Analysis: Methodology and methods: Qualitative audiovisual data analysis in sociology*. Frankfurt a.M. et al.: Peter Lang.

Luckmann, Thomas, 1981: Hermeneutics as a paradigm for social science? In: Michael Brenner (ed.), *Social method and social life*. London et al.: Academic Press.

Luckmann, Thomas/Peter Gross, 1977: Analyse unmittelbarer Kommunikation und Interaktion als Zugang zum Problem der Entstehung sozialwissenschaftlicher Daten. In: Hans-Ulrich Bielefeld (ed.), *Soziolinguistik und Empirie. Beiträge zu Problemen der Corpusgewinnung und –auswertung*. Wiesbaden: Athenaion, 198-207.

Mondada, Lorenza, 2006a: Video recording as the reflexive preservation and configuration of phenomenal features for analysis. In: Hubert Knoblauch/Bernt Schnettler/Jürgen Raab/Hans-Georg Soeffner (eds.), *Video Analysis: Methodology and methods: Qualitative audiovisual data analysis in sociology*. Frankfurt a.M. et al.: Peter Lang, 51-67.

Mondada, Lorenza, 2006b: Participants' online analysis and multimodal practices: projecting the end of the turn and the closing of the sequence. In: *Discourse Studies*, 8, 1, 117-129.

Mondada, Lorenza, 2007a: Operating together through videoconference: Members' procedures for accomplishing a common space of action. In: Stephen Hester/David Francis (eds.), *Orders of ordinary actions. Respecifying sociological knowledge*. Aldershot: Ashgate, 51-76.

Mondada, Lorenza, 2007b: L'interprétation *online* par les co-participants de la structuration du tour *in fieri* en TCUs: évidences multimodales. In: *Travaux neuchâtelois de linguistique*, Numéro 47, Institut de linguistique, Université de Neuchâtel.

Mondada, Lorenza, 2008: Pratiques de transition: Resources multimodales pour la structuration de l'activité. In: Françoise Détienne/Véronique Traverso (eds.), *Méthodologies d'analyse de situations coopératives de conception*. Nancy: PUN, in press.

Raab, Jürgen, 2007: Die «Objektivität» des Sehens als wissenssoziologisches Problem. In: *Sozialer Sinn. Zeitschrift für hermeneutische Sozialforschung*, 2, 287-304.

Raab, Jürgen/Dirk Tänzler, 2006: Video Hermeneutics. In: Hubert Knoblauch/Bernt Schnettler/Jürgen Raab/Hans-Georg Soeffner (eds.), *Video Analysis: Methodology and methods: Qualitative audiovisual data analysis in sociology*. Frankfurt a.M. et al.: Peter Lang, 85-97.

Sacks, Harvey/Emanuel Schegloff/Gail Jefferson, 1974: A simplest systematics for the organiyation of turn taking for conversation. In: *Language,* 50, 4, 696-735.

Schegloff, Emanuel A., 1992: Repair after next turn: the last structurally provided defense of intersubjectivity in conversation. In: *American Journal of Sociology*. Volume 97, Number 5 (March 1992), 1295-1345.

Schegloff, Emanuel A., 1996: Confirming Allusions: Toward an Empirical Account of Action. In: *American Journal of Sociology*, Volume 102, Number 1 (July 1996), 161-216.

Schütz, Alfred, 1962: *Collected papers I: The problem of social reality*. The Hague: Martinus Nijhoff.

Simmel, Georg, 1923: *Philosophische Kultur*. Potsdam: Klinkhardt.

Soeffner, Hans-Georg, 1989: *Auslegung des Alltags – Der Alltag der Auslegung. Zur wissenssoziologischen Konzeption einer sozialwissenschaftlichen Hermeneutik*. Konstanz: UVK.

Soeffner, Hans-Georg, 2004: *Auslegung des Alltags – Der Alltag der Auslegung. Zur wissenssoziologischen Konzeption einer sozialwissenschaftlichen Hermeneutik*. Konstanz: UVK, 2nd edition.

Suchman, Lucy, 1987: *Plans and situated actions: the problem of human-machine communication*. Cambridge: Cambridge University Press.

Linguistic Anthropology and Conversation Analysis

Charles Goodwin

Video and the analysis of embodied human interaction[1]

To demonstrate for this volume the importance of using video to analyze human action, including the detailed organization of talk and language structure, I am using an analysis of embodied argument by girls playing hopscotch. To describe how action is built in these data it is necessary to investigate a range of different kinds of semiotic phenomena in diverse media that mutually elaborate each other to create a whole that is not only different from, but goes beyond, any of its constituent parts. Such analysis, and the models of action and context it develops, would not be possible without ways of recording data that maintain the detailed sequential organization of not only talk, but also the mutual organization of living, bodies within interaction, and relevant features of the material environment that the participants are attending to. Though by no means perfect, audio-video recording does provide us with tools that enable us to begin to explore such issues.

This paper proposes and develops an approach to the analysis of action within human interaction that takes into account the simultaneous use of multiple semiotic resources by participants (e.g., a range of structurally different kinds of sign phenomena in both the stream of speech and the body, graphic and socially sedimented structure in the surround, sequential organization, encompassing activity systems, etc.). It is argued that actions are both assembled and understood through a process in which different kinds of sign phenomena instantiated in diverse media, what I call semiotic fields, are juxtaposed in a way that enables them to mutually elaborate each other. A particular, locally relevant array of semiotic fields that participants demonstrably orient to (not simply a hypothetical set of fields that an analyst might impose to code context) is called a *contextual configuration*. As action unfolds, new semiotic fields can be added, while others are treated as no longer relevant, with the effect that the contextual configurations that frame, make visible and constitute the actions of the moment undergo a continuous process of change. From a slightly different perspective contextual configurations provide a systematic framework for investigating the public visibility of the body as a dynamically unfolding, interactively organized locus for the production and display of meaning and action.

When action is investigated in terms of contextual configurations, domains of phenomena that are usually treated as so distinct that they are the subject matter of entirely separate academic disciplines, e.g., language and material structure in the environment, can be analyzed as integrated components of a common proc-

---

[1] This paper is drawn from a section of «Action and embodiment within situated human interaction» 2000, *Journal of Pragmatics* 32: 1489-1522.

ess for the social production of meaning and action. This also provides an alternative geography of cognition to one that views all cognitive phenomena as situated within the mental life of the individual. Here cognition is a reflexively situated process that encompasses both 1) the sign making capacity of the individual, for example through the production of talk, and 2) different kinds of semiotic phenomena, from sequential organization to graphic fields, lodged within the material and social environment. This emphasis on cognition as a public, social process embedded within an historically shaped material world is quite consistent with both Vygotskian perspectives and recent work in the social and anthropological study of scientific and workplace practice, which Hutchins (1995) in a groundbreaking study has called «cognition in the wild», but adds to such perspectives an equally strong focus on the details of language use and conversational organization.

A central question posed for the analysis of how social action is constructed and understood through talk is determining what it is relevant to include within such a study. Frequently scholars with an interest in pragmatics have focused almost exclusively on phenomena within the stream of speech, or in the mental life of the speaker. Thus in Searle's (1970) analysis of speech acts the hearer exists only as a figment of the speaker's imagination, not as an active co-participant in her own right, e.g. someone who herself engages in conduct that contributes to the constitution and ongoing development of the action(s) being accomplished through the talk of the moment. In the human sciences in general language and the material world are treated as entirely separate domains of inquiry. Thus within anthropology departments one finds one group of scholars which focuses on language as the defining attribute of the human species working in happy isolation from archaeologists down the hall who argue that what makes human beings unique is the capacity to reshape the material environment in ways that structure human action on an historical time scale. Each of these proposals about what makes human beings a distinctive species is at best a partial truth. A theory of action must come to terms with both the details of language use and the way in which the social, cultural, material and sequential structure of the environment where action occurs figure into its organization.

The accomplishment of social action requires that not only the party producing an action, but also that others present, such as its addressee, be able to systematically recognize the shape and character of what is occurring. Without this it would be impossible for separate parties to recognize in common not only what is happening at the moment, but more crucially what range of events are being projected as relevant nexts, such that an addressee can build not just another independent action, but instead a relevant coordinated next move to what someone else has just done.[2] The necessity of social action having this public,

---

[2] The study and theoretical formulation how such multi-party social action is recognized and accomplished has been a major topic in conversation analysis. See for example Schegloff's (1968) early formulation of *conditional relevance*, the analysis of adjacency pairs in Sacks

prospectively relevant visibility, so that multiple participants can collaborate in an ongoing course of coordinated action, casts doubt on the adequacy of any model of pragmatic action that focuses exclusively on the mental life of a single participant, such as the speaker. Within this process the production of action is linked reflexively to its interpretation; to establish the public, recognizable visibility of what they are doing speakers must build action that takes into account the particulars of what their addressees can and do know. This does not by any means ensure that congruent interpretation will automatically follow, or that relevant participants positioned at different perspectives will view events in the same way (see Goodwin 1995) for analysis of how the accomplishment of ongoing collaborative action can on occasion systematically require that different kinds of participants view the same event in alternative ways. However the organization of talk-in-interaction provides for the contingent achievement of relevant intersubjectivity through the continuing availability of processes such as repair (Schegloff 1992; Schegloff, et al. 1977). When the term action is used in this paper it should be understood as encompassing this interactively organized process of public recognition of meaningful events reflexively linked to the ongoing production of these same events through the use of appropriate semiotic resources within an unfolding temporal horizon.

In this paper it will be suggested that a primordial site for the analysis of human language, cognition and action consists of a situation in which multiple participants are attempting to carry out courses of action in concert with each other through talk while attending to both the larger activities that their current actions are embedded within, and relevant phenomena in their surround. Using as data video recordings of young girls playing hopscotch it will be argued that the production and interpretation of human social action is built through the simultaneous deployment of a range of quite different kinds of semiotic resources. Talk itself contains multiple sign systems with alternative properties. Strips of talk gain their power as social action via their placement within larger sequential structures, encompassing activities, social structural arrangements, and participation frameworks constituted through displays of mutual orientation made by the actors' bodies. The body is used in a quite different way to perform gesture, again a class of phenomena that encompasses structurally different types of sign systems. Both talk and gesture can index, construe, or treat as irrelevant, entities in the participants' surround. Moreover, material structure in the surround, such as graphic fields of various types, can provide semiotic structure without which the constitution of particular kinds of action being invoked through talk would be impossible. In brief it will be argued that the construction of action through talk within situated interaction is accomplished through the temporally unfold-

---

(1995) and Schegloff and Sacks (1973), the study of how hearers make projections about what is about to happen in an unfolding utterance in Jefferson (1973) and Goodwin and Goodwin (1987), and much other work in the field (see Heritage 1984; 1989) for descriptions of work in the field, and the theoretical issues being dealt with).

ing juxtaposition of quite different kinds of semiotic resources, and that moreover through this process the human body is made publicly visible as the site for a range of structurally different kinds of displays implicated in the constitution of the actions of the moment.

Talk-in-interaction

To explore some of the different kinds of phenomena implicated in the organization of face-to-face interaction within a setting that is the focus of the participant's orientation, I'll use the following brief dispute which occurred while three young girls were playing hopscotch. One of the girls, Rosa, played only a peripheral role in the events that will be examined here, and analysis will focus on the actions of the other two. I'll call the party whose actions are being challenged Diana (i.e. the Defendant), and her Challenger Carla. In hopscotch players jump on one foot through an ordered grid of squares drawn on the ground. If the player's foot touches a line, or if she fails to land on the correct square she is «out» and her turn is over. A player is prohibited from landing on a square with a marker, such as a stone or a beanbag on it. After a successful jump through the grid, the next jump is made more difficult by throwing markers on squares in a particular sequence.[3] The dispute being examined here begins when Diana stands at the top of the hopscotch grid (she has already successfully navigated the entire grid from the bottom), throws her beanbag into a particular square, and starts to hop through the grid. Right after the beanbag lands (in what will be argued to be the wrong square) and as Diana starts to jump Carla walks into the grid, physically stops Diana from continuing, and then argues that Diana has made an illegal move by throwing her beanbag onto the fifth square instead of the fourth. (Note that the squares could have become confused if Diana, who is

---

[3] For more detailed exposition of the rules of hopscotch see Marjorie H. Goodwin (1998). Girls games, such as hopscotch, have traditionally been offered as evidence that girls' social organization, capacity to deal with rules, and ability to successfully engage in disputes is inferior to that of boys (see for example Lever 1978). For example it is argued that a game such as football has more players who occupy an array of structurally different positions than hopscotch or jumprope. Note that if this stereotype is true, girls, and the women they become, should be less fit than men to engage in the dispute forums, such as the legal system and politics, that define power in a society. Marjorie H. Goodwin's studies of girls actual interaction in the midst of games strongly contradicts such a view. She demonstrates that the disputes that systematically emerge within a game such as hopscotch provide girls with a rich arena for the analysis of each other's actions in terms of rules, with a place where rules can be challenged and negotiated, and with an opportunity to develop an embodied habitus of power as girls use the full resources of forceful argument to oppose each other's positions. See for example Marjorie H. Goodwin (1985; 1994; 1995; 1998; 1999). Carla's actions in the present data are certainly consistent with such an argument. In a more general study of the social worlds built by children through their talk-in-interaction on the street, Marjorie H. Goodwin (1990b) found that some of the dispute processes of girls, such as the He-Said-She-Said, were in fact far more extended and complex than those of boys.

throwing from the top of the grid, instead of the usual throwing position at the foot (start) of the grid, had assigned numbers to the row in dispute so that they read from her current left to right, and thus failed to take into account that she was now looking at the grid from a reverse angle).

Here is a transcript of the talk that occurs here, with an English translation on the right[4], and a diagram of how the participants have been numbering the squares in the grid in their current game (the actual grid on the ground contains no numbers, only blank squares):

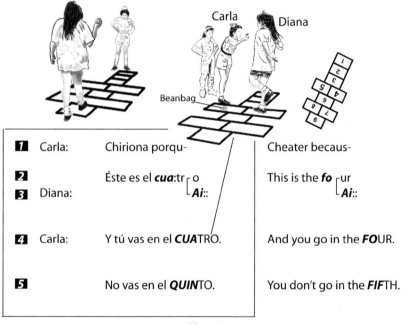

1	Carla:	Chiriona porqu-	Cheater becaus-
2		Éste es el *cua*:tr⌈o	This is the *fo* ⌈ur
3	Diana:	⌊*Ai*::	⌊*Ai*::
4	Carla:	Y tú vas en el *CUA*TRO.	And you go in the *FO*UR.
5		No vas en el *QUIN*TO.	You don't go in the *FIF*TH.

Figure 1

---

[4] Talk is transcribed using a slightly modified version of the system developed by Gail Jefferson (see Sacks, Schegloff/Jefferson 1974: 731-733). Talk receiving some form of emphasis (e.g., talk that would be underlined in a typewritten transcript using the Jefferson system) is marked with **bold italics**. Punctuation is used to transcribe intonation: A period indicates falling pitch, a question mark rising pitch, and a comma a falling contour, as would be found for example after a non-terminal item in a list. A colon indicates the lengthening of the current sound. A dash marks the sudden cut-off of the current sound (in English it is frequently realized as glottal stop). Comments (e.g., descriptions of relevant nonvocal behavior) are printed in italics within double parentheses. Numbers within single parentheses mark silences in seconds and tenths of a second. A degree sign (°) indicates that the talk that follows is being spoken with low volume. Left brackets connecting talk by different speakers mark the point where overlap begins.

A number of different kinds of phenomena have to be taken into account in order to describe the interactive organization of the dispute that is occurring here. I want to focus on how some of these phenomena consist of sign systems that are built through use of the distinctive properties of a specific medium. For example spoken language builds signs within the stream of speech, gesture uses the body in a particular way, while posture and orientation use the body in another, etc. To have a way of talking about these subsystems I'll refer to them as ***semiotic fields***. The term *semiotic* is intended to note the way in which signs are being deployed while *field* provides a rough term for pointing to the encompassing medium within which specific signs are embedded. What I want to demonstrate now is that the action that occurs here is built through the visible, public deployment of multiple semiotic fields that mutually elaborate each other. Subsequent analysis will investigate the way in which additional fields with distinctive properties are added to this mix.

Carla builds her action by deploying a number of different semiotic fields simultaneously. First, the lexico-semantic content of the talk provides Carla with resources for characterizing her opponent, *Chiriona*, (*cheater* line 1)[5] and for formulating the squares on the grid as particular kinds of entities, *el* ***Cuatro*** (*the four* line 4) and *el* ***Quinto***, (*the fifth* line 5). A term such as *the fifth* explicitly constitutes the square being talked about as a consequential item within a larger sequence of similar items. Second, these descriptions are embedded within larger syntactic structures that contrast what Diana actually did with what she should have done. Moreover this contrast is made more salient, and indeed shaped as a contrast, by the reuse of a common syntactic frame (e.g «*Y tú* ***vas en*** *NUMBER// No* ***vas en*** *NUMBER*»), which highlights as significantly different both the negation at the beginning of the second unit, and the numbers being disputed which occur in the same slot at the end of each unit. Third, prosodically the numbers being disputed are further highlighted by the heightened, contrastive stress that each receives within a larger framework of parallelism displayed by producing each line with the same pitch contour: Thus in both lines 4 and 5 Carla's pitch makes a high jump just after *vas*, then falls over *en el*, then raises over the first syllable of each number, the space where contrast is being marked, and finally falls over the final syllable of the number, which is also the final syllable of the breath group. (See figure 2)
In building her utterance Carla combines lexico-semantic content, a common syntactic frame, and the reuse of a rhythmic pitch contour capable of vividly highlighting the central point of an argument being built through contrast to tell Carla why what she has done is wrong.

---

[5] Norma Mendoza-Denton (personal communication 1995) points out that this example shows how the bilingual phonology of the children operates, taking the English word ***cheater*** and codeswitching in the middle of it at a morphological boundary by changing the /t/ of *cheat* to /r/. Although the vowel quality is primarily Spanish, the word has an English phonologial process operating within it, with the intervocalic flapping of /t/.

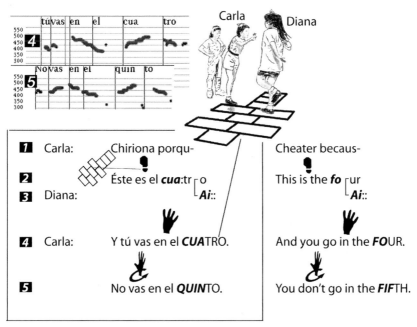

Figure 2

Fourth, this exchange is embedded within a larger course of action within a particular activity, playing hopscotch. Carla begins the dispute by using her own body to stop Diana's movement through the grid. The characterization of Diana as a *Cheater* uses the game-relevant action that Diana has just performed as the contextual point of departure for the current action and characterization.[6] Carla's subsequent talk provides a warrant for why she is entitled to both provide such a categorization, and prevent Diana from continuing. She argues that Diana has just made an illegal move. Note that grammatically in Spanish, a pro-drop language, the second person pronoun found in line 4 *tú* (*you*) is not required, and indeed no such pronoun occurs in the almost identical syntactic frame produced a moment later in line 5. The fact that the pronoun is being produced when it could have been omitted suggests that it is doing some special work. One component of this may be rhythmic, and indeed dropping the pronoun when *No* occupies the same slot, — just before *vas*— at the beginning of line 5, enables

---

[6] The way in which utterances derive both their meaning, and their status as particular kinds of actions from their placement within larger sequences, has long been the subject of sustained analysis within conversation analysis. See for example Sacks, Schegloff and Jefferson (1974), Schegloff (1968), and Heritage (1984).

Carla to build a pair of parallel utterances. However the pronoun may also help to shape the talk beginning at line 4, not as a *description* of what Diana just did (e.g. «You went in the Five»), but instead as an utterance that carries a *deontic* force, i.e. an argument about how her actual behavior contrasts with what was called for by the rules of the game in progress («You [should] go in the Four. Don't go in the Fifth»), with the *tú* perhaps referencing not Diana as a unique individual, but instead a player in her position who should act in a particular way. Through such structure in the talk the game in progress is formulated as a rule governed institution with normative consequences for discriminating permitted from illegal behavior. The structure of the encompassing activity is thus explicitly oriented to, and drawn upon as a resource for the constitution of action, within the detailed structure of the talk itself. The talk that occurs here is thus built in part through the use of the resources provided by an encompassing activity, while simultaneously constituting action within it, e.g. denying Diana the opportunity to complete her turn.

Fifth, this talk occurs within a particular participation framework (Goodwin 1981; Goodwin 1990a; Goodwin 1997; Heath 1986; Kendon 1990). With both their bodies and their gaze Carla and Diana orient toward each other. Note that this framework is not itself a speech act, such as a challenge. Instead it builds through the embodied stance a public field of mutual orientation within which a wide variety of speech acts can occur. Rather than being itself a momentary action within an exchange, it constitutes part of the interactive ground from which actions emerge, and within which they are situated (see also Kendon 1990). However, as we shall see later in this sequence this framework is built and sustained through the visible embodied actions of the participants. As such it, like the actions that occur within it, is open to challenge, negotiation and modification. Though it surrounds larger strips of diverse individual actions, it is itself a dynamic, interactively organized field.

Sixth, this framework of embodied mutual orientation makes it possible for sign systems other than talk to also function. As Carla pronounces *Cuatro* and *Quinto* she displays these same numbers with handshapes: Unlike many gestures, which display aspects of meaning that are not present in the stream of speech (Kendon 1997; McNeill 1992), these hand gestures provide visual versions of the numbers being spoken by Carla, i.e., *Cuatro* and the simultanous four fingered handshape and are alternative instantiations of a common lexical item, the number *four*. This tight overlap makes it possible to investigate with clarity one issue posed for the analysis of embodied action. If one conceptualizes action as the communication of propositional content, and/or with providing the addressee with the resources necessary to recognize some action being instantiated in the current talk (for example something that might be very loosely glossed here as a challenge), then the hand gesture is entirely redundant with the information provided in the stream of speech, and thus need not be taken into account in the analysis of the action occurring here; embodiment except in the stream of speech is irrelevant.

In opposition to such a position it will be argued here that the handshapes displaying the numbers present in the accompanying speech are not simply a visual mirror of the lexical content of the talk, but a semiotic modality in their own right. Analytically, it is not sufficient to simply characterize their **content** with a lexical gloss that describes the handshapes as redundant versions of the numbers in the talk (e.g. as alternative signifiers for a common signified such as *Five*). Instead the issues posed for a participant attempting to use such signs to build social action involve the organization of relevant phenomena within specific media, e.g. Carla has to use her body in a quite precise way while taking into account the visible body of her co-participant. She is faced with the task of using not only her talk, but also her body, to structure the local environment such that her gestures can themselves count as forms of social action. What precisely does this involve? Unlike talk gestures can't be heard. In looking at the data we find that Carla actively works to position her hand gestures so that they will be perceived by Diana. Unlike many accompanying gestures, Carla's hand is explicitly positioned in Diana's line of sight. Indeed the work of thrusting the gesturing hand toward Diana's face twists Carla's body into a configuration in which her hand, arm and the upper part of her torso are actually leaning toward Diana.

Carla's gesture is thus organized with reference to a specific embodied configuration, one that includes not only her own body, but also that of her addressee. Though the content being displayed here is congruent with what is being said within the talk, a quite different kind of work, involving the precise deployment of semiotic resources with properties quite unlike the structure of speech, is required in order to build social action with the gesturing hand. This same process of making visible congruent meaning through the articulation of different kinds of semiotic materials is also found in the production of the contrast found in lines 4 and 5. The number handshapes are framed by contrastive movements of Carla's arm and hand.[7] As Carla says «Y tú vas en el *Cua*tro» she stretches her arm forward with the palm toward Diana. However as she begins the next phrase she turns her hand around, while keeping the elbow which anchors the gesturing arm in the same position, and moves the upper arm to a new position closer to her own body, while still maintaining the forward thrust of her torso. By using the visual and rhythmic structure of her moving body Carla is able to establish a contrast within a larger gestural frame that parallels the one produced through reuse of common syntactic and prosodic frames in the talk. In brief, Carla is performing her action not only vocally, but also through a simultaneous sequence of gestural and body displays. Though done with quite different media these displays make visible the same two numbers that occur in the vocal stream, and highlight the contrast between them through a congruent

---

[7] Describing these movements in writing is not entirely effective. The rhythmic and visual patterning of these movements can be seen much more clearly on the video. Ideally I would like to be able to include video clips in a paper like this.

display of contrastive items within a larger framework of parallel equivalence (e.g. the common syntactic frame in the talk, and the arm and torso establishing the variable handshapes as alternative values within a common framework of visible, embodied action)[8].

Given all of this embodied organization, the question still remains: why isn't the action that Carla is performing done entirely within the stream of speech? Why does she go to all of this extra semiotic work? Within interaction participants don't produce talk or build action into the air, but instead actively work to secure the orientation of a hearer (Goodwin 1981), and design the current action and utterance in fine detail for the particularities of the current addressee (Goodwin 1981; Sacks, et al. 1974). What Carla is doing here will fail as a form of pragmatic action if Diana does not take it into account. Through the use of the gesture Carla is able to specifically organize central components of her current action with reference to Diana's current visible orientation, i.e. positioning them right in Diana's line of sight. The gestures provide Carla with a semiotic modality for **insisting** that Diana take what she is doing and saying into account, indeed a way of quite literally getting into Diana's face with the particulars of the action. The way in which Carla thrusts her gestures toward Diana's face, as well as her walking into the grid when Diana is in the process of making a jump, help constitute what she is doing as a challenge to Diana. Carla's thrusted gestures are a proxemic challenge to Diana's personal space, as is her incursion into the game relevant territory of the grid in the course of Diana's attempt to move through it. These proxemic and territorial dimensions may be quite consequential in that Diana has actively attempted to continue her movement through the hopscotch grid despite Carla's challenge by continuing to jump until Carla pushes her in line 2. During the talk being examined here Diana is still standing on one foot, a posture that could allow her to pursue her turn at jumping further. On another level the gestural movements enhance and amplify the indignant force of the action.

In brief, talk and gesture mutually elaborate each other within 1) a larger sequence of action and 2) an embodied participation framework constituted through mutual orientation between speaker and addressee. It would seem that something like this set of concurrently relevant semiotic fields is what is being pointed to by the phrase «face-to-face interaction». However this is by no means a fixed array of fields. Thus on many occasions, such as phone calls, or when participants are dispersed in a large, visually inaccessible environment (e.g., a hunting party, or a workgroup interacting through computers), visible coorientation may not be present. I'll call some particular subset of possible fields that is being oriented to at a particular moment as relevant to the organization of a particular action a **contextual configuration**.

---

[8] This contrast is also displayed through crucial rhythmic components (Erickson 1992) of both the talk and the gesturing arm. I am not however able to capture this in the transcript.

Changing contextual configurations

What happens next provides the opportunity to investigate in more detail how the shape of the current contextual configuration has consequences for the organization of action. As Carla says *«QUINTO» in* line 5, Diana looks down, moving her gaze away from Carla's face and gesturing hand, and toward the grid.

Figure 3

The participation framework which provided an essential ground for Carla's use of her gesturing hand is no longer operative. When Diana looks away Carla finds herself in the position of looking and gesturing toward someone who is now publicly disattending her. Such phenomena demonstrate how any participation framework is an ongoing contingent accomplishment, something not under the control of a single party (who can at best make **proposals** about the structure of participation that should be operative at the moment), but rather something that has to be continuously achieved through public displays of orientation within ongoing processes of interaction.

Not only the gesture but also the action Carla is performing, the challenge to Diana, is called into question by virtue of the way in which Diana is no longer visibly acting as a recipient to it. Let me note in passing that here, unlike some approaches to «speech acts» action is being analyzed here as a multi-party interactive phenomenon.

Does Carla in fact analyze these events in this way? Does she treat what Diana has done as undermining her current action, and if so what can she do about this?

Without the slightest break in her fluent, dynamic production of speech Carla restates the argument she has just made in a different way with a different kind of gesture. As Diana's head moves downward Carla drops her gesturing hand. However she now uses her foot to do a deictic stomp at a place constituted by the intersection of three different, mutually relevant, semiotic fields:

- First, the place where Diana is now looking, the target of her gaze and thus the place that she is visibly displaying to be the current focus of her orientation and attention.
- Second, one of the squares in the hopscotch grid that is the focus of the current dispute, indeed the square where Diana threw her beanbag
- Third, a square that is explicitly being talked about within Carla's current speech.

The structure of Carla's talk also changes in ways that adapt it to this new configuration of orientation and gesture. In lines 4 & 5 Carla used numeric expressions functioning as names to specify the entities being disputed: *el **Cuatro*** and *el **Quinto***. Such language talked about these phenomena, but did not in any way presuppose that the participants were actually looking at the grid squares being talked about. Though available in the local scene the grid was not being put into play as something that had to be actively attended to and scrutinized in order to properly constitute the actions in progress at the moment. One could look elsewhere, and indeed this is precisely what Carla and Diana both did by gazing toward each other, and it was this structure of mutual orientation that Carla exploited by placing her numeric handshapes directly in Diana's line of sight.

By way of contrast, after Diana looks down Carla uses the deictic expressions *Éste* (*this*) and *ese* (*that*) (lines 6-7) to specify the particular squares at issue while using numbers to propose how they should be categorized.[9]

Such deictic expressions presuppose that their addressee is positioned to see what is being pointed at (which is being further specified by the concurrent foot point), and indeed the entities being pointed to are located precisely at the target of Diana's gaze. Orientation to the grid is now an explicit, crucial component of the operations that have to be performed to properly constitute the action currently in progress. The grid as something to be actively scrutinized is now in play as a relevant semiotic field implicated in the organization of the actions of the moment in ways that it wasn't a moment earlier.

---

[9] Carla also used a deictic stomp accompanied by *éste* in line 2 to indicate a relevant square in the grid. At this point Carla is actually pushing Diana in an attempt to stop her progress through the grid. As the two moved apart Carla switched to the iconic handshapes thrust into Diana's face, an action that had the effect of leading Diana to gaze up toward Carla and her outstretched hand.

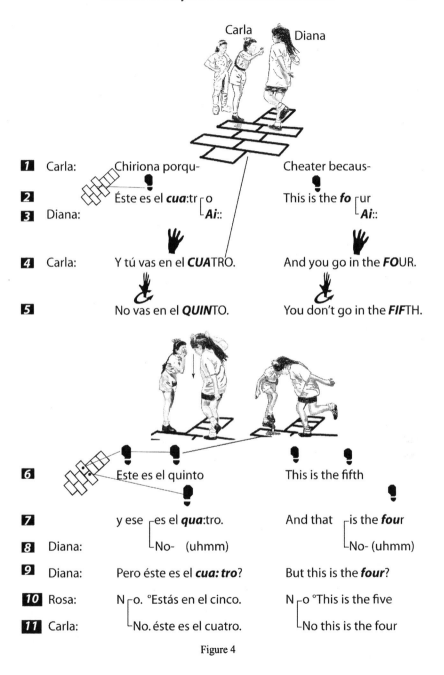

Figure 4

In brief, what one finds within this single turn at talk is a switch from one contextual configuration to another.[10] The second contextual configuration contains a new semiotic field, the grid as something to be looked at, that wasn't necessary for the first. Despite the addition of this field, most of the semiotic fields in play during lines 4-5 remain relevant. The way in which contextual configurations are constituted through specific, somewhat contingent mixes of particular semiotic fields provides for the possibility of underlying continuity even while relevant change is occurring (e.g., sets of fields can overlap from one configuration to another). Rather than replacing one perceptual world with an entirely different one, there is relevant change in a continuing contextual gestalt as configurations are reconfigured. Despite this continuity the shifts that do occur are both significant and consequential for how participants build appropriate action. Thus the shift in focus to the grid that occurs here also involves changes in the kinds of sign systems, in both talk and gesture, used to refer to the entities being talked about. Though Carla is still pursuing her challenge, there has been a change in context or more precisely the particular contextual configuration of relevant semiotic resources that are providing the organization of the action of the moment.

The most crucial property relevant to the organization of action displayed through what happens here is *reflexive awareness*. Central to Carla's construction of action is the ongoing analysis of how her recipient is positioned to co-participate in the interactive frameworks necessary for the constitution of that action. When Diana looks away Carla takes into account what Diana is doing and reorganizes her action in terms of it (see also Goodwin 1981). This reflexive awareness is not simply an «interior» element of the mental processes necessary for defining the action (as it could be analyzed for example within traditional speech act analysis) but a public, visible component of the ongoing practices used to build the action, something that leads to systematic, relevant changes in the shape of the action. Moreover, within this process the addressee, as an embodied actor in her own right, is as crucial a player as the speaker.

One of the things required for an actor to perform such rapid, reflexive adaptation is access to a set of structurally different semiotic resources, each of which is appropriate to specific contextual configurations. Here Carla is able to refer to and identify the same entities — specific positions in the hopscotch grid — with a number of different sign systems each of which has quite distinctive properties. These include numeric linguistic expressions functioning as names (which do not require looking at the entity being referred to – lines 4-5, though this can

---

[10] See Goodwin (1981) for analysis of how ongoing talk is reorganized to make it appropriate to a new contextual configuration defined by a structural change in the type of recipient located as the addressee of the moment. See Hanks (1996a; 1996b) for analysis of both deixis and the relevance of the organization of spaces in the environment to the organization of action. For an analysis of narrative spaces relevant to the organization of pointing see Haviland (1996). The issue of relevance, posed by the pervasive possibility of alternative categorizations of the same entity, has long been a central theme of work in conversation analysis. See for example Schegloff (1972).

be built into their structure through syntactic affiliation with a deictic expression – lines 6-7), iconic hand gestures (which presupposed orientation toward the hand rather than the entity being described through the hand), deictic linguistic expressions and deictic or indexical gestures (both of which make relevant gaze toward the entity being pointed to). Not all of these resources are relevant and in play at any particular moment. However the ability to rapidly call upon alternative structures from a larger, ready at hand tool kit of diverse semiotic resources, is crucial to the ability of human beings to demonstrate in the ongoing organization of their action reflexive awareness of each other and the contextual configurations that constitute the situation of the moment.

Looking at these same phenomena from another perspective we find that the analyst cannot simply take an inventory of all semiotic resources in a setting that could potentially be brought into play, and use this inventory as a frame to describe a relevant context. As these data demonstrate, not all possible and relevant resources are in play at any particular moment. Indeed what happens here depends crucially on the way in which the grid **replaces** the hand displaying numbers and focus on each other's face as what is being oriented to at the moment. To describe the context we have to track in detail the temporal unfolding of the interaction, while attending to what the participants themselves are constituting for each other as the phenomena to be taken into account for the organization of the action of the moment (Sacks, et al. 1974). We are thus faced with the task of describing both the larger set of possibilities from which choices are being made, and the way in which alternative choices from that set structure the events of the moment in consequentially different ways.

Semiotic structure in the environment

Another crucial component of this process is the hopscotch grid being talked about and pointed at. The grid differs radically from both talk and gesture in many important respects. Unlike the fleeting, evanescent decay of speech, which disappears as material substance as soon as it is spoken (unless captured in another medium such as writing or tape recording), the hopscotch grid has both an extended temporal duration — it is there in exactly the same form throughout the game, and in the present case of a painted grid on a playground, day after day for new games — and is built of concrete material so durable that it can support the weight of multiple actors jumping through it. Rather than constituting a mental representation, it is as corporeal, solid, and enduring as the ground the players are walking upon. However it is simultaneously a thoroughly semiotic structure. Indeed it provides crucial frameworks for the building of action that could not exist without it, such as successful jumps, outs, fouls, etc. The actions that make up the game are impossible in a hypothetical «natural environment» unstructured by human practice, e.g. a field without the visible structure provided by the gridlines. Simultaneously the game is just as impossible without embodiment of the semiotic structure provided by the grid in a medium that can be actually jumped on. The notion that the primary focus for the analysis of human action should be the isolated mental states of individual actors here becomes impossible. As demonstrated quite powerfully in the work of Hutchins (1995), human cognitive activity is situated within historically shaped social systems that encompass both actors and crucial semiotic artifacts such as the maps needed to navigate ships.

Conclusion

Despite its simplicity, the mix of semiotic fields found in a scene such as the hopscotch game locates a perspicuous site for developing an approach to the analysis of human action that takes into account simultaneously the details of language use, the semiotic structure provided by the historically built material world, the body as an unfolding locus for the display of meaning and action, and the temporally unfolding organization of talk-in-interaction.

Analyzing action as something accomplished through the temporally unfolding juxtaposition of multiple semiotic fields with quite diverse structures and properties, has a range of consequences. First, the analytic boundaries between language, cognitive processes and structure in the material world dissolve. The actions made visible in Carla's talk were not constituted in any single field, such as the talk, but rather within a larger configuration in which a range of different fields (the talk, the pointing foot or finger, the semiotic structure provided by the grid, the larger encompassing activity, etc.) mutually elaborated each other.

This framework is analytically different from many approaches to both cognition and embodiment that focus primarily on phenomena lodged within the individual. For example, much study of metaphor has taken as its point of departure the embodied **experience** of the speaker, e.g. the way in which metaphor emerges from the structure of the human body, its position in a world structured by phenomena such as gravity (e.g. the pervasive relevance of *Up* and *Down* in human cognition and language) and «preconceptual structures of experience» (Johnson 1987: 15). While providing valuable insight into many kinds of conceptual organization, such focus on the interior life of a single actor does not develop a systematic framework for investigating the **public** visibility of the body as a dynamically unfolding, interactively organized locus for the production and display of relevant meaning and action. Crucial to the organization of the events being investigated here is the ability of **other** participants to systematically see how a co-participant's body is doing specific things by virtue of its positioning within a changing array of diverse semiotic fields.[11] Diana is seen to be following or not following the rules of the game in progress by virtue of how

---

[11] Such public visibility and construal of relevant events is crucial to many areas of human social life. See Goodwin (1994) for analysis of how such public practices for organizing vision enabled lawyers defending the policemen who beat Rodney King to shape what the jury saw on the tape in a way that exonerated the policemen while shifting the focus of attention to Rodney King's actions.

her body is positioned within the hopscotch grid. Such actions are public and accountable (as demonstrated by Carla's challenge and attempt to prevent Diana from continuing). Their analysis requires a framework that focuses not primarily on Diana's interior life (though what she wants to do is visible to all), but instead on the visible juxtaposition of her body and the grid, within a recognizable course of activity. Human cognition encompasses, and is embedded within, the semiotic structure provided by historically shaped frameworks for action, instantiated in both material media, and the systematic practices of a group performing the activities that constitute its lifeworld. Such public visibility is also crucial to analysis of how the body is used to perform action within interaction. Carla takes into account the patterns of orientation visibly displayed by Diana's gaze and posture by changing her own actions in response to them. Central to what is occurring in these data (and in face-to-face interaction in general) are socially organized, interactively sustained configurations of multiple participants who use the public visibility of the actions being performed by each others' bodies, the unfolding sequential organization of their talk, and semiotic structure in the settings they inhabit to organize courses of action in concert with each other.

The human body is unlike most other phenomena in the scene. Within interaction the body is a dynamic, temporally unfolding field that displays a reflexive stance toward other coparticipants, the current talk, and the actions in progress. Moreover the actions made visible by the body are quite diverse. Some, such as a display of orientation toward another participant or a relevant feature of the surround have a temporal organization that extends over multiple actions occurring within an extended strip of interaction. Gestures, including both iconic representations such as the numeric handshapes and the deictic points found here, can have a far shorter temporal duration. Moreover these two kinds of action function at different levels of organization. Gestures can carry propositional information and function as individual actions, or components of multimodal actions. By way of contrast the displays of postural orientation used to build participation frameworks help establish the interactive ground that frames and makes possible the production, reception and joint constitution of a variety of different kinds of action built through gesture and talk. The body functions in yet another way when prosody and intonation are used to display alignment and stance (Couper-Kuhlen/Selting 1996; Goodwin 1998). Rather than locating a homogeneous field for analysis, the notion of embodiment encompasses many different kinds of phenomena.

As the rearrangement of contextual configurations in the hopscotch data demonstrated, context is not simply a set of features presupposed or invoked by a strip of talk, but is itself a dynamic, temporally unfolding process accomplished through the ongoing rearrangement of structures in the talk, participants' bodies, relevant artifacts, spaces and features of the material surround that are the focus of the participants' scrutiny. Crucial to this process is the way in which the detailed structure of talk, as articulated through sequential organization, provides for the continuous updating and rearrangement of contexts for the production and interpretation of action. Within the rich matrix of diverse semiotic resources that create relevant contextual configurations, action, setting and the meaningful body reflexively constitute each other through temporally unfolding processes of situated human interaction.

References

Couper-Kuhlen, Elizabeth/Margret Selting, 1996: *Prosody in conversation: Interactional studies.* Cambridge: Cambridge University Press.
Erickson, Frederick, 1992: They know all the lines: Rhythmic organization and contextualization in a conversational listing routine. In: Peter Auer/Aldo Di Luzio (eds.), *The contextualization of language.* Amsterdam et al.: John Benjamins, 365-397.
Goodwin, Charles, 1981: *Conversational organization: Interaction between speakers and hearers.* New York: Academic Press.
Goodwin, Charles, 1994: Professional vision. In: *American Anthropologist* 96, 3: 606-633.
Goodwin, Charles, 1995: Seeing in depth. In: *Social Studies of Science* 25, 237-274.
Goodwin, Charles/Alessandro Duranti, 1992: Rethinking context: An introduction. In: Alessandro Duranti/Charles Goodwin (eds.), *Rethinking context: Language as an interactive phenomenon.* Cambridge: Cambridge University Press, 1-42.
Goodwin, Charles/Marjorie Harness Goodwin, 1987: Concurrent operations on talk: Notes on the interactive organization of assessments. In: *IPrA Papers in Pragmatics* 1, 1, 1-52.
Goodwin, Marjorie Harness, 1985: The serious side of jump rope: Conversational practices and social organization in the frame of play. In: *Journal of American folklore* 98, 315-330.
Goodwin, Marjorie Harness, 1990a: Byplay: Participant structure and the framing of collaborative collusion. In: Bernard Conein/Michel de Fornel/Louis Quéré (eds.), *Les Formes de La Conversation,* Vol. 2. Paris: CNET, 155-180.
Goodwin, Marjorie Harness, 1990b: *He-Said-She-Said: Talk as social organization among black children.* Bloomington: Indiana University Press.
Goodwin, Marjorie Harness, 1994: Ay chillona!: Stance-taking in girls' hop scotch. In: Mary Bucholtz/Anita C. Liang/Laurel A. Sutton/Caitlin Hines (eds.), *Cultural performances: Proceedings of the third Berkeley Women and Language Conference.* Berkeley: Berkeley Women and Language Group, Linguistics Department, UC-Berkeley, 232-241.
Goodwin, Marjorie Harness, 1995: Co-construction in girls' hopscotch. In: *Research on Language and Social Interaction* 28, 3, 261-282.
Goodwin, Marjorie Harness, 1997: By-play: Negotiating evaluation in storytelling. In: Gregory R. Guy/Crawford Feagin/Deborah Schiffrin/John

Baugh (eds.), *Towards a social science of language: Papers in honor of William Labov 2: Social interaction and discourse structures*. Amsterdam et al.: John Benjamins, 77-102.

Goodwin, Marjorie Harness, 1998: Games of stance: Conflict and footing in hopscotch. In: Susan M. Hoyle/Carolyn T. Adger (eds.), *Kids' talk: Strategic language use in later childhood*. New York: Oxford University Press, 23-46.

Goodwin, Marjorie Harness, 1999: Constructing opposition within girls' games. In: Mary Bucholtz/Anita C. Liang/Laurel A. Sutton (eds.), *Reinventing identities: From category to practice in language and gender research*. New York: Oxford University Press, 388-409.

Hanks, William F., 1996a: Exorcism and the description of participant roles. In: Michael Silverstein/Greg Urban (eds.), *Natural histories of discourse*. Chicago: The University of Chicago Press, 160-202.

Hanks, William F., 1996b: *Language and communicative practices*. Boulder et al.: Westview Press.

Haviland, John B., 1996: Projections, transpositions, and relativity. In: John J. Gumperz/Stephen C. Levinson (eds.), *Rethinking linguistic relativity*. Cambridge: Cambridge University Press, 271-323.

Heath, Christian, 1986: *Body movement and speech in medical interaction*. Cambridge: Cambridge University Press.

Heritage, John, 1984: *Garfinkel and ethnomethodology*. Cambridge: Polity Press.

Heritage, John, 1989: Current developments in conversation analysis. In: Derek Roger/Peter Bull (eds.), *Interdisciplinary approaches to interpersonal communication*. Clevedon: Multilingual Matters, 21-47.

Hutchins, Edwin, 1995: *Cognition in the wild*. Cambridge et al.: MIT Press.

Jefferson, Gail, 1973: A case of precision timing in ordinary conversation: Overlapped tag-positioned address terms in closing sequences. In: *Semiotica* 9, 47-96.

Johnson, Mark, 1987: *The body in the mind: The bodily basis of meaning, imagination, and reason*. Chicago: University of Chicago Press.

Kendon, Adam, 1990: Behavioral foundations for the process of frame-attunement in face-to-face interaction. In: Adam Kendon (ed.), *Conducting interaction: Patterns of behavior in focused encounters*. Cambridge: Cambridge University Press, 239-262.

Kendon, Adam, 1997: Gesture. In: *Annual Review of Anthropology* 26, 109-128.

Lever, Janet Rae, 1978: Sex differences in the complexity of children's play and games. In: *American Sociological Review* 43, 471-483.

McNeill, David, 1992: *Hand & Mind: What gestures reveal about thought*. Chicago: University of Chicago Press.

Sacks, Harvey, 1995: *Lectures on conversation*. Edited by Gail Jefferson. Vol. I + II. Oxford: Basil Blackwell.

Sacks, Harvey/Emanuel A. Schegloff/Gail Jefferson, 1974: A simplest systematics for the organization of turn-taking for conversation. In: *Language* 50: 696-735.
Schegloff, Emanuel A., 1968: Sequencing in conversational openings. In: *American Anthropologist* 70, 1075-1095.
Schegloff, Emanuel A., 1972: Notes on a conversational practice: Formulating place. In: David Sudnow (ed.), *Studies in Social Interaction.* New York: Free Press, 75-119.
Schegloff, Emanuel A., 1987: Between macro and micro: Contexts and other connections. In: Jeffrey C. Alexander/Richard Münch/Bernhard Giesen/Neil J. Smelser (eds.), *The micro-macro link.* Berkeley: University of California Press, 207-234.
Schegloff, Emanuel A., 1992: Repair after next turn: The last structurally provided defense of intersubjectivity in conversation. In: *American Journal of Sociology* 97, 5, 1295-1345.
Schegloff, Emanuel A./Gail Jefferson/Harvey Sacks, 1977: The preference for self-correction in the organization of repair in conversation. In: *Language* 53, 361-382.
Schegloff, Emanuel A./Harvey Sacks, 1973: Opening up closings. In: *Semiotica* 8, 289-327.
Searle, John R., 1970: *Speech acts: An essay in the philosophy of language.* Cambridge: Cambridge University Press.

Marjorie Harness Goodwin

Constructing inequality as situated practice

Introduction

My interest as a linguistic anthropologist is with documenting how talk is used to build social organization within face-to-face interaction. I have principally been involved in looking at how human activity and forms of basic human sociality are co-constructed through talk-in-interaction. I've investigated forms of language-in-interaction within the peer group, the work group, and in the family. Critical to this work is examining the embodied practices through which participants in interaction build their local activities. I consider it crucial to document how talk, intonation, *and* the body (as well as artifacts and features of the local setting) mutually elaborate one another in the construction of action among the people I am studying, and to that end make use of video recordings in my work. This is because I wish to describe rigorously, systematically, and empirically the array of resources utilized by participants to build their ongoing social organization as the situated product of interactive practices. By using video recordings I make available to other researchers the data my descriptions of interactive practices are based upon.

A central concern of mine relates to models of female voice and language in psychology and linguistics. Traditional studies of girls groups have focused on orientations towards an ethic of care, empathy, collaboration and wanting to form connections with others. Psychologists (Leaper 1994; Maccoby 1998) and sociologists (Adler/Adler 1998) up until the 90's promoted the notion of «separate worlds» of girls and boys, the view that boys are competitive while girls are cooperative. Adler and Adler (1998: 55), for example, argue that boys «gain status from competitive and aggressive achievement-oriented activities», while girls value «social and nurturing roles». Carol Gilligan, author of best-selling book *In a different voice,* whose work has influenced a great number of researchers, argues that males are oriented towards a «justice orientation» (concern with equality, reciprocity, and fairness) while females are oriented towards a «care orientation» -- the idea of attachment, loving, and being loved, listening and being listened to, responding and being responded to. Remarkably this view of female psychology persisted even when in psychology in the 90's researchers began investigating forms of social aggression among females. In fact, later psychological work on aggression (Crick/Grotpeter 1995; Grotpeter/Crick 1996; Brown 2003; Underwood 2003) provides dichotomies similar to those of earlier psychologists such as Maccoby: boys are characterized as physically aggressive, while girls are seen as socially or relationally aggressive. These types of dichotomized orientations are current in popular media as well. In *As good as it gets*, a young secretary asks author Melvin Udall played by Jack Nicholson «How do you right women so well?» His response is «I think of a man. And I take away reason and accountability».

As a feminist researcher I make use of a methodology that combines analysis of talk in interaction with ethnography to provide a more informed picture of girls' lives than exists in either social science or popular literature. Stereotypes of girls as having little concern with an ethic of justice or as all-embracing of an ethic of care fall apart when we examine through extensive ethnography in conjunction with talk-in-interaction how girls actually orchestrate their lived social worlds.

Among the Philadelphia children I studied in the 1970's (Goodwin 1990), extended he-said-she-said political processes were initiated with utterances using indirect speech (such as «And <u>Tan</u>ya said that <u>you</u> said that I was showin <u>off</u> just because I had that <u>blouse</u> on».). Such utterances were used to reconstitute the local social order, usually as a leveling process, in response to someone putting herself above others.

He-Said-She-Said Accusations

Annette to Benita: And *Tan*ya said
that *you* said
that *I* was showin' off
just because I had that *bl:*ouse on.

Bea to Annette: Kerry said
*y*ou said that (0.6)
I wasn't gonna go around *Pop*lar no more.

Barbara to Bea: *T*hey say
y'all say
I wrote *e*verything over there.

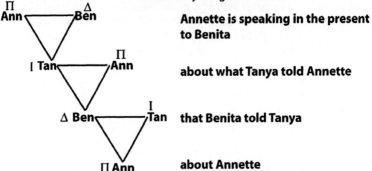

Annette is speaking in the present to Benita

about what Tanya told Annette

that Benita told Tanya

about Annette

Figure 1: He-Said-She-Said diagram

Regardless of the particular participants, there was a regular rotation of positions within this structure. The party who initiated the story of the offense (someone saying something about someone in one's absence) had heard about it in the past and reports it to the offended party with the expectation that she will take action and confront the offending party. In response to accusations, denials either deny that the action occurred, or claim that the intermediate party is lying, trying to start a fight. A single utterance creates a coherent domain of action, a small culture, including identities, actions, and biographies as well as a relevant past that warrants the current accusation. In essence this form of statement constitutes a vernacular legal process.

In his book *The essential difference: The truth about the male and female brain* Simon Baron-Cohen (2003), director of the autism research center at Cambridge University, argues that males have a stronger drive to systemize, and females to empathize. He states that this is because the female brain is hard wired for empathy. In order to problematize this claim I now turn to a three-year study I conducted at a progressive elementary school in Los Angeles, one that included children of multiple ethnicities as well as a range of social classes, to look at how girls manage their social relations.

Constructing difference in a girls' friendship group

Differentiation in terms of social class was not salient in the working class Philadelphia community I studied (Goodwin 1990). However, it was central to my fieldwork among peers (1997-1999) on the playground in Los Angeles (Goodwin 2006). Among a multi-ethnic, primarily upper middle class clique I studied, children made use of signs – participation in elite sports, family real estate, foreign travel, and Cotillions -- to reference their social position; through this sign use they constructed a field that positioned people with respect to their recognition of and access to particular signs. Children replicated in situ the class differences that organized their larger society. Here I will be concerned with the linguistic, intonational and corporeal resources through which girls practice forms of status differentiation and social exclusion in their spontaneous play.

A pervasive feature of girls' social organization in my later field study on the playground was open attack on one another's face and construction of inequality. The first group of sequences I will discuss provide examples of how girls constructed Angela, an African American working class girl, as socially different from other girls. Next I will investigate how girls sanction girls who think they are superior to others and police the local social order.

The following occurs as girls are preparing to get a jump rope to play. When Angela, a peer who was not fully accepted by members of a small clique of fourth grade friends, makes a bid for her place in the game she is told she can't play. Data are transcribed according to conventions in Conversation Analysis developed by Jefferson (Sacks/Schegloff et al. 1974: 731-733).

Example 1: Treating Angela as nonpresent

```
            Girls are sitting at the lunch table
1 Lisa:     I'm gonna go get the jump ropes.
2 Janis:    °You're last. ((to Angela))
3 Angela:   I'm first.
4 Lisa:     No.
5 Janis:    NO::.
6 Lisa:     [You're not here.
7 Aretha:   [You're not even here!
8 Angela:   °Go:d.
```

Immediately after Angela makes her bid to play jump rope, both Lisa and Janis make their refusals with loud «No's». Lisa and Aretha produce degrading depictions of Angela, describing her as someone who is «not even here». That Angela treats such depictions as inappropriate is hearable from her softly spoken «God». response.

In the next example girls collaborate in the active exclusion of Angela as she approaches them while they are eating. Through their talk they build a form of social order that displays disdain and disgust for a peer.

Example 2: Dismissive greeting and farewell to Angela

```
              ((Angela approaches the group of girls dis-
              cussing an absent party of their friendship
              group))
1 Ruth:       A- much (.) worse (.) fight.
2 Janis:      What did she say.
3 Ruth:       Hi Angela! Bye Angela! ((waving hand
              «Bye»))
4 Lisa:       Shoo shoo shoo::!
5             ((Angela does not move))
6 Janis:      What did she say.
7 Ruth:       HI::. Eh heh heh! ((to Angela))
8 Aretha:     Nothing.
9 Melissa:    She was angry at me first.
10 Lisa:      She was?
11            ((Angela goes away running))
```

Supportive rituals like greetings and farewells provide ritual brackets around a spate of joint activity (Goffman 1971). However, when Angela approaches a group of girls as they are discussing a potential fight between two friends, Ruth gives a greeting «Hi Angela!» This is followed immediately by a farewell: «Bye Angela». Lisa says «Shoo shoo shoo::.» These types of actions are used to dismiss younger children, pets, or pests. After Ruth's perfunctorily produced «hi», she turns to her playgroup, the girls resume talk about an absent party, and Angela runs away. Here the rituals of greeting and farewell are not intended to affirm the presence of the approaching party, but rather to dismiss her.

Angela on occasion is made to confess her position as someone who «tags along» with the others and is not a full-fledged member of the group. In the next example (Example 3) Sarah asks Angela to admit that she's a tagalong (lines 14-15), and prompts her what to say (lines 17-20). When she delivers the lines Sarah prompts her to say in line 21 («I'm a tagalong»), she is praised, in much the same way one would address a dog (line 23).

Example 3: Angela confesses her «tagalong» status

```
 1 Angela:  I- I mean like- you guys are like-
 2          I don't judge anybody because you guys
            know,
 3          that like I just, you know, follow you
            guys.
 4          ((shoulder moves in time with words))
 5          [wherever you guys go, but um,
 6 Sarah:   [You're like a tag. You tag along. ((left
            palm extended with arm bent towards An-
            gela))
 8          Basically-    [Angela tags along.=
 9 Angela:                [So,
10 Sarah:   That's it.=right?
11 Angela:  So li   [ke- Yeah. ((shoulder shrug))
12 Sarah:           [Right Angela? Admit it. eh heh heh!
13 Angela:  Yeah like-    [whatever.
14 Sarah:                 [ADMIT IT ANGELA!
15 Sarah:   [ADMIT IT! ((extends arms palm up to An-
            gela))
16 Angela:  [OKAY! ((leaning towards Sarah))
17   Sarah: Say it. «You:: (.) are:: (.) I: am a: (.)»
18          ((using hands as if conducting on each
            beat,))
19          then extends hands palm up towards Angela
20          as if asking her to complete the utter-
            ance))
21 Angela:  I'M A TAG-ALONG °girl°! ((jerks body in
22          direction of Sarah))
            (0.4)
23 Sarah:   Good girl! eh heh!
24 Angela:  °°I'm gonna get you! ((play fight))
25 Sarah:   heh-heh Oka(hh)y.
26          heh-heh [hmh-hmh-hnh-hnh-hnh!
27 Angela:          [Okay!
```

Other ways in which girls displayed relative social ranking was through intrusions into what Goffman (1971) has described as «territorial preserves». A group of sixth graders regularly invaded the younger (fourth grade) girls' play space during jump rope games and eating space during lunch. In this sequence we can see repetitive attempts by Dionne to place herself in a position of relative superiority. When Dionne initially approaches the girls, she avoids any of the conventional ways of bracketing entry into an interaction, demanding, «Where's Aretha».

Example 4:   Sixth grader invades fourth graders' lunch boxes

```
          ((Dionne approaches a group of five fourth graders
          who are seated eating lunch. She asks where one of
          their group members is.))
 1  Dionne:  Where's Aretha.
 2  Janis:   She's-
 3  Melissa: In the [art room.
 4  Janis:         [At-
 5  Janis:   the art room.
 6  Lisa:    [Why:.
 7  Dionne:  [Don't talk to me Janis.
 8  Dionne:  Can I see what you have in your lunch?
 9           (0.6) ((reaching into Lisa's lunch bag))
10  Lisa:    °Mm hm.°
11  Dionne   Oh my go:sh.
12           [Can I have this? ((taking drink bottle
             from Lisa))
13  Sarah:   [((collusive mouth wrinkle toward Janis))
14  Lisa:    No. ((taking bottle back))
15  Dionne:  You smell.
16  Dionne:  Okay.=What do you have in your lunch.
17           ((looking in Melissa's empty lunch box))
18  Sarah:   Dionne you're such a big bully.
19  Dionne:  Did you see us-
20           that milk commercial last night?
21           (1.5)
22  Dionne:  [Do you watch tv?
23  Sarah:   [((eyes look down))
24           Yes. I do. ((raising eyes)) °But I couldn't
25           leave it on for the milk commercial.°
26  Dionne:  °I'm sorry Sarah.° ((bends puts hands on
             knees))
27  Sarah:   °Hmph.° ((nodding two small nods)) Now go!
28           ((points towards another part of play-
             ground))
29  Sharie:  eh heh      [heh heh!
30  Lisa:                [hnh hnh hnh hnh!
31  Janis:   GO BACK TO YOUR-
             ((palm opens, points to Dionne))
32  Janis:   ((extends arm, points towards where
33           Sarah had previously))
33  Dionne:  SHUT UP [ JANIS.
34  Janis:           [(°over there°.)
35  Dionne:  I don't like talking to you any more.
36  Sarah:   [Eh uhm ((throat clear))
37  Janis:   [(°           °)
```

```
38 Dionne:  After what you said lastertime when y-
39          yesterday-
40          [last week.
41 Sarah:   [EH UHM! ((stands up, facing Dionne,
42          spreading arms out as if a road block))
43 Dionne:  Sarah, ((stands up, extending arms with
            palms up))
44          [eh heh heh heh
45 Sharie:  [eh heh heh!
46 Dionne:  [And nobody here has a good lunch.
            ((hands on hips))
47 Melissa:[((stands up spreading hands imitating
            Sarah's roadblock))
48 Dionne:  And where's Aretha.
```

Dionne attempts to establish her position through (1) trying to take food from girls' lunch boxes, (2) insults («You smell») in line 15, and (3) lines 19-20 making reference to her celebrity status as an actress. («Did you see us- that milk commercial last night?») in order to justify her intrusions.

How do the girls interpret such actions? The girls treat these actions as objectionable in several ways: (1) They speak to her with bald imperatives (lines 27, 31), («Now go!» and «GO BACK TO YOUR-») (2) Sarah addresses Dionne with a negative person descriptor, calling her a «big bully» in line 18. In response to this negative categorization, she alludes to her status as a commercial celebrity (by asking if Sarah had seen her in a milk commercial the night before) positioning herself with reference to something this group treats as a valued sign.

The girls make reference to valued symbols of the materialistic Hollywood world they embrace in their conversations. They frequently position themselves with respect to knowledge about elite activities of the upper middle class. In the midst of the activity of playing house at lunchtime, when fourth grade girls elaborate their job, many choose the role of actress.

Example 5: Girls describe their identity in the game of «house»

```
1 Janis:  My name is Becky.
2         I drive a: a:
3         A purp- a silvery purple Mustang.
4         And I'm sixteen years old,
5         And my job is,
6         I'm a famous actress.
```

Here the construction of identity is an ongoing project, created in the midst of the ongoing talk. In defining their roles the girls describe the types of cars they own by making use of formats supplied by prior speakers to closely tie their talk to the talk of prior speaker. For example, girls use the format «I got a» or «I have a» and fill in a car model and car color.

Example 6: Girls describe their cars in «house»

```
1 Janis:   I have a purple silver Porsche.
2 Ruth:    I have a black Corvette.
```

Here as decisions are being made about ages and cars, the girls define themselves in terms of what luxury items they own in the play realm. Their statements about their cars create a field that makes relevant particular types of next moves. As the girls begin to specify the cars they have, Sarah states that she has a Miata. Immediately Janis counters «No you don't ah ha hah! Heh heh!»

Example 7: Deciding car types during playing «house»

```
 1 Sarah:    Wait. Everybody who's playing come here!
 2           All right. Listen.
 3           These are the two-
 4 Lisa:     I got a Nisan convertible.
 5           No I- I GOT A GREEN MUSTANG!
 6 Janis:    I got a silver Mus-
 7           I got purple- silver Mus-
 8           Purple-    [glitter Mustang.
 9 Sharie:              [I wanna be sixteen?
10 Sarah:    I have a Miata.
11 Janis:    No you don't. ah hah hah! Heh heh!
12 Lisa:     [She has a Miata. ((pointing to Ruth))

           ((several lines omitted))

25 Janis:    I have [a- I have a sparkly- purple-
26 Sarah:           [It's- (.) purple and blue Miata.
27 Janis:    I have a sparkly purple Mus [tang.
28 Ruth:                                 [A Miata?
29 Sarah:    Miata,
30 Janis:    Sparkly purple Mustang.
31 Belicia: [And I have a- And I have a Ghia.
32 Ruth:    [And I have a- I have a- sparkly blue-

33 Gloria: [You guys? This's all I'm sayin.=
33 Ruth:   [You do? That's the stinkiest car.

34          [The Miata. ((tapping Sarah's shoulder))
35 Lisa:    [Oh! I-
36          I have the newest Mustang.
37          It has like a snake in front of it?
```

Sarah elaborates features of her car with «I have- It's purple and blue Miata.» (line 25) Ruth counters with «A Miata?» (line 28) and Sarah responds by repeating «Miata.» (line 29) Ruth, putting her hand on Sarah's shoulder, subsequently

Constructing inequality as situated practice 49

counters Sarah's choice of car with «You <u>do?</u> That's the <u>stink</u>iest car, the Miata.» (lines 33-34).

The girls hold one another accountable for being able to recognize and produce appropriate types of signs. The car one selects is evaluated with respect to a measure of one's cultural competence. Janis and Ruth openly critique and ridicule Sarah's selection of the category Miata: (1) through Janis's opposition («<u>No</u> you don't.» line 11) and laughter and (2) through Ruth's turn prefaced with a partial repeat produced with challenging intonation («A Mi<u>a</u>ta?» line 28 and «You <u>do</u>?» line 33). This type of preface is often used by children in aggravated opposition moves (Goodwin 1983). Ruth's move is followed by a negative assessment: «That's the <u>stink</u>iest car, Mi- the Miata.» (lines 33-34) Here the car that is selected is treated as an inappropriate sign in the language game the children are playing. Through interactive games of this sort girls construct a shared vision of the world. They establish what categories, objects and events in the world are to be considered of value, and display who has access to them. With each turn judgments can be made about someone's taste and ability to make appropriate discriminations. Participants are positioned in the local interaction with respect to meanings in the larger cultural system of value and preparing themselves for their future role as consumers.

Alignment while sanctioning peers

Girls like Janis, who position themselves above others, are not, however, immune from critique. During fifth grade, when excluded from a baseball game by Janis' boyfriend (allowing only Janis and her two best friends to play) Sarah, Aretha, and Angela (the African American working class girl who is generally marginalized in the group) articulated for each other their derogatory opinions about Janis and the material basis she used to define herself. As we will see, although Angela joins gossiping about the absent party who offended her, her participation is in many ways still peripheral to the group.

In Example 8 Aretha states, «Janis thinks she's popular because she stays up to date.» (lines 2-3). The preface «she thinks» displays how the girls read the intentionality or status claims that underlie the use of particular signs (in this case, wearing clothes that are trendy).

Example 8: Critiquing a friend who excluded girls from baseball

```
1 Aretha:  No, you know what?
2          Janis thinks she's popular
3          Because she stays up to date.
4          She likes the Spice Girls,
5          She has Spice Girls everywhere.    *hh
6          She- [wears the most popular clothes-
7 Sarah:        [Look!  You see this shirt?
8          I GOT THIS THREE YEARS AGO.
```

```
 9            I don't really care. ((looking at Angela))
10 Angela:    Neither do I. ((looks down at her shirt))
11            I had this last year. And I don't really
              care about it.
12 Sarah:     BECAUSE I AM NOT TREN DY::::!
              ((taps Aretha's knee))
13            People like me for who I am and not how I
              look.
14            Girlfriend! Gimme some-  ((arm around Are-
              tha))
15            ((assumes glamour girl pose, hand behind
              head))
16            Gimme some sugah.
17            ((drapes arm over Aretha)
18 Aretha:    Gimme some- Gimme some dap!
19            ((Aretha and Sarah do a 3-beat hand clap
              game))
20 Sarah:     Here's the sugar.
21            Here's the su[gar! eh heh-heh!
22 Angela:                 [Woe woe! Woe woe!
              ((A and A clap))
23            Woe- woe-Ow!
24 Aretha:    eh heh heh!!
25 Sarah:     Neh neh!  [ow:::::!((Angela and Sarah clap))
26 Angela:              [Ow:::[:! !
27 Aretha:                    [Eh heh-heh! heh-heh!
```

Girls talk about the mental life of an actor as displayed through their sign use and they provide accounts for the figure's cited belief about status – the types of sign displays that she makes. The following provides a diagram of the reading and challenging of status claims made by Speaker A to her Recipient B as in the following examples from the Hanley School and Maple Street children.

```
A → B:    Janis thinks
                she's popular
                    because she stays up to date
                        She likes the Spice Girls
                        She has Spice Girls everywhere
                        She   wears   the   most   popular
                        clothes-

A → B:    she think
                she so big
                    just because um,
                    Miss Smith let her work in the kitchen
                    for her one time.

A → B:    She think
```

Constructing inequality as situated practice 51

```
                    she cute
A → B:   Janis thinks that
                    she's so popular
                    'Cause she stays up to date.
```

Through the embedded «she think» simultaneously a judgment is made about the character of the person who would make such claims through the use of particular signs – undercutting and problematizing the claim. Through these structures and actions speakers construct actors with a complex mental life construed through their use of signs, and hold them accountable.

By attending to what assessments and activities are located within this frame, peers learn how evaluations of their local environment are to be produced.

Example 9: Continuing the critique of the excluding girl, Janis

```
 1 Angela:  Tell me naturally
 2          [Do you really like Janis?
 3 Aretha:  [Janis does everything that's trendy.
 4          She thinks that she's so popular
 5          ['Cause she stays up to date.
 6 Sarah:   [Look at her pants.
             (2.0)
 7 Sarah:   I don't like being trendy.
 8 Angela:  She's not even matching
 9          To tell [you the truth.
10 Sarah:           [I got this three years ago.
11 Sarah:   Trust [me.
12 Aretha:        [I HATE THOSE PANTS!
             (0.8)
13          THEY'RE UGLY!!
             (0.8)
14 Sarah:   Ooooo! Girlfriend!
15 Aretha:  They are! Look at 'em!
16          They look like some boys' shorts.
17 Angela:  They look-
18 Angela:  Okay.
19          They [look like- Shaka Zulu.
20 Aretha:       [You know how boys wear their shorts?
21          They look like she's trying to be like-
22          She wants to- *h match Sean! ((eyeball
             roll))
             (0.8)
23          So she's wearing some tren[dy-
24 Sarah:   ((chanting))              [Sean has a shirt
             like that!
25          Sean has a shirt like that!
26          ((high fives Aretha)) Girl! Girl! Girl!
             (0.4)
```

```
27            Girl! Girl! (0.3) Girl! eh heh-heh!
28            Gi(hh)rl// friend!
29 Angela:    eyeah:::!Yeah!
```

Aretha begins the critique of Janis (line 3), saying, «Janis does everything that's trendy. She thinks that she's so popular 'cause she stays up to date.»
Sarah aligns with Aretha. She undercuts the idea that wearing trendy clothes is desirable with «Look at her pants» (line 6) and «I don't like being trendy» (line 7) and then adding that her pants are three years old. Aretha takes up the topic of Janis's pants and directs an insult towards Janis (line 12): « I HATE THOSE PANTS! THEY'RE UGLY!»

Aretha's activity of insulting Janis is positively evaluated by Sarah with «Ooooo! Girlfriend!» Expressions such as «Oooooo!» are a form of response cry; they express heightened appreciation for what has just been said. The term «Girlfriend!» demonstrates Sarah's alignment as a close friend with Aretha.

An important way to examine alliance formation is to look at who's attended to and who is ignored. When Angela attempts to enter with a statement that they look like «Shaka Zulu» (line 19), she is ignored. Instead Aretha expands her own commentary on Janis, rather than sequencing to Angela, with «You know how boys wear their shorts?» (line 20). In addition, she provides a commentary on why Janis is wearing the clothes she selects: she aspires to look like her boyfriend: «She wants to- *h match Sean!» ((eyeball roll))

As Sarah provides a next move to Aretha's condemnation of Janis, she states «Sean has a shirt like that!» Next she repeats «Girl!» six times (lines 26-27) and then uses the membership category «Gi(hh)rlfriend!» (line 28) «Girl» functions as a post completion stance marker (Schegloff 1996:90). Both the word «girl», as well as the handclaps that accompany it, display a celebratory stance towards the congruent disapproval of Sean.

Aretha and Sarah display to each other their convergent similar assessment of Janis with a celebratory handclap. Angela, for her part, attempts to join in the handclap reaching over Sarah to attempt to slap Aretha's and Sarah's raised celebratory fists, saying «Yeah» (line 29) rather than «girlfriend», a term indicating friendship.

All of the events are densely layered. The bodies of participants create a framing where other actions can occur. Friendship between Aretha and Sarah is made visible through the orientation of their bodies as well as their talk. While Aretha and Sarah are situated vis-à-vis one another, Angela is positioned behind Sarah. She is the last to join in fist pounding or hand clapping, activities that celebrate a congruent worldview with respect to the kids who have excluded the girls from the game. Moreover, as soon as she reaches over Sarah, both Aretha's and Sarah's arms go down to their laps, as if exiting from any possible reading that Angela is aligned with them. Clearly the use of the body here is critical for displaying stance and alignment. In the midst of negative assessment about an of-

Constructing inequality as situated practice 53

fender, differentiated forms of participation make visible local forms of social organization in the group.

Figure 2: Girls celebrate common view about an excluding girl by fist pounding

Figure 3: Angela is last to join in celebratory fist pounding

Frequently facing formations and bodies as well as the talk of participants to interaction make visible local alignments. Across a range of social encounters, Angela is spatially positioned at the margins of the social group she attempts to affiliate with. While the girls have lunch inside the classroom and all sit around a small table talking animatedly, Angela sits on a table at some distance from the primary group.

Figure 4: Angela sits at some distance from other girls at lunch

In a next example we find negative assessments made not in the absence of the target (as in Example 9), but rather in the presence of the target. Again we will find that multiple participants ratify the particular version of events that is presented. In this example Angela is seated across the table from the other girls. Negative assessments of Angela's behavior provide a particular way the girls treat her as deviant. At lunch Angela's resistance to complying with traditional norms is frequently sanctioned. For example in the midst of having lunch girls comment on the way she eats chocolate pudding without a utensil. They first ask her to leave and eat at another table. Then the girls take up a position vis-à-vis Angela's activity of using her tongue rather than a spoon through an explicit assessment statement, «Oh that's disgusti:::ng!» (line 9). As she continues to eat, not heeding their requests or listening to their assessment they produce loud, extended response cries (lines 12 –14) that are accompanied by nonvocal movements that themselves mark disgust. The girls put their hands to their closed eyes as they rapidly turn their backs on the table so they are no longer facing Angela (line 12-13).

Example 10: Girls turn away from Angela in disgust

```
                Aretha, Janis, Lisa, and Angela are at lunch
 1 Lisa:        If you're gonna have to eat that
 2              Could you go like-
 3              Go to that table? ((pointing to the side))
 4 Angela:      ((turns away from picnic table while eat-
                ing))
 5 Aretha:      Janis? ((lifts up Janis' plastic food
                bag))
 6 Lisa:        Not to be mean
 7              But we don't want to see chocolate with
                carrots.
 8 Janis:       [Now plea::se-
 9 Aretha:      [Oh that's disgusti:::ng! ((closes eyes))
10              She has chocolate pudding on- get-
11 Angela:      ((begins to eat with her tongue))
12 Aretha:      OU::: [::::::: ((Girls turn away in dis-
                gust))
13 Janis:             [OH::::! ((turning away in disgust))
14 Janis:       Oh!=
15 Aretha:      ANGELA!= ((slaps hands to lap))
16 Janis:       Oh my god. ((raises hands to head, lowers
                head with eyes shut))
17 Aretha:      You just-
18 Lisa:        Can  [I-
19 Aretha:           [AH::::::: ((eyes closed))
20 Lisa:        I- I need to go to the room. ((starts to
                walk away))
```

Their bodies as much as their words portray their alignment.

Figure 5: Girls turn away from Angela in disgust

With these examples we saw how through commentary, and in particular, assessments, participants take up a stance or evaluative position with respect to some object and an alignment with respect to a participant. In Example 10, forms of talk and body alignment by the group position the target as someone who has deeply offended the local social order.

Conclusion

In the midst of talk peers police the local social landscape, and make evaluative commentary to one another with respect to what they consider the valued signs in their larger social universe that are linked to social status. Peers hold one another accountable for recognizing the meaning of signs, such as cars that are luxurious, and being able to produce appropriate moves within a language game, such as playing house. Through constructions using mental state verbs, («think she popular») children, as cognitively complex actors, read the intentionality or claims that underlie the use or display of particular signs by an actor and assess the character of the person making such claims.

I have also examined a number of activities in which peers quite openly produce attacks on another's face, through territorial invasions and negative assessments, and exclusion (not being entitled to participate in play activities, or, when participating, being a marginal rather than fully ratified participant – in other words, a tagalong). While the school with its progressive ideals, including a multi–class population as well as a multi ethnic one, was envisioned as an institution where children of diverse social classes could meet to foster mutual understanding, what happens is that interaction leads to an increase in differentiation between children.

In this article I have examined how a group of girls conduct talk-in-interaction as recipients and producers of relations of inequality. My data demonstrate a preference for disagreement rather than a preference for agreement (Sacks 1987 [1973]) and an orientation towards sustaining opposition. The larger patterns of power and domination that constitute the concerns of critical discourse analysis (van Dijk 1993) can be examined in my data; they also constitute the major concerns of participants in the interactions, as is made visible through how participants respond to their invocation. Fieldwork over a three-year period permitted the assemblage of examples demonstrating how micro processes of interaction produce the local social organization that articulates with concerns of the larger society.

While most studies of asymmetries of power have focused analysis on interaction in male or mixed sex groups, in this paper I have examined forms of domination with respect to girls' groups. Forms of ridicule in girls' groups call into question the notion that girls are fundamentally interested in cooperative interaction and a morality based on principles of relatedness, care, equity, and responsibility. While there are strong displays of within-group solidarity, particularly in the midst of gossip, these are coupled with equally strong forms of degradation and attacks upon parties constituted as outsiders.

Appendix Transcription Conventions

Data are transcribed according to a modified version of the system developed by Jefferson and described in Sacks, Schegloff, and Jefferson (1974: 731-733).

Cut offs: A dash (-) marks a sudden cut-off of the current sound.

Underlining: Underlining (___) indicates some form of emphasis.

Overlap Bracket: A left bracket ([) marks the point at which the current talk is overlapped by other talk.

Overlap Slashes: Double slashes (//) provide an alternative method of marking overlap.

Lengthening: Colons (::) indicate that the sound immediately preceding has been noticeably lengthened.

Intonation: Punctuation symbols are used to mark intonation changes rather than as grammatical symbols: A period indicates a falling contour. A question mark indicates a rising contour. A comma indicates a falling-rising contour.

Inbreath: An h preceded by an asterisk (*h) marks an inbreath.

Comments: Double parentheses (( )) enclose material that is not part of the talk being transcribed, frequently indicating gesture or body position.

Silence: Numbers in parentheses (0.6) mark silences in seconds and tenths of seconds.

Increased Volume: Capitals (CAPS) indicate increased volume.

Breathiness, Laughter: An h in parentheses (hhh) indicates plosive aspiration, which could result from breathiness or laughter.

Problematic Hearing: Material in single parentheses indicates a hearing the transcriber was uncertain about.

Italics: Italics are used to distinguish comments in parentheses about nonvocal aspects of the interaction.

References

Adler, Patricia A./Peter Adler, 1998: *Peer power: Preadolescent culture and identity.* New Brunswick et al.: Rutgers University Press.

Baron-Cohen, Simon, 2003: *The essential difference: The truth about the male and female brain.* London: Penguin.

Brown, Lyn M., 2003: *Girlfighting: Betrayal and rejection among girls.* New York: New York University Press.
Crick, Nicki R./Jennifer K. Grotpeter, 1995: Relational aggression, gender, and social-psychological adjustment. In: *Child Development* 66, 710-722.
Goffman, Erving, 1971: *Relations in public: Microstudies of the public order.* New York: Harper and Row.
Goodwin, Marjorie H., 1983: Aggravated correction and disagreement in children's conversations. In: *Journal of Pragmatics* 7, 657-677.
Goodwin, Marjorie H., 1990: *He-Said-She-Said: Talk as social organization among black children.* Bloomington: Indiana University Press.
Goodwin, Marjorie H., 2006: *The hidden life of girls: Games of stance, status, and exclusion.* Oxford: Blackwell.
Grotpeter, Jennifer K./Nicki R. Crick, 1996: Relational aggression, overt aggression and friendship. In: *Child Development* 67, 2328-2338.
Leaper, Campbell, 1994: Exploring the consequences of gender segregation on social relationships. In: *New Directions for Child Development* 65, 67-86.
Maccoby, Eleanor E., 1998: *The two sexes: Growing up apart, coming together.* Cambridge et al.: Harvard University Press.
Sacks, Harvey, 1987 [1973]: On the preferences for agreement and contiguity in sequences in 'conversation. In: Graham Button/John Lee (eds.), *Talk and social organisation.* Clevedon: Multilingual Matters: 54-69.
Sacks, Harvey/Emanuel A. Schegloff/Gail Jefferson, 1974: A simplest systematics for the organization of turn-taking for conversation. In: *Language* 50, 696-735.
Underwood, Marion K., 2003: *Social aggression in girls.* New York: Guilford Press.
van Dijk, Teun A., 1993: Principles of critical discourse analysis. In: *Discourse and Society* 4, 2, 249-283.

Antonia L. Krümmheuer

Conversation analysis, video recordings, and human-computer interchanges

Introduction[1]

This paper will show how conversation analysis (in the following abbreviated as CA) can be adopted for the interpretation of video recordings of human-computer interchanges. CA is often misunderstood to focus on spoken conversation only. However, CA has sociological origins: through the analysis of social events as they occur, CA aims to understand how social order and mutual intelligibility are accomplished, including verbal and nonverbal aspects. Traditionally CA is used to understand human interaction. In this paper CA is adopted to analyze human-computer interchanges. Thereby, human beings and computers are not put together on one level. On the contrary, the analysis aims to localize the specific character of human-computer interchanges in contrast to human interactions. Therefore, an excerpt of a human-computer interchange (a teasing sequence) will be analyzed by conversation analytical means. The focus will be on the verbal and nonverbal interplay during its sequential development and its comparison to human interaction.

The analysis is based on a research project which questions whether the sociological term interaction can be used to describe human-computer interchanges. As the term interaction is scrutinized, the paper refers to human-computer interchanges and not – as traditionally done – to human-computer interaction. Looking at the «interactive» capacities of artifacts, this study contributes to a sociological and philosophical discourse in which the question of technical agency is debated controversially (Collins/Kusch 1998; Dreyfus 1979; Latour 1988, 2005; Pickering 1995; Rammert/Schulz-Schaeffer 2002b; Searle 1990; Weizenbaum 1976). In contrast to an ontological view, in which the scientist determines whether an artifact can act or not, the ethnomethodological and conversation analytical view analyzes if and how the *participants* distinguish between whether their co-partner is a human or a technical artifact (such as a computer) (Hutchby 2001; Suchman 1987, 2007; Wooffitt et al. 1997). To gain a better understanding of the «interactive» character of human-computer interchanges, video recordings were made at an event where computer scientists pre-

---

[1] I am indebted to Christian Greiffenhagen, Stephan Windmann, Claudia Küttel and Ulrike Tikvah Kissmann for commenting on prior versions of this paper. I also want to thank Karen Meehan for proof-reading the text and Christian Becker-Asano, Stefan Kopp, Marc Latoschik, Matthias Rehm and Ipke Wachsmuth for their patient explanations of the inner workings of agent systems.

sented an embodied conversational agent. This virtual agent is a personified software program which is supposed to be able to «interact» in a human-like fashion, and visitors at the event were able to «talk» with it (Cassell et al. 2000; Kopp et al. 2003).[2]

To exemplify how these recordings can be analyzed by conversation analytical means, firstly, the conversation analytical view on interaction as well as the methodological background will be introduced. Secondly, the theoretical and empirical background of the research will be described. The main part of this paper will be concerned with the analysis of a brief extract from a human-agent interchange in which a human user teases a virtual agent. The teasing sequence will be compared to human teasing sequences. The analysis will emphasize differences in the sequential organization of the interchange, focusing on the so called «next-turn proof procedure» (Hutchby/Wooffitt 1998: 15, in detail Sacks et al. 1974: 728-279). Thereby the audiovisual analysis will point out the specific hybrid character of the interchanges, which is based on an asymmetric participation framework and an asynchronous and determined turn-taking organization.

Conversation analysis

Traditional studies on human-computer «interaction» (HCI) are mainly concerned with the usability and design of computer based tools and software programs (Helander et al. 1997). They focus on the user's cognitive capacities and how these affect the use of computer programs. The concept of interaction is based on a cognitive and psychological model of interaction, the *planning model* (described and criticized by Hutchby 2001; Suchman 1987, 2007; Wooffitt et al. 1997). Within this model, interaction is conceptualized as the interchange of actions between two individuals. The actions derive from the mental plan of an individual who aims at achieving a certain goal. In order to execute the plan he will carry out certain actions. The other party to the interaction determines the meaning of these actions by inferring from them the actor's plans and thus discovering the actor's goals. The empirical studies, like usability-tests, are based on the quantitative evaluation of laboratory-framed experiments that test special variables of the human-computer interchange, such as the acceptance or the speed of task solving (Rubin 1994). While the cognitive model focuses on the

---

[2] From a sociological view the description and analysis of human-computer interchanges is based on a dilemma. On the one hand, activities of a software program need to be described that simulates conversational «behavior», which the engineers (and often even the artifact itself) refer to as «interactive», «emotional», «intelligent», etc. On the other hand, adopting this terminology would be inadequate as sociological and IT terms are based on different theoretical assumptions. As the agent is supposed to simulate human-like behavior, in the following, the descriptions of the interchange between human and system will go along with this conception and treat the agent as if it were an actor. The analysis, in contrast, will focus on the technical origin of the agent.

mental processes of interacting individuals, CA explores the observable interactive processes through which participants coordinate their actions. Sense-making is thereby not seen as an isolated cognitive process but as a mutual and situated accomplishment of the interaction partners.

Talk-in-interaction

CA was founded as a field of study in the 1960s by Harvey Sacks and Emanuel Schegloff (Sacks et al. 1974; Schegloff 1972; Schegloff/Sacks 1973; see also Sacks 1992).[3] The term *conversation* analysis is misleading. CA is not interested in a linguistic understanding of talk only, but has a sociological footing (Heritage 1984), which is mainly based on phenomenologically oriented work (for example by Alfred Schütz), the ethnomethodological concepts of Harold Garfinkel, and Goffman's studies on interaction. CA is concerned with the question of how social order is established. Despite other sociological traditions (such as Parsons' structural functionalistic concepts), CA asks how people accomplish social order and mutual understanding through their actual actions, and aims to describe the member's practices «in doing social life» (Sacks 1984: 21). Therefore, audio or video recordings of actual and naturally occurring interactions are analyzed (Sacks et al. 1974; Schegloff/Sacks 1973).

The analysis of those recordings revealed that the organization of talk (and social action) is not only orderly, but that this orderliness is a mutual accomplishment of the participants themselves who display an orientation to this orderliness. As Schegloff and Sacks (1973: 290) point out:

«If the materials (records of natural conversations) were orderly, they were so because they had been methodically produced by members of the society for one another, and it was a feature of the conversations that we treated as data that they were produced so as to allow the display by the coparticipants to each other of their orderliness, and to allow the participants to display to each other their analysis, appreciation, and use of that orderliness.»

Thus orderliness is not seen as a fixed and/or mental structure participants orient to, but as an interactive achievement of the participants in the situation which can be observed by the participants and by others (e.g. scientists).

According to ethnomethodological assumptions, CA is based on an indexical and reflexive understanding of actions and meaning. The meaning of an action (or an object in action) is indexical, that is, the understanding of it can vary according to the situation in which it occurs. Furthermore, the meaning has

---

[3] For introductory literature see Atkinson/Heritage 1984; Bergmann 2000; ten Have 1990, 1999; Heritage 1984, Hutchby/Wooffitt 1998; Psathas 1995; especially for video-based research see Heath 1997; Jordan/Henderson 1995).

a reflexive character, that is, the comprehension of an action is shaped by the actual situation, and at the same time the understanding of the actual situation is shaped by this and prior actions (for a detailed interpretation of those terms see Lynch 1993). Thus, an action is always «context-shaped» and «context-renewing» (Heritage 1984: 242).

While participants accomplish their activities, they make those activities «accountable» (Garfinkel 1967: vii). This means that participants provide a kind of explanation for what they are doing in the way they accomplish their actions. They render their actions «visibly-rational-and-reportable-for-all-practical-purposes» (Garfinkel 1967: vii). Although participants give accounts of their actions, the meaning of an action is based on a «specific vagueness» (Garfinkel 1972: 6) which is necessarily unsolved. The production and interpretation of actions is shaped by common-sense knowledge and background expectancies.[4] As participants do not (and often cannot) explicate all the information which underlines their actions, they assume a shared understanding, unless problems occur.

To describe the members' methods of doing social life, CA focuses on the mutual and observable actions and their interpretations which are produced by members during the course of interaction. Therefore, the sequential organization of talk-in-interaction is analyzed. The early studies showed that the social organization of talk is based on a «turn-by-turn basis» (Sacks et al. 1974: 725). Conversational turn-taking systems consist of single turns and a rule-set for the allocation of those turns (Sacks et al. 1974: 702-706).[5] The construction of a turn as well as turn-taking is seen as an interactive phenomenon. Every turn which does not open or end a conversation is sequentially embedded in a series of others. Participants regularly orient the production of their turn to its sequential relation to a former and later turn: They address its relation to a prior turn, make a contribution and show an orientation to the next turn («three-part structure», Sacks et al. 1974: 722). As every next turn displays the second speaker's interpretation of the prior turn, the first speaker can receive proof of how his turn is understood by the other («next-turn proof procedure», Hutchby/Wooffitt 1998: 15; in detail Sacks et al. 1974: 728-279). The first speaker can accept the second speaker's interpretation and continue the conversation or initiate a repair.[6] Thus, sense-making is seen as an interactive and observable accomplishment which is continuously open to changes. Thereby, the meaning of an utterance is not decided by the scientist, but mutually constructed by the participants

---

[4] This knowledge is embedded in the actions of the actors. However, it is mostly unspoken. Garfinkel (1972: 6) calls them the «seen but unnoticed features of common discourse».

[5] A turn is constructed by one or more unit-types (such as sentential, clausal, phrasal, and lexical constructions). Unit-types project a possible completion of a turn and thus a «transition relevant place» where a turn-taking can happen (Sacks et al. 1974: 702-703). Goodwin (1981) shows that even the production of a turn is interactively coordinated as speakers orient their talk according to the behavior (such as the gaze or bodily orientation) of the other.

[6] Repair and repair initiation are described in (Schegloff et al. 1977; Schegloff 1992).

themselves. However, the scientist can use the sequential character of talk for the analysis.[7]

The first studies in CA were based on audio recordings and thus the analysis was focused on talk only. The technological development of handheld cameras (and nowadays camcorders) opened the way to audiovisual recordings as well. Researchers such as Goodwin (1981) and Heath (1986) started to work with video data, and their studies emphasize the interplay of gaze and bodily direction in the production of talk. The analysis of video recordings opened new areas of research. While the first studies analyzed mundane and institutional interaction, in recent decades especially workplace studies focused on the interactive interplay of institutional action and technical and/or virtual artifacts (Heath/Luff 2000; Luff et al. 2000). Within this field of study CA was also adopted to analyze human-computer interchanges, computer supported cooperative work and the design of computer based artifacts (Luff et al. 1990; Suchman 1987, 2007; Wooffitt et al. 1997).[8]

Collecting and analyzing audiovisual data

CA is based on the ethnomethodological premise of the «unique adequacy requirement of methods» (Garfinkel/Wieder 1992: 182), that means data collection and analysis as well as other methodological issues should be «adequate for the materials at hand and for the problems one is dealing with» (ten Have 1990: 24). Thus, the literature on CA provides no step-by-step instructions on how to analyze the data. This does not mean that the researcher can feel free to do anything he likes. There are some principles CA is oriented to, which are outlined in the following:[9]

1. Data analysis is based upon recordings of naturally occurring data. Thus, the analysis is not based on experimental settings, interviews, protocols or imagined interactions. Audio(visual) recordings enable a detailed analysis of single episodes of an interaction to be reviewed, paused or played in slow motion. The decision whether to use audio or video recordings depends upon the field to be recorded as well as the scientist's research interest (it is useless to analyze audio recordings to get a better understanding of spatial interactions). As audiovisual data seem to record the situation as it happens, the researcher

---

[7] As Sacks et al. (1974: 729) point out, «But while understandings of other turns' talk are displayed to co-participants, they are available as well to professional analysts, who are thereby afforded a proof criterion (and a search procedure) for the analysis of what a turn's talk is occupied with. Since it is the parties' understandings of prior turns' talk that is relevant for their construction of next turns, it is *their* understandings that are wanted for analysis. The display of those understandings in the talk of subsequent turns affords both a resource for the analysis of prior turns and a proof procedure for professional analyses of prior turns – resources intrinsic to the data themselves».
[8] For a critical view on this development see Button 1990 and Button/Sharrock 1995.
[9] For introductory literature see footnote 3.

should consider that even the «objective» view of a camera has a certain perspective toward the situation and that it generates a special kind of data.[10] Questions of when, where, what and who should be recorded require careful consideration. In order to ensure the quality of the data the researcher should also be acquainted with the technology.

2. The recorded interactions are transcribed.[11] Transcripts are written documents of the sequential course of interaction. They «freeze» the interaction and enable a detailed analysis of the development of action and interaction over time. Special attention is given to the realization of verbal and nonverbal action, i.e. how a word is pronounced or stressed, overlaps in talk, gaze, gestures and bodily direction.[12] The analysis of interaction is always based on transcriptions in conjuncture with the recordings.

Transcribing interaction always means making a choice: on the one hand, the transcription of data should be oriented to Sack's (1984: 22) maxim «that there is order at all points», thus, every detail of interaction should be transcribed. On the other hand, the transcript should be readable and thus not all aspects can be included. As transcripts are reductions, they are not seen as substitutes for the recordings, but as their «representations» (Hutchby/Wooffitt 1998: 74). Depending on the amount of data, time limitation and the precision of transcripts the recording can be transcribed as a whole or in selected parts.[13]

The transcription of data fulfills two purposes. Firstly, transcripts are part of the analysis and thus should be done by the analyst in person. The *process* of transcribing helps the researcher to become familiar with the data and its inher-

---

[10] A researcher can for example explore the field with a handheld camera and focus on certain aspects of a situation or the camera can be installed at a certain point of a room and focus on the whole setting. Furthermore, the view onto the situation will be technologically shaped, as for example, the camera angle determines what can be seen and what cannot, smell and heat cannot be recorded, a fixed camera cannot move to look behind a blocking body, and a defect during the recording can go along unnoticed, producing useless material (see also Jordan/Henderson 1995: 53-56; for a discussion of the influence of the recording equipment on the ongoing interaction see Krummheuer 2005; Lomax/Casey 1998).

[11] As recordings provide data of singular events which cannot be repeated, a prior step should be to create security copies of each record. If possible they should be digitalized to allow them to be played on the computer or to include them in presentations or articles. It is also helpful to write a content log of the recordings, including time, place, persons and activities. The content log is useful to get an overview of the recorded data and helps to locate certain activities or situations (see also Jordan/Henderson 1995: 43).

[12] There are different conventions for transcribing interaction. These variations can be explained, as the conventions are adapted to the special research problems one is dealing with as well as the particularities of the data themselves (for example audio recordings of face-to-face conversations or video recordings of mediated interactions). English transcripts are mostly based on a system developed by Gail Jefferson (described for example in Hutchby/Wooffitt 1998: vi-vii, 73-92, for German transcripts see Selting et al. 1998).

[13] Transcribing is also very time-consuming. Depending on the precision of the transcript and the type of recording (audio or video) it can take as much as five hours to transcribe (and «proof-listen») one minute of interaction.

ent structures. He can investigate the data and thereby develop the analysis. Secondly, the *product* of the transcription can be shared with other researchers – who can consequently disagree with the researcher's analysis.

3. The analysis is based upon the sequential development of situated activities. Actions (for example utterances, gestures, bodily movements) and the interaction they emerge from are points of departure for the analysis. The selection of episodes to be analyzed can vary. One can focus, for example, on certain sections of talk, such as, the opening and closing, the structures and segmentation of a certain event, the organization of repairs, the bodily and visual orientation of participants, the interplay of activities and artifacts, etc. (ten Have 1990; Jordan/Henderson 1995: 56-79).

The analysis can be done by single case analysis or collection studies. In the latter one searches for recurrent interactive structures, compares them and analyzes how the participants treat those structures as relevant and orderly themselves. Thus, the researcher always looks for order and then tries to account for that order on the basis of the participant's actions and interpretations (in detail see Sacks 1992: 291-302).

Special attention is also given to deviant cases. Those cases can be very useful as they show that the usual accomplishment of orderliness is based upon background expectancies which are seen to be mutually shared. Breakdowns in routine show some of those background expectancies which are taken for granted (see for example Schegloff 1972: 355-359). Furthermore, if the actors treat the interactions as deviant, they reveal an orientation to those background expectancies themselves.

Background: research project, field, and data

Embodied conversational agents are personified and interactive software programs with artificial intelligence (Cassell et al. 2000). Like text-based dialog systems (for example online formulas for booking), they can analyze textual (sometimes even verbal) input and generate a specific reaction (output) to it. Furthermore, embodied conversational agents engage in a conversation with their virtual bodies. Thus, talk can be realized by facial expressions, gestures, gaze or bodily orientations. Embodied conversational agents are still under development, but ultimately, they should be capable of communicating with (human) users in a human-like manner with the aim of simplifying the use of computer-based technology.

While computer scientists call the human-agent interchange an «interaction», the sociological term interaction is bound to human beings only. Thus, the question arises, how the interchange between embodied conversational agent and human actor can be sociologically conceptualized. In recent decades a broad discussion about technological agency has arisen within the field of science and technology studies (Bijker/Law 1992; Rammert/Schulz-Schaeffer 2002a). Within this discussion the ontological separation of human and nonhumans is questioned. Some argue that there is no difference between human and nonhuman agency (Latour 1988, 2005), others differentiate between kinds of agency (Collins/Kusch 1998). Within this discussion Rammert and Schulz-Schaeffer (2002b) propose a change of perspectives. Instead of leaving it to the scientist to determine whether a technology can act or not, they propose to observe the interpretations of the participants dealing with those technologies. This perspective is similar to the conversation analytical approach to interaction which focuses on the member's practices and interpretations. When applying this perspective to the analysis of human-agent interchanges the question is not «Can the agent interact?» but «Do human and agent treat the interchange as an interaction, and do they treat each other as interacting partners?». To answer these questions, several interchanges between human users and the embodied conversational agent, Max, were video recorded and analyzed by conversation analytical means.

The embodied conversational agent Max

The embodied conversational agent, Max, was developed by the «Artificial Intelligence Group» led by Prof. Dr. Ipke Wachsmuth at the Faculty of Technology at Bielefeld University.[14] In the version I recorded, Max «works» as a presenter (Kopp et al. 2005). He can provide information about himself, the working group which built him, and the event he was presented at. As well as presenting, Max can also play a game and engage in small talk.

Figure 1: Video recording at «Campus:City!» (credit: Ipke Wachsmuth).

---

[14] For further information see http://www.techfak.uni-bielefeld.de/~skopp/max.html.

Max is a human-sized agent which can be seen on a huge screen (see fig. 1). His actions are generated by a software program «behind» the figure. Although it appears that Max is looking directly at the user, he cannot really see him. He can only adjust his eyes to fix upon a point which the system hopefully has identified as the user's location. In order to communicate with Max, users send messages to the agent by typing text on a keyboard in front of the screen. The actual production of the text can be seen in the white space at the bottom of the screen. After they press Enter, the text is sent to Max and can be seen in the grey space above the other space. Max's dialogue system then searches the user's text for key symbols and grammatical phrases – special words or a question mark, for example. Based on its findings, the dialog system assigns a *single functional* purpose to the message and selects – according to special rules – a preprogrammed utterance combined with a bodily reaction (movement of lips, facial expression, gestures, etc.). Thus, the agent always reacts after a message is entered and every message is bound to a communicative function and treated as complete and intelligible (Gesellensetter 2004; Kopp et al. 2003, 2005).

Data collection

The interchanges between the users and Max were videotaped at an event called «Campus:City!» in February 2004. At this event, scientists from Bielefeld University presented their projects to the public in various streets and shopping malls in the town-center. The event meant that the campus moved into the everyday life of the city and it offered people the opportunity to gain an insight into scientific research. The agent's technological equipment was set up on the ground floor of a shopping center in front of the electronics department (fig. 1). People were able to volunteer to «talk» to Max or observe others «communicating» with Max.

The interchanges were videotaped using two cameras. One recorded the screen, the other the situation in front of the screen (user and audience). The event lasted seven hours and over 50 interchanges with Max were recorded. Out of this data 29 interchanges between adults and Max were analyzed. Interchanges of children with Max as well as interchanges between Max and the computer scientists who developed the agent were left out.

To get a better understanding of how CA can be adopted to the analysis of video data on human-agent interchanges, one of those interchanges will be analyzed in the following. The example shows how the user Rosemary (like many other users) teases the embodied conversational agent Max. The analysis investigates the interplay of verbal and nonverbal phenomena, focusing on the sequential organization and the participation framework of the situation. By comparing the teasing sequence of Rosemary and Max with findings from teasing sequences in human interactions, the specific character of the human-agent interchange will be elaborated.

Analyzing a sequence: an example

Rosemary has already been talking to Max for a while. The agent has just offered to explain something about Artificial Intelligence (AI) to her. Rosemary accepted the offer, and Max gave her some information about AI in general. In his presentation, the agent claims to be an example of AI himself. As the presentation comes to an end, Rosemary looks at the keyboard (fig. 2) and asks Max who coded his program:[15]

Transcript part 1[16]

```
Max ends his presentation and Rosemary looks at the keyboard
and types her text, which she sends to the program (fig. 2):

1.  txR   w h o ~ c o d e d ~ y o u r ~ p r o g r a m /
2.  TX    *who coded your program*
3.  R     ((looks at Max))
4.  M     <<tilts his head sideways, starts scratching
5.        his head, simultaneously jerks his right arm briefly>

6.  M     nobody> ((looks down)) knows that [exactly.
7.  R                                       [((raises her
8.                                            eyebrows, smiles))

9.  R     ha ha ha:: ((takes a breath while laughing)) (fig. 3)
10. R     <<quietly> hehehe> ((looks at Max, smiles broadly))

11. M     [((puts his arm down, looks straight ahead))
12. R     [((looks at KB))
13. P     [((looks at Rosemary and smiles))

14. txR   [a r e ~ y o u ~ s t u p i d [/
15. R     [((looks at KB with a smile  [looks at TX))

16. TX    *are you stupid*
17. R     ((licks her lips, tips her head back with a slight
18.       bouncing movement, looks at Max))

19. R     [((sways gently))
20. M     [((moves his hands up to his shoulders with his
21.          palms facing forward)) (fig. 4)

22. M     I H'OPe ((puts his hands down)) you don't mean THAT
23.       seriously
24. txR   [w h y ~ n o t                           [/
25. R     [((looks at KB, types with a smile;  [looks at TX, then
26.          at Max))
```

---

[15] See appendix 1 for notation conventions.
[16] See appendix 2 for the German original.

```
27. TX    *why not*

28. M     [<<moves one hand briefly in front of his body>
29. R     [((smiles, sways slightly from side to side))

30. M     why do you have to PROBE my>
31.       ONE vulnerable SPOT.
32. R     ((laughs, nods her head, puts her tongue between her
33.       lips, looks at KB, smiles, moves her fingers over KB,
34.       stops smiling))
```

Figure 2

Figure 3

Figure 4

After Max claims to be an example of AI, Rosemary asks him who coded his program (l. 1-2). The message is formulated as a first part of the «adjacency pair» (Schegloff 1972; Schegloff/Sacks 1973: 295)[17] question-answer and thus establishes the expectation of an answer. Max starts scratching his head and states that «nobody knows that exactly» (l. 6). The utterance treats Rosemary's former message as a question: it refers to a piece of information Rosemary asked for and thus delivers the second part of the adjacency pair. While Max is speaking, Rosemary raises her eyebrows, starts laughing and then writes «are you stupid» (l. 7-16). Her reaction treats Max's answer as unexpected and deviant. Her interpretation is also shared by the audience: a man next to Rosemary smiles and looks at her (l. 13). He seems to share her interpretation. Her message itself is a provocation which relates Max's prior statement of being an example of AI to being stupid. Rosemary's reaction to Max's utterance shows that she seems to treat his response as evidence of the fact that the system did not «understand» her question («who coded your program», l. 2). Although the system treated Rosemary's first message as a question, Rosemary treats Max's utterance as an inadequate answer.

Thereupon Max raises his hands in defense and rebuts her accusation, hoping that she does not mean it seriously (l. 20-23). Thus, the agent aligns to Rosemary's attack, and reaffirms the provocation. But, similar to his prior statement the agent seems to be *context-blind* as he does not react to the playful

---

[17] Adjacency pairs are two follow-up utterances produced by different speakers, such as greetings or question-answer sequences. The first and second parts of the sequence are normatively organized. After the first part is produced the production of the second part is «conditionally relevant» (Schegloff 1972: 364), that is, the production of a second part is not obligatory, but its absence will be noticed. Thus, the first part implicates the next turn, but does not determine it. Thereby, an utterance 'in itself' cannot be identified e.g. as a question. It is the production of the second part that makes a prior utterance into a first part: By answering the prior turn, the prior turn becomes a question.

framing of her accusation. This can be explained by the system's inability to «see» Rosemary's nonverbal activities. Despite Max's rejection, Rosemary continues teasing Max by asking a seemingly innocent question with a smile, «why not» (l. 24-27). Max again tries to evade the attack (l. 28-31).

The example above reveals similarities to a certain form of human talk: teasing. This communicative form is described and analyzed in various scientific studies (for example Drew 1987; Günthner 1996, 1999). Günthner (1996, 1999) describes teasing – in German «frotzeln» – as a playful provocation. Teasing is regularly based by the participants upon a certain participation framework[18] and a teasing sequence which is bound to certain situated and interactive roles of the participants. The participation framework of teasing is created by the interactive roles of a teaser or attacker («teasing subject»/«Frotzelsubjekt») and the recipient of the teasing («teasing object»/«Frotzelobjekt») (Günthner 1996: 83). Often, this attack is launched in front of an audience, which influences the performance of the attacker and the attacked and which can also be actively involved in the teasing sequence.

The communicative structure of the teasing sequence evolves in three steps (Günther 1996: 83-84; see also Drew 1987: 232-243):
1. The object's prior action
2. The teasing attack launched by the attacker
3. The object's reaction to the attack.

The teasing attack is always aligned to another person's prior action. Thereby the utterance attributes a known aspect of the person's identity and combines it with a deviant character (Drew 1987: 243-247; Günthner 1999: 310). Thus, the person is constructed as a teasing object. The teasing attack has a dual character. On the one hand, it implies provocation or criticism. On the other hand, this provocation is mitigated by playful or humorous elements. This playful framing can be displayed, for example, by intonation, nonverbal activities, laughter or exaggerated formulations (Drew 1987: 219; Günthner 1996: 84-92).

The attacked person usually reacts upon the dual character of the teasing attack. He denies or corrects the deviant attributions and shows an orientation towards the playful framing of the criticism, for example by talking in a laughing voice which indicates that the object has recognized the playful character of the attack (Drew 1987: 221-230; Günthner 1996: 92-94). Thus, he confirms the teasing character of the first utterance and recreates himself as teasing object,

---

[18] The term «participation framework» was developed by Goffman (1981) in his work on «footing» and adopted to conversation analysis by different scholars (Goodwin 1981, Goodwin 1990). The term footing emphasizes that participants align to their actions and those of others in different ways (Goffman 1981: 128). The relation of one participant to a certain action is called «participation status» (Goffman 1981: 137), for example being a «ratified participant» of an interaction or a «bystander». The alignment of all participants of a situation at a certain moment can be described by the «participation framework» (Goffman 1981: 137). These terms are based on a dynamic understanding of those relations, thus the participation status of a person can change during the course of interaction.

which has been attacked. Of course the attacked object can only react to one aspect of the dual attack. It can play along with the teasing or just defend itself. But, Günthner (1996: 93) points out that a person who does not respond to the humorous character of the tease risks being portrayed as a bad sport.

Similar to the structures described in human interaction, Rosemary classifies Max's answer as deviant and combines this deviant behavior with his identity. Akin to teasing in human interaction, the provocation is mitigated. This can be observed in the shift of context. While Rosemary writes her first utterance («who coded your program» l. 1-2) in a serious manner, she then laughs and types with a smile on her face (fig. 2-4). The playful framing of her utterance can also be seen in her body movements. She licks her lips, leans back and sways while smiling (l. 15-19). Rosemary is playfully challenging the agent and awaits his answer. But in contrast to human face-to-face interaction, the mitigation is one-sided: Max cannot recognize the user's facial expressions and Rosemary does not translate her mitigating reactions into text – she could have typed a smiley, for example. Although Max does not «orient» to the playful framing of the teasing, his reaction can be interpreted as a «po-faced receipt of teasing» (Drew 1987), a typical behavior in the light of a teasing attack.[19] But this performance has a specific hybrid character which distinguishes the interchange from human teasing sequences.

The participation framework of a hybrid interchange

The participation framework of the example above features different participating parties: firstly, Max and Rosemary, who are involved in a mutual interchange; secondly, several persons standing in the background who are observing the interchange and who are thus presenting themselves as an audience; thirdly, persons who are involved in other conversations or bystanders who can see and hear the interchange but show – unlike the audience – no special interest in the hybrid interchange between Rosemary and Max (see fig. 2-4).

A specific feature of the participation framework of this situation is based on the *hybrid* character of the interchange: on the one hand, the design of the agent simulates a face-to-face interaction. Max can be seen on the screen facing the user and talking to him. The user is also facing the agent. Thus, Max and the user show a bodily orientation towards each other. On the other hand, the participants occupy two worlds. Thus, the user and Max are engaged in a mutual interchange. However, they are situated in different places. Similar to other mediated communication such as a telephone conversation «there are two «theres» there» (Schegloff 2002: 287). Unlike human telephone conversations, the interchange is firstly accomplished by two different entities (human and software

---

[19] Similarly Bergmann (1988: 309) observes that pets are often teased. He argues that the ignorance of the pet towards the teasing attack can be nicely interpreted as a po-faced receipt and thus as a human-like behavior towards teasing.

program) and secondly, these entities exist in different worlds (the virtual world of the agent and the socio-material world of the user). The user enters the virtual world of the agent through text-messages written on the screen and sent to the agent. The agent enters the world of the user as a bodily representation of an actor on the screen and his utterances are amplified by speakers. Thus, the system recognizes the user as text and analyzes it based on preprogrammed rules. The user can hear and see the agent and analyze the interchange according to its situated development and his background knowledge. Similar to Suchman's (1987: 119) findings on human-machine interchanges we can distinguish not only two different «theres», but beyond this, two different situations: the «situation of the machine» and the «situation of the user».

Due to the different situations the user and the agent do not share a common understanding of the actual participation framework. While the system is based upon the assumption of a dialog with an isolated user, the user is socially situated in a room with other persons. The data show that users often demonstrate a split-orientation to Max and the audience. The users often accomplish their nonverbal actions in a slightly exaggerated manner.[20] Rosemary for example frames her message to Max with nonverbal behavior. She licks her lips, leans backwards and sways a little (l. 15-19). Thus, she frames her action towards the audience as non-serious, while the agent cannot recognize this nonverbal framing.[21]

The hybrid character of the turn-taking system

The hybrid character of the interchange can also be seen in the organization of turns and turn-taking. In the example above, Rosemary and Max are engaged in a recurring exchange of turns. In contrast to human face-to-face interaction the interchange evolves at a low speed, as Rosemary has to type her text and Max's speech-synthesis is relatively slow. The central feature of the hybrid interchange is its asynchronous and determined character. The interchange is *asynchronous* as the user and the agent produce their own, and interpret each other's actions without the other. The agent is excluded from the user's text production and analyzes the user's input and generates a preprogrammed output. The user cannot interfere in the production of the agent's utterance and interprets the finished utterance of the agent without the agent (sometimes together with the audience). In contrast to human interaction the production of turns and turn-taking is therefore not a synchronous production and interpretation by the conversation partners.

---

[20] With these nonverbal actions the users frequently distance themselves from their «interactive» role of a person who seriously speaks with an agent, and they frame the interchange with the agent as not serious. (The term «role distance» was developed by Goffman (1972)).

[21] It cannot be said whether Rosemary knows that Max cannot recognize her nonverbal behavior. But whether or not this is the case, the slightly exaggerated accomplishment of her nonverbal behavior shows her orientation to the audience as well.

Furthermore, the system *determines* the turn-taking and the meaning of its own actions and those of the user and cannot negotiate the meaning together with the user. In the example above Max and Rosemary share a different understanding of the situation. While Max rejects an accusation, Rosemary teases him in a playful manner. Thereby both participants do not seem to cooperate with the situated interpretations of the other: Max does not understand the playful framing of Rosemary's provocation (l. 20-23) and Rosemary continues to tease Max (l. 24-27 «why not»). Thus, in contrast to human interaction, the meanings of the user's and the agent's actions are not confirmed in every next turn and thus not mutually negotiated. This can also be seen in the further development of the teasing sequence in the following excerpt:

Transcript part 2

```
35. txR    d o n ' t ~ b e ~ s i o -o- -i- o ~ h u
36.        f f y /
37. R      ((looks at TX))
38. TX     *don't be so huffy*
39. R      ((looks at Max, leans slightly forward))

40. M      wha:t do you mean by [tha:t?
41. R                           [((looks at KB))

42. txR    y o u ~ a r e ~
43. R      ((bites briefly her lips, looks up))
44.        e:::hm:::  (fig:5)
```

Figure 5

```
45. R      ((looks at KB))

46. txR    v e r y ~ s e n s i t i v [e /
47. R                                [(((looks at TX then to Max))
```

```
48. TX    *you are very sensitive*
49. M     interESting viewpoi[nt ros'MARY-
50. R                   [<<laughing> phk'ou>
```

After a pause Rosemary asks Max to tell her something, he offers several suggestions.

After Max rejects her teasing message again (see transcript part 1), Rosemary tells him not to be huffy (l. 35-38). Max asks her what she means by that (l. 40). Rosemary rewrites her first message (l. 42-48). Thus, she treats Max's utterance as a repair initiation and tries to solve the source of trouble.[22] But, the agent treats Rosemary's new message as an interesting piece of information (l. 49). Rosemary appears to be astonished (l. 50). Again, she treats Max's utterance as evidence that Max did not understand her prior message and shortly afterwards initiates a change of topic. Thus, not only does the repair fail, but also the teasing sequence fades away, too, because Rosemary cannot base her actions on a shared understanding of the situation. The system, on the other hand, is not «aware» of a problem at all.

The ambiguous character of the hybrid interchange

Teasing is a means of criticizing a person whilst saving her face. Günthner (1999: 320) emphasizes that in her data, teasing only occurred between people who shared a long-standing and intimate relationship. She argues that on the one hand this relationship enables the subject to attribute the action to the identity of the other, on the other hand teasing reconstructs and strengthens the intimate relationship in two ways. Firstly, by teasing the object, the subject refers to some shared knowledge about the object and thus recreates and strengthens the intimate relationship. Secondly, by framing the provocation in a playful manner, the subject shows an orientation to saving the face of the other. The subject demonstrates that it cares for the other and therefore creates and recreates an intimate relationship (Günthner 1996: 99-100, 1999: 319-320).

The example of Max and Rosemary shows that Rosemary adapts communicative resources known from human interaction to the human-agent interchange. But when comparing them to human interaction we can observe an *ambiguous and hybrid character of this interchange*. On the one hand, Rosemary attributes social aspects to Max. She engages in an interchange with the system. And this interchange shows similarities to the turn-taking system which can be observed in human interactions. Teasing Max demonstrates the assumption that Max is someone or something that cannot only communicate but someone who can be teased as well. Mapping deviant action onto Max's identity means that he is treated as something with some form of identity. Although Rosemary pro-

---

[22] For repair in human conversation see Schegloff et al. (1977) and Schegloff (1992); for repair in human-agent interchanges see Krummheuer (in print).

vokes Max in front of the audience, she also saves his face by mitigating her attack. Through these actions she treats Max as something more than a technical artifact. With regard to the question whether user and agent treat the interchange as interaction and each other as interaction partners, Rosemary seems to treat Max as social actor of an interaction.

On the other hand, Max is excluded from major parts of the interchange. In front of the audience Rosemary demonstrates her action as playful teasing. However, she does not use digital strategies to «translate» her performance for the agent, such as a written smiley.[23] Although, when the agent rejects her teasing attack, she continues teasing it. She seems to be testing the agent's communicative and social abilities to prove its teasing behavior. Thus, Max is not treated as an equal partner of an interaction which emphasizes the ambiguous and hybrid character of the interchange.

Discussion

This paper aimed to adopt CA to video recordings of human-agent interchanges. The analysis focused on the sequential organization (especially the next-turn proof procedure) of the interchange and compared it to human interaction in order to acquire a better understanding of the specific character of human-agent interchanges.

Firstly, the audiovisual analysis reveals a hybrid participation framework of the interchange which influences the human-agent interchange in special ways, an aspect which would be missed by an audio analysis only. In contrast to human face-to-face interaction the interchange is constructed by different entities «inhabiting» separate worlds. The user and the agent are furthermore involved in the interchange in different ways, and therefore perceive the interchange from totally different situations. Furthermore, the participation framework shows that in contrast to the traditional cognitive model (planning model) of human-computer interchanges, the user is not necessarily isolated. In many situations it is likely that the user is involved in a complex situation with other participants who influence the user's interpretation of the agent's activities (for example, shared office situations or vending machines in public places). Moreover, the user bases his actions and interpretations in accordance with the situated development of the interchange.

Secondly, the audiovisual analysis is able to focus on bodily orientations, gestures and facial expressions. Thereby it can be seen that an analysis of the textual interchange misses an important framing of the situation as Rosemary frames her actions nonverbally in a playful manner.

---

[23] It cannot be confirmed whether Rosemary knows that the agent can «see» her nonverbal behavior or not. But as the agent does not react to it (for example, he does not smile when she smiles), she could be aware of the absence of reactions.

Thirdly, the analysis shows a specific hybrid character of this interchange. The analysis of a transcript shows that the user and the system interpret the hybrid interchange according to their respective perceptions of the situations and their communicative abilities. Thereby the system simulates interactive rituals, for example, bodily orientation towards the user, the simulation of a kind of turn-taking, which generates verbal and nonverbal output. Also, the user seems to play along with the idea of an «interaction» with the agent. Rosemary looks at the agent, reacts to it, and teases the agent. However, the analysis of the teasing sequence reveals that the hybrid interchange is based on an asynchronous and determined turn-taking system and is often not based upon a shared interpretation of the situation. The user and the agent can frequently not negotiate a mutual understanding of the interchange. These differences appear at every next turn. The agent and the user react upon each other's actions but they do not mutually show whether they share a common interpretation of the other's actions. Thus, in contrast to human interaction the hybrid interchange is not based on a mutual negotiation and confirmation of meaning.

References

Atkinson, Maxwell J./John Heritage (eds.), 1984: *Structures of social action. Studies in conversation analysis*. Cambridge: Cambridge University Press.
Bergmann, Jörg R., 2000: Konversationsanalyse. In: Uwe Flick/Ernst von Kardorff/Ines Steinke (eds.), *Qualitative Sozialforschung. Ein Handbuch*. Reinbek bei Hamburg: Rowohlt, 524-537.
Bergmann, Jörg R., 1988: Haustiere als kommunikative Ressourcen. In: *Soziale Welt*. Sonderband 6, edited by Hans- Georg Soeffner, *Kultur und Alltag*, 299-312.
Bijker, Wiebe E./John Law (eds.), 1992: *Shaping technology/building society: Studies in sociotechnical change*. Cambridge et al.: The MIT Press.
Button, Graham, 1990: Going up a blind alley. Conflating conversation analysis and computer modelling. In: Paul Luff/Nigel Gilbert/David Frohlich (eds.), *Computers and conversation*. London: Academic Press, 67-90.
Button, Graham/Wes Sharrock, 1995: On simulacrums of conversation: Toward a clarification of the relevance of conversation analysis for human-computer interaction. In: Peter J. Thomas (ed.), *The social and interactional dimensions of human-computer interfaces*. Cambridge: Cambridge University Press, 107-125.
Cassell, Justine/Joseph Sullivan/Scott Prevost/Elizabeth Churchill (eds.), 2000: *Embodied conversational agents*. Cambridge et al.: The MIT Press.
Collins, Harry M./Martin Kusch, 1998: *The shape of actions. What humans and machines can do*. Cambridge et al.: The MIT Press.
Drew, Paul, 1987: Pro-faced receipts of teases. In: *Linguistics* 25, 219-253.
Dreyfus, Hubert L., 1979: *What computers can't do – The limits of artificial intelligence*. New York: Haber & Row.

Garfinkel, Harold, 1967: *Studies in ethnomethodology*. Englewood Cliffs: Prentice-Hall.
Garfinkel, Harold, 1972: Studies of the routine grounds of everyday activities. In: David Sudnow (ed.), *Studies in social interaction*. New York: The Free Press, 1-30. (Orig.: 1964, in: *Social Problems* 11, 3, 225-250).
Garfinkel, Harold/D. Lawrence Wieder, 1992: Two incommensurable, asymmetrically alternate technologies of social analysis. In: Graham Watson/Robert M. Seiler (eds.), *Text in context. Contributions to ethnomethodology*. Sage: London, 175-206.
Gesellensetter, Lars, 2004: *Ein planbasiertes Dialogsystem für einen multimodalen Agenten mit Präsentationsfähigkeit*. Master thesis at the Faculty of Technology at Bielefeld University.
Goffman, Erving, 1981: Footing. In: Erving Goffman (ed.), *Forms of talk*. Philadelphia: University of Pennsylvania, 124-159. (Orig.: 1979, in: *Semiotica* 25, 1-29).
Goffman, Erving, 1972: Role distance. In: Erving Goffman (ed.), *Encounters. Two studies in the sociology of interaction*. Harmondsworth: Penguin Books, 71-134. (Orig. 1961, Indianapolis: Bobbs-Merrill).
Goodwin, Charles, 1981: *Conversational organization. Interaction between speakers and hearers*. New York: Academic Press.
Goodwin, Marjorie H., 1990: *He-Said-She-Said. Talk as social organization among black children*. Indiana University Press: Bloomington.
Günthner, Susanne, 1996: Zwischen Scherz und Schmerz – Frotzelaktivitäten in Alltagsinteraktionen. In: Helga Kotthoff (ed.), *Scherzkommunikation. Beiträge aus der empirischen Gesprächsforschung*. Opladen: Westdeutscher Verlag, 81-108.
Günthner, Susanne, 1999: Frotzelaktivitäten in Alltagsinteraktionen. In: Jörg Bergmann/Thomas Luckmann (eds.), *Kommunikative Konstruktion von Moral. Band 1: Strukturen und Dynamiken der Formen moralischer Kommunikation*. Wiesbaden: Westdeutscher Verlag, 300-322.
Heath, Christian, 1986: *Body movement and speech in medical interaction*. Cambridge: Cambridge University Press.
Heath, Christian, 1997: The analysis of activities in face to face interaction using video. In: David Silverman (ed.), *Qualitative research. Theory, method, practice*. London: Sage, 183-200.
Heath, Christian/Paul Luff, 2000: *Technology in action*. Cambridge: Cambridge University Press.
Helander, Martin G./Thomas K. Landauer/Prasad V. Prabhu (eds.), 1997: *Handbook of human-computer interaction*. Amsterdam: Elsevier, 2nd edition.
Heritage, John, 1984: *Garfinkel and ethnomethodology*. Cambridge: Polity Press.
Hutchby, Ian, 2001: *Conversation and technology. From the telephone to the internet*. Cambridge: Polity Press.

Hutchby, Ian/Robin Wooffitt, 1998: *Conversation analysis: Principles, practices and applications.* Cambridge: Polity Press.
Jordan, Brigitte/Austin Henderson, 1995: Interaction analysis: Foundations and practice. In: *The Journal of the Learning Sciences* 4, 1, 39-103.
Kopp, Stefan/Lars Gesellensetter/Nicole C. Krämer/Ipke Wachsmuth, 2005: A conversational agent as museum guide – design and evaluation of a real-world application. In: Themis Panayiotopoulos/Jonathan Gratch/Ruth Aylett/Daniel Ballin/Patrick Olivier/Thomas Rist (eds.), *Intelligent virtual agents. Proceedings of the 5th International Working Conference IVA 2005 in Kos, Greece.* Berlin: Springer, 329-343.
Kopp, Stefan/Bernhard Jung/Nadine Leßmann/Ipke Wachsmuth, 2003: Max – A multimodal assistant in virtual reality construction. In: *Künstliche Intelligenz* 4, 11-17.
Krummheuer, Antonia L., 2005: Shifting the focus: The impact of recording equipment on the ongoing interaction. In: Cor Van Dijkum/Jörg Blasius/Claire Durand (eds.), *Recent developments and applications in social research methodology. Proceedings of the RC33 Sixth International Conference on Social Science Methodology, Amsterdam 2004.* Opladen: Barbara Budrich. (CD-Rom)
Krummheuer, Antonia L.: Zwischen den Welten. Verstehenssicherung und Problembehandlung in künstlichen Interaktionen von menschlichen Akteuren und personifizierten virtuellen Agenten. In: Herbert Willems (ed.), *Weltweite Welten. Internet-Figurationen aus wissenssoziologischer Perspektive.* Wiesbaden: VS Verlag, in print.
Latour, Bruno, 1988: Mixing humans and nonhumans together: The sociology of a door-closer. In: *Social Problems* 35, 3, 298-310. (Article published under the name of Jim Johnson.)
Latour, Bruno, 2005: *Reassembling the social. An introduction to actor-network-theory.* Oxford: Oxford University Press.
Lomax, Helen/Neil Casey, 1998: Recording social life: Reflexivity and video methodology. In: *Sociological Research Online* 3, 2. <http://ideas.repec.org/a/sro/srosro/1998-74-1.html, 3.3.2003>
Luff, Paul/Nigel Gilbert/David Frohlich (eds.), 1990: *Computers and conversation.* London: Academic Press.
Luff, Paul/Jon Hindmarsh/Christian Heath (eds.), 2000: *Workplace studies. Recovering workpractice and informing system design.* Cambridge: Cambridge University Press.
Lynch, Michael, 1993: *Scientific practice and ordinary action. Ethnomethodology and social studies of science.* Cambridge: Cambridge University Press.
Pickering, Andrew, 1995: *The mangle of practice. Time, agency, and science.* Chicago: University of Chicago.
Psathas, George, 1995: *Conversation analysis. The study of talk-in-interaction.* London: Sage.

Rammert, Werner/Ingo Schulz-Schaeffer (eds.), 2002a: *Können Maschinen handeln? Soziologische Beiträge zum Verhältnis von Mensch und Technik.* Frankfurt a.M.: Campus.

Rammert, Werner/Ingo Schulz-Schaeffer, 2002b: Technik und Handeln. Wenn soziales Handeln sich auf menschliches Verhalten und technische Abläufe verteilt. In: Werner Rammert/Ingo Schulz-Schaeffer (eds.), *Können Maschinen handeln? Soziologische Beiträge zum Verhältnis von Mensch und Technik.* Frankfurt a.M.: Campus, 11-64.

Rubin, Jeffery, 1994: *Handbook of usability testing. How to plan, design, and conduct effective tests.* New York: John Wiley & Sons.

Sacks, Harvey, 1984: Notes on methodology. In: Maxwell J. Atkinson/John Heritage (eds.), *Structures of social action. Studies in conversation analysis.* Cambridge: Cambridge University Press, 21-27.

Sacks, Harvey, 1992: *Lectures on conversation.* Vol. I & II. Oxford: Blackwell.

Sacks, Harvey/Emanuel A. Schegloff/Gail Jefferson, 1974: A simplest systematics for the organization of turn-taking for conversation. In: *Language* 50, 4, 696-735.

Schegloff, Emanuel A., 1972: Sequencing in conversational openings. In: John J. Gumperz/Dell Hymes (eds.), *Directions in sociolinguistics. The ethnography of communication.* New York: Holt, Rinehart and Winston, 346-380. (Orig.: 1986, in: *American Anthropologist* 7, 6, 1075-1095).

Schegloff, Emanuel A., 1992: Repair after next turn: The last structural provided defense of intersubjectivity in conversation. In: *American Journal of Sociology* 97, 5, 1295-1345.

Schegloff, Emanuel A., 2002: Beginnings in the telephone. In: James E. Katz/Mark Aakhus (eds.), *Perpetual contact: Mobile communication, private talk, public performance.* Cambridge: Cambridge University Press, 284-300.

Schegloff, Emanuel A./Gail Jefferson/Harvey Sacks, 1977: The preference for self-correction in the organization of repair in conversation. In: *Language* 53, 2, 361-382.

Schegloff, Emanuel A./Harvey Sacks, 1973: Opening up closings. In: *Semiotica* 8, 289-327.

Searle, John R., 1990: Minds, brains, and programs. In: Margaret A. Boden (ed.): *The philosophy of artificial intelligence.* Oxford University Press: New York, 67-88.

Selting, Margret et al., 1998: Gesprächsanalytisches Transkriptionssystem (GAT). In: *Linguistische Berichte* 173, 91-122.

Suchman, Lucy, 1987: *Plans and situated actions: The problem of human-machine communication.* Cambridge: Cambridge University Press.

Suchman, Lucy, 2007: *Human-machine reconfigurations. Plans and situated actions.* Cambridge: Cambridge University Press.

Ten Have, Paul, 1990: Methodological issues in conversation analysis. In: *Bulletin de méthodologie sociologique* 27, 23-51.

Ten Have, Paul, 1999: *Doing conversation analysis. A practical guide.* London: Sage.
Weizenbaum, Joseph, 1976: *Computer power and human reason. From judgement to calculation.* San Francisco: Freeman.
Wooffitt, Robin/Norman M. Fraser/Nigel Gilbert/Scott McGlashan, 1997: *Humans, computers and wizards. Analysing human (simulated) computer interaction.* London: Routledge.

Appendix 1: Notation Convention:

To get a better understanding of the interchange, the textual/verbal interchange is emphasized by bold letters. Keyboard is abbreviated as KB.

'Actors'
R	Rosemary (user)
M	Max (agent)
P	Person in the audience
txR	Text written by Rosemary
TX	Text which is sent to the system and appears in the upper text field

Writing in the text field
h e l l o	The text production of the user in the text field is displayed in single letters in the same order as it was typed
~	A swung dash indicates a space between letters
-t-	A letter between hyphens indicates a deleted letter
/	Slash means that Enter has been pressed, the text is sent to Max
hello	Text between stars is sent to Max and can be read in the upper text field of the screen

Verbal and nonverbal keys
stress	Capital letters indicate a stressed syllable or word(s)
:, ::, :::	Colon indicates an extension of the sound or syllable (number of colons indicate the length of the extension)
((laughs))	Double brackets are used for nonverbal actions
<<nodding> yes>	Angle brackets indicate how specific words are uttered or what actions took place while they were uttered
[hello] [yes] I do	Square brackets show where utterances/actions overlap

(-), (--), (---)   Hyphens within brackets stand for brief in-
                   tervals heard between utterances ranging
                   from 0.25 to 0.75 seconds
(2.0)   Estimated pauses over 1.0 seconds are writ-
                   ten in single brackets

Appendix 2: Original German Transcript:

```
1.  txR   w e r ~ h a t ~ d i c h ~ p r o g r a m m i e r t /
2.  TX    *wer hat dich programmiert*
3.  R     ((Blick: Max))
4.  M     <<legt den Kopf schief, beginnt sich den Kopf
5.        zu kratzen, zuckt dabei kurz mit dem rechten Arm>

6.  M     das weiß keiner> ((blickt nach unten)) [so: genau.
7.  R                                            [((zieht die
8.                                    Augenbrauen hoch, lächelt))

9.  R     ha ha ha:: ((atmet lachend ein)) (Abb. 3)
10.       <<leiser> hehehe> ((schaut breit lächelnd zu Max))

11. M     [((nimmt Arm runter, schaut nach vorn))
12. R     [((Blick zur TS))
13. P     [((schaut lächelnd zu Rosemary))

14. txR   [b i s t ~ d u ~ d o o f    [/
15. R     [((schaut lächelnd auf TS, [dann auf TX))

16. TX    *bist du doof*
17. R     ((leckt sich die Lippen, legt mit einer federnden
18.       Bewegung den Kopf leicht nach hinten, blickt zu  Max))

19. R     [((wippt leicht mit dem Körper))
20. M     [((hebt die Hände vor den Körper,
21.          Handflächen nach außen)) (Abb. 4)

22. M     ich H'OFFe ((nimmt Hände runter)) du meinst die FRAge
23.       nicht ernst

24. txR   [w i e s o ~ n i c h t          [/
25. R     [((blickt auf TS, tippt lächelnd; [Blick: TX dann
26.          zu Max))

27. TX    *wieso nicht*

28. M     [<<hebt linken Arm kurz an>
29. R     [((lächelt leicht, schwingt leicht mit dem Körper))

30. M     warum muss man den fINger jetzt so ti:ef in meine>
31.       EINzige WUNDE bo:hren.
32. R     ((lacht und nickt kurz, legt Zunge zwischen die
```

```
33.         Lippen, blickt auf TS, lächelt, bewegt Finger über TS,
34.         das Lächeln verschwindet))
35. txR     s e i ~ n i c h t ~ s i o -o- -i- o ~ e i n g e s c h
36.         n a p p t /
37. R       ((Blick: TX))
38. TX      *sei nicht so eingeschnappt*
39. R       ((schaut zu Max, wippt leicht mit dem Körper))
40. M       wa:s meinst du da:[mit?
41. R                          [((Blick: TS))

42. txR     d u ~ b i s t ~
43. R       ((beißt sich kurz auf die Lippe, schaut nach oben))
44.         ä:::hm::: (Abb. 5)
45.         ((blickt auf TS))

46. txR     s e h r ~ e m p f i n d l i c [ h /
47. R                                     [((Blick: TX, dann Max))

48. TX      *du bist sehr empfindlich*

49. M       interessAN:ter gesichtspun[kt ros'MARie-
50. R                                 [<<lachend> phk'häu>
```

Sociological Hermeneutics

Ulrike Tikvah Kissmann

How medical forms are used: The study of doctor-patient consultations from a sociological hermeneutic approach

With the growing attention to coding and classification and the attempts to produce an electronic medical record, sociological and anthropological research has increasingly focused on hand-written medical forms (cp. Berg 1996; Berg/Bowker 1997; Heath/Luff 2000). Although earlier studies by Garfinkel (1967) and Freidson (1975) emphasized the role of record keeping for the organization of medical work, medical forms have recently become a central topic in the discussion on the impact of standardization. For that research purpose, sociologists and anthropologists have used video-taped interactions and transcribed conversations as well as the analysis of documents that are in use. One can distinguish on the one hand the research that deals with work practices in relation to medical records. Marc Berg (1996), for example, elaborated on how the practices of reading and writing bring the record into being. Whereas Marc Berg and Geof Bowker (1997) analyzed how the patient's body is mediated through record keeping and the underlying work practices. However, none of these studies explain how medical records influence or structure concrete doctor-patient interactions.[1] On the other hand, doctor-patient interactions have been studied in, for example, Wodak (1997), Bahrs/Matthiessen (2007) and Heath (2002). However, the role of medical forms has been neglected in these approaches. It remains unclear when and how doctors use medical records during the concrete consultation. What and how do forms contribute to the doctor-patient interaction? To put it in the words of Charles Goodwin and Marjorie Harness Goodwin (1997): What do doctors *see* when they collect data on a patient and fill out forms? How are language, documents and human interaction interdigitated?

The following essay will describe the interpretations of medical forms that doctors provide in the preoperative admission of patients to a hospital. Through the analysis of video recordings it will examine misunderstandings in doctor-patient consultations and reconstruct the interpretative achievements of the personnel that are necessary to fill out medical forms. It has been a longstanding concern in sociology, anthropology and other social sciences to analyze breaches and breaks in routines in order to understand the taken-for-granted everyday world (cp. Schütz 1962; Garfinkel 1963). This ethnomethodological approach was adopted by conversation analysis to elaborate on breaches in doctor-patient conversations (cp. Ten Have 1990; Maynard 2003). In this paper, I will

---

[1] The work done by Heath/Luff (2000) is an exception.

use misunderstandings in video-taped doctor-patient interactions in order to study the taken-for-granted interpretations of doctors when they use medical records. I will ask how, when a communication problem crops up, doctors deal with it and how forms are brought into the interaction. As we will see, I adopt the sociological hermeneutic method that is based on Hans-Georg Soeffner (1989 and 2004) and that was further developed by, for example, Jürgen Raab (2002).

The essay also draws on discussions in sociology of technology (such as, for example, Schmiede 2006; Böhle et al. 2004; Rammert 1992) in which knowledge is no longer formulated as «the opposite» of technology but in which knowledge and technology are increasingly linked. In these debates, new types of knowing, such as, application and orientation knowledge gain in importance compared to «old», theoretically based, disciplinary knowledge (see, for example, Degele 2000). Non-explicit and subjective stocks of knowledge also count in these new types of knowing that are necessary to use technoscientific objects such as medical records. They are acquired through lifelong experience and, therefore, can constitute biographical knowledge or, as Hubert Knoblauch (2005: 147) puts it, «biographical articulation» of knowledge. As I have previously shown for nuclear technology, biographical experiences and occasionally also the family history influence the way experts deal with technology (Kissmann 2002 and 2007). This suggests for our case that the same body of medical knowledge can be applied differently according to individual experiences. To this end, I will finally address the question whether the use of medical forms during doctor-patient consultations differs individually among physicians.

Firstly, I will introduce the sample and the role of the in-house continuing education workshop in which I presented a selection of video situations. Secondly, I will describe one example of «normal» misunderstanding and the technoscientific script «administrative duty» that is in use in this specific doctor-patient consultation. Thirdly, a break in routine will be described and the underlying technoscientific script «signpost» will be portrayed. Fourthly, I will compare the behavior of the doctor during the break in routine to the findings of the narration analysis of his biographical interview.

The sample

Before routine operations take place, such as the implantation of hip or knee prostheses, the preoperative admission or indication consulting hour represents the patient's first contact with the hospital. In the case of more complicated illnesses, the patient first attends one of the special consulting hours of the head physician in the department and assistant medical director instead before attending the preoperative admission and answering the remaining standard questions. The result of this arrangement is that the doctor-patient conversations during the indication consultation follow fixed routines of questions and answers, while the special consulting hours offer a certain creative latitude. This different subjection to routines also reveals itself in the fact that during preoperative admission the conversation takes as its basis the forms that must be filled out during the interaction. However, no forms are used during special consultations. In the latter case, the diagnosis reached after the doctor-patient conversation is recorded on a dictaphone and typed out by the head physician's secretary.

Altogether 39 interactions were filmed during the preoperative admission. These included the conversations that anesthesiologists and surgeons conducted with patients as well as the interactions that outpatient nurses had with patients. To provide a basis for comparison, 8 videos were made of doctor-patient conversations during the special consultation sessions. Of these 47 videos, I chose excerpts in which the patients or the staff signal a lack of understanding or a misunderstanding by showing, for example, no reaction to a question. A selection of video situations in which – in my view – a misunderstanding cropped up was shown to the hospital personnel during an in-house continuing education session[2]. The staff classified the conversation practices exhibited there as «normal». They saw no break in communication in such situations but more a routine for follow-up questioning. Only in one interaction did the hospital personnel perceive a break, which led to an unusual, even exceptional, approach by the doctor. The break in communication was seen as such because it lead to a deviation from routines. The described surgeon then proceeded differently than usual and commented upon the change.

In the following two chapters, I will present one example of a «normal» misunderstanding and the break in routine. The former took place during the anesthesiological and the latter during the surgical indication consultation. In contrast to the special consulting hours, the work practices during the preoperative admission or indication consulting hour are extremely standardized. The doctor-patient consultations held by anesthesiologists and surgeons in the preoperative admission only last 20 minutes each. During that time the anesthesiologists must read the anaesthesiological patient consent form that the patients completed previously, and additionally they must fill out the anaesthesiological record[3]. In the surgical preoperative admission the surgeons have to complete

---

[2] The in-house continuing education workshop had the role of a feedback workshop where I presented a selection of my findings and discussed them with the hospital staff. Moreover, such workshops also serve to validate the findings as shown in, for example, Karasti (2001).

[3] The doctors who attend the anesthesiological preoperative admission fill out one form only: the anesthesiological record. A second form, the anesthesiological patient consent form, has previously been handed to the patient by a nurse. After having been filled out, the patient brings this anesthesiological patient consent form to the consulting hour. It contains previous illnesses and serves to explain the narcosis to the patient. This completed patient consent form lies in front of the anesthesiologist during the consulting hour. In order to make sure that the form is filled out correctly, the doctor starts asking questions about the patient's previous illnesses. This new information by mouth together with the information provided by the clarification form serve to complete the first page of the anesthesiological record that consists of altogether three pages. (The two other pages are filled out during and after the operation). When it is completed, the doctor turns again to the consent form in order to explain the narco-

two medical forms: the admission sheet and the surgical patient consent form[4]. Notwithstanding the slight differences between the forms of the two professions, their work practices are very similar. In 20 minutes both anesthesiologists and surgeons, have to gather the necessary information and to reach the decision whether the patient can be narcotized or operated, respectively. When that decision is made, the risks have to be explained to the patient and the respective patient clarification form is signed.

The «normal» misunderstanding as well as the break in routine will show us what is taken-for-granted by the doctors that attend the preoperative admission. «Normal» means that this approach to record keeping would have stayed unnoticed to the staff, if I had not presented it in the in-house continuing education session. The interpretative achievement that is necessary to fill out the forms during the «normal» misunderstanding is called «administrative duty». In contrast to this, the analysis of the break in routine will render visible a second type of record keeping which is called «signpost». The presented breach contains a deviation from routines and, therefore, cannot stay unnoticed.

A «normal» misunderstanding

To start the analysis of a doctor-patient interaction, I watched the whole consultation from the beginning to the end several times and I looked for misunderstandings that occurred during the consultation. The selected misunderstandings were studied in more detail together with the beginning and the end of the doctor-patient consultation. Firstly, this means that I analyzed the selected situations in 5-second steps. This step-by-step interpretation was done according to the sociological hermeneutic methodology as presented in Soeffner (1989 and 2004).[5] In order to maintain the sequentiality of events, I always started with the beginning and then proceeded to the misunderstandings of the doctor-patient consultation. The principle of sequentiality is used in all approaches to video interaction analyses (see, for example, Heritage 1984). In the sociological her-

---

sis to the patient. As for the surgical consent form, at the end of the conversation both partners of the interaction must sign the clarification form.

[4] In consultation with the patient, the doctors who attend the surgical preoperative admission fill out two standard forms. At the beginning of each surgeon-patient interaction, the doctor processes the admission sheet. The patient is asked about his or her ailments, the diagnosis is recorded and the indication to operate is given or not given. In addition, the doctor must ask about, and record information about possible previous illnesses or allergies. In order that the form be filled out correctly, the patient is also given a brief examination and his or her X-ray pictures are inspected. When the admission sheet is completed, the surgeon turns to the surgical patient consent form. While the standardized admission form is created in the hospital itself, the patient consent form is published by the professional association of surgeons. The clarification form serves to explain to the patient the operation procedure and its associated risks. At the end of the conversation, both partners in the interaction must sign this form.

[5] An example of the individual analytic steps can be seen at http://www2.hu-berlin.de/computerisiertes-wissen/Video-Auswertung/.

meneutic approach it is primarily based on Dilthey (1976) and Weber (1973). Sequentiality in hermeneutic video analysis is discussed in, for example, Raab (2002). Secondly, my analysis was done separately for the nonvocal interaction, the transcribed conversation and finally for the verbal interaction as a concerted activity. This multimodal approach is currently practiced by authors that draw on linguistics (as, for example, Goodwin 2006; Mondada 2004). But also Raab/Tänzler (2002) use scores that show all verbal and nonvocal parts arranged one below the other and that make a separate analysis possible. Raab (2002: 474) points out that the hermeneutic interpretation can be done separately for the nonvocal interaction and the transcribed conversation. However, it always has to be undertaken in the light of their interrelations. I chose this approach because one can notice gestures and gazes in the nonvocal interaction that one would have skipped over in the verbal interaction. The nonvocal interaction and the transcribed conversation were finally joined together and analyzed as a concerted activity.

The following excerpt is the beginning of a doctor-patient consultation. The «normal» misunderstanding occurred right at the beginning. It consisted of the fact that the anesthesiologist («A») first had the wrong patient consent form. By addressing the patient («P») with her family name, the doctor did not only demonstrate politeness, but also made sure that she had the right medical record. In so far, we are dealing with a «normal» misunderstanding which means, in this example, a routine necessity for checking the congruence of the paper form with the patient.

```
A: ((clacking⁶ sounds)) So: Ms. Müller [anonymized], everything
   has been written out here, the clarification was on the Au-
   gust the eighteenth a-
P:                      Liebig [anonymized] is my name, al-
   right?
A:     Yesyes, (2) aha your name is Liebig, because the other
                        ▲
       Anesthesiologist exchanges the patient consent form
   was already lying here so well
P:                              Liebig Gertrud
A:                                        then we will do
   o- we will of course take Ms. Liebig, good, I already won-
                        ▲
           Anesthesiologist turns patient consent form twice
   dered why he is called Liebig=and you Müller
                        ▲
Anesthesiologist holds the form upside down and emphatically
looks at the patient's companion, then at the patient
P: ((Laughter))
```

---

⁶ The transcription rules are at the end of the document. The doctor-patient consultations were conducted in German. For the purpose of this article the presented excerpts were translated by a native speaker.

At the point in the interaction when the anaesthesiologist said, «I already wondered why he is called Liebig and you Müller» a transition in interaction took place. The doctor had turned the consent form twice and finally held it upside down. At that moment the doctor-patient relation became less tense. This became obvious, for example, through the patient's laughter. The analysis of the video sequence before the transition in communication revealed that the medical forms were in the center of the interaction and that they established a strong doctor-patient hierarchy. They supported the doctor's position of authority, whereas the patient was left with a marginal position. The maintenance of asymmetry in doctor-patient consultations has been discussed in, for example, Heath (1992). In the presented example we see that the forms serve to support that asymmetry. Moreover, they encouraged the doctor's relentless attitude and helped to shape the strong doctor-patient hierarchy. Below in figure 1 the correct patient clarification form was in the doctor's right hand and with the left she pushed the pile with the wrong form away from her. The anesthesiologist occupied the whole table whereas the patient tried to put the envelope with her X-ray pictures on the table. Unfortunately, the patient did not succeed in doing so. The doctor did not notice her, nor did she support her. She was occupied with the medical forms and by that means established herself as an authority and a competent doctor. Her attitude was rigid and relentless. By contrast, the use of the medical forms gave the patient a marginal position.

In addition to the discussion on the asymmetry in doctor-patient relations, the application of medical forms also meant for the anesthesiologist to have a blinded view on the patient. She only was attentive to her whenever the form

Figure 1: The patient occupies a marginal position

Figure 2: The anesthesiologist holds the clarification form upside down: The strong hierarchy has dissolved.

was concerned. But beyond the necessities of the form the doctor neglected the individual needs of the patient. She could have taken, for example, the envelope with the X-ray pictures right from the beginning of the conversation. After the transition in interaction the strong hierarchy turned upside down as much as did the patient clarification form. In that situation, the anesthesiologist lost her blinded view on the patient and was able to express empathy. This became clear in the sequence in which she attentively and emphatically looked at the patient and her companion. The atmosphere in the doctor-patient relationship became relaxed at that point in the interaction and the patient was not marginal anymore. Instead, she became the center of the doctor's interest. During the rest of the consultation the doctor turned to the forms again and the empathic attention towards the patient's situation vanished again.

One can conclude from this transition in interaction that for the anesthesiologist the use of medical forms was equivalent to a blinded view on the patient and a loss of empathy. By contrast, as soon as the medical forms became unimportant for the interaction, she expressed empathy and oriented herself to the patient's needs. The interpretative achievement that was necessary to fill out the form during the «normal» misunderstanding is therefore based on the assumption that social competency and medical forms are mutually exclusive. For this reason, this type of record keeping is called «administrative duty». Either the patient was in the center of the doctor's interest or the medical forms were in her focus with the consequence that the patient was marginalized.

Using Timmermans and Berg (1997) I describe the doctor's interpretative achievement as a «technoscientific script». The choice of this term indicates that properties are inscribed in the medical form whose meanings can only be deciphered by going beyond the mere form itself. By referring to Timmermans and Berg I distinguish this notion of script from the use that Barley (1986) makes of it. The latter described scripts as «recurrent patterns of interaction that define, in observable and behavioral terms, the essence of actor's roles» (1986: 83). In contrast to this, the script of a technoscientific object, such as, a medical record represents the background framework for its *potential* meanings. To put it differently, it offers certain roles to the actors but does not determine them. Timmermans and Berg laid the emphasis on the interpretative candor of medical records that enables them to function. The standards registered in paper forms, therefore, are not an instrument of power that subordinate users to external instructions. In our case, the technoscientific script of the patient clarification form that was used by the anesthesiologist during the presented «normal» misunderstanding consisted in the «administrative duty». She drew upon *one possible* meaning how medical forms can be completed, i.e. without social competency. As we will see in the next chapter, the next doctor drew on a different meaning than the presented anesthesiologist. He used the technoscientific script «signpost».

The break in routine

In this section, a surgeon-patient interaction with Martin Zeinert (anonymized) and another patient will be portrayed. The surgeon Martin Zeinert decided to leave the normal alignment of the doctor-patient consultation. That break in routine appeared after 1 minute and 30 seconds. By this time, the problems cumulated and made the surgeon resort to a verbal response that lay outside the normal routine. The result was that the remaining 18 minutes were problem-free. Before I will present an excerpt from this conversation at the time of this change, the beginning of the doctor-patient consultation will be described briefly.

Through the video interaction analysis, it became clear that the first seconds of the conversation were already unusual. The patient's behavior made the conversation take a complicated direction. She was controlling and dominant, whereas the doctor Martin Zeinert tried to find an appropriate reaction to her particularities. He sometimes appeared insecure and sometimes self-assured. A power skirmish took place between the doctor and the patient. Despite his occasional insecurity, the surgeon remained friendly. The patient took on the role of the doer and the doctor the role of the one who lets her have her way. On the part of the doctor, this speaks for a principally egalitarian, but atypical doctor-patient relationship. It is to be expected that these structures will be repeated at later stages of the conversation. As one will see, the break in routine is structured so that the patient («P») is active and «goes toward» the surgeon («S») while the surgeon reacts to the unusual behavior and must find an adequate way of dealing with it.

```
S: Okaa:y (5) ((sheets of paper rustling in the background))
   good, did he already tell you something about the operation?
P: No:, to be perfectly frank
S:                                    Mmm
P:                          I also don't really want to
   know
S:      Aaa:h, good
P:                  (4) It's enough for me to know, umm, snip-
   ping out ((claps hands)), somehow ((loud clapping of hands))
   getting the whole thing together again
S:                                    Mmm
P:                          I mean I=cannot=move
   =now nor=can=I=move=afterwards so it's all the same to me if
   it becomes stiff
S:         Mmm
P:                 And then I'll wake up and then the world
   will be in order again
S:                          Okay, so
P:                          Except what you have to say
   to me, then I'll also listen
S:                          We'll still do a little
   anamnesis, as preparation, and for planning the
                            ▲
   Surgeon points at the admission sheet
   operation, and umm then we'll speak briefly about the
   operation and if it's enough for you, just say stop
                            ▲
   Surgeon points to the clarification form
```

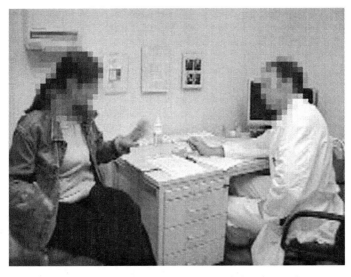

Figure 3: The surgeon points at the admission sheet and
says «we'll still do a little anamnesis»

In the in-house continuing education session, the hospital personnel that was present described the patient's behavior as uncooperative. The surgeon's tasks consisted among other things of informing the patient about the operation. It is problematic and uncooperative when the patient, as in the above case, refuses the information. On the other hand, one must give her credit for saying what she wanted for the first time in the interaction. The patient might have refused to listen by saying «I also don't really **want** to know», but at the same time she limited her refusal and concluded with: «Except what you **have** to say to me». For the first time, she gave the doctor the chance to respond to her sensitivities and demands, which was not the case previously. While she did not give the doctor a chance to understand what she wanted during the first one and a half minutes, shortly before the break in routine she was more open. The doctor reacted to her openness and offered her the chance to help shape the situation. In the first place, he said, «We'll do...» and not, «I'll do such-and-such with you....» Thus, the surgeon included the patient in shaping the conversation. In the second place, with the statement «If it's enough for you, just say stop», he signaled that he is prepared to respond to the patient and to conduct the conversation in a non-routine fashion. This was the difference from the beginning of the consultation when the power skirmish took place. After his initial insecurity, the doctor returned to the routines again. That was different now, because now the departure from routine was implemented with, «If it's enough for you, just say stop». In this way, the surgeon may have directed the conversation, but the patient had the possibility to intervene and to help shape it.

When one compares the conversation excerpt with the video, one sees that the doctor was referring to the admission sheet when he said «anamnesis» and to the patient clarification form when he said «operation» and in each case pointed to it with his pencil. That means that the consultation consisted not only of filling out both forms but of addressing their medical content. Instead of «admission sheet», the doctor talked about the «anamnesis», in other words the patient's case history. His choice of words revealed that he was not just concerned with checking off questions. Instead, the patient's medical history was his focal point. Thus, in the case of breaks in routine, the surgeon referred to his status as a doctor. In a similar way, instead of naming the clarification sheet, he said, «speak briefly about the operation». From his point of view, the actual content of the operation was the focal point, not legal duties. What matters to the doctor was his *true* function as a doctor. Here, *true* means establishing contact with the patient as a socially skilled doctor. The surgeon might have referred to his status as a doctor and stressed his medical competence. However, at the same time he gave proof of his people skills by giving the patient a chance to help shape the conversation. This egalitarian bent could be established from the entire previous interaction and was a structural property of the conversation. Now it becomes clear that the forms are also given this meaning. The surgeon used them for the anamnesis as well as for describing the operation and not for the collection of data or for patient clarification. In this way, he gave expression to his ideas about how to lead a medically and socially skillful consultation. The technoscientific script for his actions is formed by ideas about original medical values, which consist of medical and people skills as well as of responsible conduct.

To sum up, I discovered that a change took place in the conversation due to the break in routine, and that the following 18 minutes proceeded without disruptions. The break in routine was recognizable through the surgeon's pointing to the admission sheet and the patient clarification form, indicating a direction for the interaction. This is the reason why I called the technoscientific script «signpost». Both forms had a direction-indicating meaning and were offering an orientation to the patient. Through this they represent original medical values and hence guarantee a medically grounded as well as socially skillful doctor-patient consultation. The doctor reacted to the disruptions of the first one and a half minutes by diverging from the question-answer routine and making it clear that, for him, what was really important was the *true* medical function. With, «If it's enough for you, just say stop», he was also indicating that the patient can intervene.

The biographical interview with Martin Zeinert (anonymized)

The technoscientific script «signpost» that is used by Martin Zeinert during the break in routine draws on the ideal of the *good* doctor. As we will see, this ideal receives its strength and authenticity through biographical experiences. The surgeon constructed his life story around his motivation to become a doctor. However, he did not present a black and white world with *good* doctors as inevitable models. Instead, the way he recollected and narrated his experiences made it clear that he is aware of the grey zones of *good* conduct in a doctor and that he judges himself to be fallible. In the following citation, Martin described his own experiences as a patient, when medical forms were the focus of the doctor-patient consultation. The presented doctor did not conform to the moral ideal of doctors as *helpers*, whose medical ability and social skills complement each other.

```
M.Z.: [...] I[7] was only a refugee like all the others too, who
were in a similar situation and u:m, um they said if you're a
refugee go there and there=that's a psychologist who'll write
you, refugee, a note you need- who who earns his money that
way, u:m by writing refugees a note so they can call in sick
and um=go there, you'll get your official excuse, go there=he
doesn't want anything=I actually wanted to talk with him but I
very quickly noticed that you've filled out your sheet of
questions, have to sit one hour in the waiting room, then you
can go in to him= >he's not interested in you< =and let's put
it this way- well okay you get your sick-leave excuse=go
```

---

[7] The biographical interview was conducted in German. For the purpose of this article some interview passages were translated by a native speaker.

In the above excerpt Martin described an example of a doctor who used medical records according to the technoscientific script «administrative duty» as much as the anesthesiologist during the «normal» misunderstanding. The doctor that was portrayed by Martin did not respond to his needs nor did he show social skills in any way. He rather was a mere assistant in filling out forms. With this example of a doctor, the surgeon made it clear that he himself disposes of moral ideals of socially skilled doctors. However, Martin could have explained how different a doctor he is. But he did not juxtapose his own conduct to that example, nor did he establish himself as superior to others who do not conform to his ideals. Instead, the above example was embedded in a life story that emphazised his own fallibility. The motto with which Martin started his narration was «I actually **always** wanted to become a doctor, that is, um=that is already as a child, a:nd somehow everything didn't **go** as it should have».

The reason why it did not go as it should was briefly elaborated upon in numerous reports that followed this introductory evaluation. Martin was born in the GDR (former East Germany) in 1969. He imparted the information that he would have liked to have studied medicine. However, because he was a church member and his parents were not considered to be from the working class, it took enormous efforts for him to achieve as much as a study place as a medical-technical assistant at a trade school. At the time, he planned to study for his secondary-school degree at a night school. In addition, he hoped to receive the chance to study medicine through his service in the East German army (the NVA). He had already begun with courses at night school when he fled to the West in summer 1989. At this point in the interview, Martin did not go into this any further and instead reported briefly about his career in the West. After he achieved his secondary-school degree late and then studied medicine, he succeeded in getting the position as a doctor in the hospital where he now works. His initial autobiographical self-presentation ended here. The interviewer only needed to ask one follow-up question and Martin delivered an almost 2-hour-long narration of his escape to the West and his professional development.

The narration of the escape began by means of a description that brought in those who experienced the events (i.e. «Ereignisträger» which means «social units», see Kallmeyer/Schütze 1977). In this case a female student of the medical trade school was suddenly arrested. This description is an example of a «Kategorie gebundene Aktivität» («activity linked to a category», see Kallmeyer/Schütze 1977): a student who, like Martin, wanted to become a doctor but was arrested. Since Martin belongs to the same category, the use of this sort of text brings home the fact that he was also threatened by arrest. The category-linked activity is an expression of the atmosphere that dominated in the medical trade school, meaning that in principle everyone could have been threatened by arrest. Martin then brought himself as a social unit into the story and described his own arrest, which, because of the previous interpretation of the text, is congruent:

M.Z.: [...] and I am then, um, on vacation in Romania, since I still (1), although I was conscripted into the NVA, could report for duty, um (1) was arrested on vacation because of the danger that I might escape u:m, I didn't want to escape, despite that (1) because I actually had somehow planned my path in the GDR

The arrest was, however, not yet the reason for his escape to the West. With the last sentence, Martin indicated a causal connection and suggested his suffering (see «Markierer», or «indicator», in Kallmeyer/Schütze 1977). In the subsequent narration, he described what he suffered and why he escaped. Martin recounted how he was arrested and imprisoned in Romania. What he suffered from most was seeing a fellow prisoner and cellmate beaten to death. The experience was especially disturbing for him, as he indicated at several different points, because he did not know the reason for his imprisonment then and does not to this day. At the time he did not know why he was in that cell and if he would be the next person to be beaten to death. A short time later, Martin was allowed to leave his cell and was brought to the train station in Bucharest. This is the location from which he escaped. As he wandered through the city, starving, a woman doctor who noticed him on the street helped him. She took him home with her and gave him something to eat. Later, after Martin went to the East German embassy, two soldiers accompanied him to the train station in order to bring him back to the GDR. When the train stopped in Budapest, Martin escaped a second time. In Budapest he reached the refugee camp that had been set up in the summer of 1989 for refugees from the GDR. He then describes his third escape, this time to Austria. He concluded this first section of his narration by taking up the thread of the medical profession:

M.Z.: [...] and I fell (1) to the ground and thanked God that I was in Austria=when I was in Austria (1) but that was not=that was so strange, somehow=the wish to become a doctor and then again and again, this meeting people that I absolutely, held in high esteem, found worthy of great respect (1) and so that was the way it wa:s the picture I had of a doctor, that was actually to:ta:lly positive, you see? I mean, not that they are superhumans=that was obvious to me um, but the picture that I so to speak acquired of a doctor was that, um, was absolutely positive, including the woman who saved my life in Romania (1) you see? That um (3) yes (2) so that is, um, positive

In this intermediate evaluation, he referred to the positive image of a doctor, which was impressed on him by, for example, the doctor in Bucharest. Of course, she did not give him medical treatment. The model of a doctor that Martin constructed in his life story received its attractiveness through the interpersonal skills that he ascribes to doctors. The way he recollected and narrated his experiences revealed that he associated the medical profession with the positive experiences he had with doctors during his escape. *Helping* people is one of the fundamental tasks of doctors. He also presented himself in the video as someone who associates *helping* and social skills with medical values. That explains why, in his video interaction with the patient, Martin attached so much importance to using the medical forms in an equitable and socially skillful way. As we can see now, the interpretative achievement that became visible during the analysis of the break in routine draws on biographical experiences.

The second narrative strand, which was developed thereafter, concerned the time after the escape, when Martin addressed the psychological and physical consequences of his imprisonment. While in the first narrative strand the positive experiences with the female doctor were very self-confidently expressed, in the second part of the narration the fallibility of the autobiographer came into view. In this «other» side of the self-presentation, the account no longer follows a straight path toward the ideal of the *good* doctor. Instead, lines of argument increasingly emerged and Martin cited the above mentioned example of the doctor in Austria who filled out the forms without being interested in him. This example was followed by a line of argument in which he stated that he felt that the doctor's behavior was appropriate at the time, but now, because of his experience, he sees it differently. During this argumentation, he compared his own trauma with wartime traumas and considered under what circumstances he himself could become involved as a perpetrator of violent situations.

```
M.Z.: […] and then I also always had the picture in my head of
this young guy who beat and kicked this man to death there in
Bucharest and um I was also very interest:ed in sport and had
um=um already done all sorts of sports in the GDR, and um, um,
then I thought, well I also would have gone into the NVA so
that I could do my three years and um then be able to
study=for this reason, right? But >on the other hand I also
then< =well um, maybe I also would have had to do something
like that
```

In other words, Martin did not set up his own medical ability as a contrast to the example of the above mentioned doctor in Austria. Instead, he reflected upon how easily he himself could have fallen into a situation in which he might have been unjust to others. The above excerpt, followed by the line of argument, gave expression to Martin's doubts about how resolute he himself would be under hierarchical conditions. In the second narrative strand, the self-confident ideals were replaced by insecurity—so much so, that Martin imagined himself in the role of the violent perpetrator. Implicit is the question of what, in addition to the obligations of military service, he would have done in the NVA in order to become a doctor.

Conclusion

By means of video interaction analyses, the article reconstructed the interpretative achievements of the personnel in doctor-patient consultations that are necessary to fill out forms. Using a sociological hermeneutic approach (Soeffner 1989 and 2004), I analyzed when and how doctors use medical records during concrete doctor-patient interactions. To this end, a selection of video situations in which a misunderstanding cropped up was shown to the hospital personnel during an in-house continuing education session. The staff classified the conversation practices exhibited there as «normal». They saw no break in communication in such situations, but more a routine for follow-up questioning. Only in one interaction did the hospital personnel perceive a break, which led to an unusual, even exceptional, approach by the doctor. In the article I described one «normal» misunderstanding and the break in routine. Both breaches served to reconstruct what is taken-for-granted by doctors who attend preoperative admission. This approach draws on ethnomethodology (Garfinkel 1963) and conversation analysis (Ten Have 1990; Maynard 2003).

This way I portrayed two ways of record keeping. During the «normal» misunderstanding the taken-for-granted assumption consisted of the fact that medical forms and social skills are mutually exclusive. The presented anesthesiologist was either interested in filling out the form and tolerated that the patient was marginalized or she expressed empathy to the patient's situation and could hardly keep track of the medical forms. This way of record keeping is called «administrative duty». Because the staff considered this misunderstanding «normal», it would have stayed unnoticed had I not presented it in the in-house continuing education session. In contrast to the «administrative duty» mode, the interpretative achievement that was necessary to fill out the forms during the break in routine is called «signpost». The presented surgeon gave the medical forms a meaning that indicated the direction of the doctor-patient consultation. He attached great importance to using the records in an equitable and socially skillful way. I showed that he conformed to the ideal of doctors as *helpers,* whose medical ability and social skills complement each other. The comparison to the surgeon's biographical interview revealed that he associates the medical profession with the positive experiences he had with doctors during his escape from the GDR in summer 1989. The interpretative achievement that became visible during the analysis of the break in routine draws on these biographical experiences.

With the application of standardized paper forms in routine work one may think that all doctors fill out the records in the same standardized way. However, I demonstrated that the use of medical forms differs individually among doctors.

For this reason, the article drew on Timmermans and Berg's work (1997) and their notion of technoscientific script. The technoscientific script of a medical record represents the background framework for its potential meanings and is a kind of screenplay for its use. Hence it limits the possible plots and actors. With «administrative duty» and «signpost» I portrayed two technoscientific scripts, i.e. two possible meanings of medical forms. My findings also made it clear that the standardized forms are always marked by an interpretative candor that enables them to function differently, depending on the situation. During the «normal» misunderstanding they facilitated the straight and quick collection of data on the patient, whereas during the break in routine the medical forms helped to provide an orientation within a problematic situation.

Acknowledgements

I would like to thank Geof Bowker who adviced me on how to organize feedback workshops for hospitals. I also wish to express my thanks to Wolfram Fischer who initially taught me the sociological hermeneutic method of video interaction analysis. I also gratefully acknowledge the support of my research team, Renate Lieb, Julia Teschlade and Siegrid Steinhauer. Finally, I wish to thank the Berlin Equal Opportunity Program (Berliner Programm zur Förderung der Chancengleichheit für Frauen in Forschung und Lehre) that financed my post-doctoral scholarship. It allowed me to begin my first study on hospitals from 2004 until 2006. As part of that study, I collected the data that was necessary for this article. It also gave me the possibility to write the application for my actual research project «The effect of computerized knowledge in the operating room from a gender perspective» which is funded by the German Research Foundation (Deutsche Forschungsgemeinschaft).

Transcription rules

(4)	= length of the pause in seconds
Ye:s	= long vowel
((laughing))	= comment by the transcriber
/	= insertion of the phenomenon commented upon
no	= emphasis
many-	= rupture
>no<	= quiet words
…	= omissions in the transcript
( )	= content of the comment is not understandable; space between parentheses corresponds approximately to the length of the comment
(he says)	= uncertain transcription
yes=yes	= quick addition
Yes so was No but	= simultaneous speech beginning with «so»

umm then   = simultaneous speech and gesture beginning with «then»
▲
doctor points to the paper form
,   = short pause

References

Bahrs, Ottomar/Peter F. Matthiessen (eds.), 2007: *Gesundheitsfördernde Praxen. Die Chancen einer salutogenetischen Orientierung in der hausärztlichen Praxis*. Bern: Huber.

Barley, Stephen, 1986: Technology as an occasion for structuring: evidence from observations of ct scanners and the social order of radiology departments. In: *Administrative Science Quaterly* 31, 1, 78-108.

Berg, Marc, 1996: Practices of reading and writing: the constitutive role of the patient record in medical work. In: *Sociology of Health & Illness* 18, 4, 499-524.

Berg, Marc/Geoffrey Bowker, 1997: The multiple bodies of the medical record: Toward a sociology of an artefact. In: *The Sociological Quarterly*, 38, 3, 513-537.

Böhle, Fritz/Annegret Bolte/Wolfgang Dunkel/Sabine Pfeiffer/Stephanie Porschen/Sevsay-Tegethoff Nese, 2004: Der gesellschaftliche Umgang mit Erfahrungswissen: Von der Ausgrenzung zu neuen Grenzziehungen. In: Ulrich Beck/Christoph Lau (eds.), *Entgrenzung und Entscheidung. Was ist neu an der Theorie reflexiver Modernisierung?*, Frankfurt a.M.: Suhrkamp, 95-122.

Degele, Nina, 2000: *Informiertes Wissen. Eine Wissenssoziologie der computerisierten Gesellschaft:* Frankfurt a.M.: Campus.

Dilthey, Wilhelm, 1976, [1958]: Entwürfe zur Kritik der historischen Vernunft. In: Hans-Georg Gadamer/Gottfried Boehm (eds.), *Seminar: Philosophische Hermeneutik*. Frankfurt a.M.: Suhrkamp, 189-220.

Freidson, Eliot, 1975: Doctoring together. A study of professional social control. New York et al.: Elsevier.

Garfinkel, Harold, 1963: A concept of, and experiments with, «trust» as a condition of stable concerted actions. In: O.J. Harvey (ed.), *Motivation and social interaction*, New York: Ronald Press, 187-238.

Garfinkel, Harold, 1967: Studies in ethnomethodology. Oxford et al.: Polity Press.

Goodwin, Charles/Marjorie Harness Goodwin, 1997: Seeing as situated activity. Formulating planes. In: Yrjö Engeström and David Middleton (eds.), *Cognition and communication at work*. Cambridge: Cambridge University Press, 61-95.

Goodwin, Marjorie Harness, 2006: *The hidden life of girls. Games of stance, status, and exclusion*. Malden et al.: Blackwell.

Heath, Christian, 2002: Demonstrative suffering: The gestural (re)embodiment of symptoms. In: *Journal of Communication*, 52, 597-616.

Heath, Christian, 1992: The delivery and reception of diagnosis in the general-practice consultation. In: Paul Drew/John Heritage (eds.), *Talk at work. Interaction in institutional settings*. Cambridge: University Press, 235-267.

Heath, Christian/Paul Luff, 2000: *Technology in action*. Cambridge: University Press.

Heritage, John, 1984: *Garfinkel and ethnomethodology*. Cambridge: Polity Press.

Kallmeyer, Werner/Fritz Schütze, 1977: Zur Konstitution von Kommunikationsschemata der Sachverhaltsdarstellung. In: Dirk Wegner (ed.), *Gesprächsanalysen. Forschungsberichte des Instituts für Kommunikationsforschung und Phonetik der Universität Bonn*, Series 1, Vol. 65. Hamburg: Helmut Buske Verlag, 159-274.

Karasti, Helena, 2001: Bridging work practices and system design: Integrating systematic analysis, appreciative intervention and practitioner participation. In: *Computer Supported Cooperative Work*, 10, 211-246.

Kissmann, Ulrike Tikvah, 2002: *Kernenergie und deutsche Biographien. Die Gegenwärtigkeit des Nationalsozialismus in biographischen Rekonstruktionen von Kerntechnik-Experten*. Gießen: Psychosozial.

Kissmann, Ulrike Tikvah, 2007: Normalizing moral dilemmas: The construction of true and false experts in german nuclear technology. In: *Science as Culture*, 16, 187-205.

Knoblauch, Hubert, 2005: *Wissenssoziologie*. Konstanz: UVK.

Maynard, Douglas W., 2003: *Bad news, good news. Conversational order in everyday talk and clinical settings*. Chicago et al.: University of Chicago Press.

Mondada, Lorenza, 2004: Interaktionale Praktiken der Forscher und Entstehung des wissenschaftlichen Wissens. Für einen Dialog zwischen interaktionaler Linguistik und Wissenschaftssoziologie. In: *Zeitschrift für qualitative Bildungs-, Beratungs- und Sozialforschung*. 5, 179-211.

Raab, Jürgen, 2002: «Der schönste Tag des Lebens» und seine Überhöhung in einem eigenwilligen Medium. Videoanalyse und sozialwissenschaftliche Hermeneutik am Beispiel eines professionellen Hochzeitsvideofilms. In: *Sozialer Sinn*, 3, 469-495.

Raab, Jürgen/Dirk Tänzler, 2002: Politik im/als Clip. Zur soziokulturellen Funktion politischer Werbespots. In: Herbert Willems (ed.), *Die Gesellschaft der Werbung*. Wiesbaden et al.: Westdeutscher Verlag, 217-245.

Rammert, Werner, 1992: Neue Technologien – neue Begriffe? In: Thomas Malsch/Ulrich Mill (eds.), *ArBYTE. Modernisierung der Industriesoziologie?*, Berlin: Sigma, 29-51.

Schmiede, Rudi, 2006: Wissen und Arbeit im «Informational Capitalism». In: Andrea Baukrowitz/Thomas Berker/Andreas Boes/Sabine Pfeiffer/Rudi

Schmiede/Mascha Will (eds.), *Informatisierung der Arbeit – Perspektiven zur Gestaltung eines gesellschaftlichen Umbruchprozesses.* Berlin: Sigma, 457-490.

Schütz, Alfred, 1962: *Collected papers I: The problem of social reality.* The Hague: Martinus Nijhoff.

Soeffner, Hans-Georg, 1989: *Auslegung des Alltags – Der Alltag der Auslegung. Zur wissenssoziologischen Konzeption einer sozialwissenschaftlichen Hermeneutik.* Frankfurt a.M.: Suhrkamp.

Soeffner, Hans-Georg, 2004: *Auslegung des Alltags – Der Alltag der Auslegung. Zur wissenssoziologischen Konzeption einer sozialwissenschaftlichen Hermeneutik.* Konstanz: UVK, 2nd edition.

Ten Have, Paul, 1990: Und der Arzt schweigt. Sprechstunden-Episoden, in denen Ärzte auf Patienteninformationen sprachlich nicht reagieren. In: Konrad Ehlich/Angelika Redder/Rüdiger Weingarten (eds.), *Medizinische und therapeutische Kommunikation. Diskursanalytische Untersuchungen.* Opladen: Westdeutscher Verlag, 103-121.

Timmermans, Stefan/Marc Berg, 1997: Standardization in action: Achieving local universality through medical protocols. In: *Social Studies of Science,* 27, 273-305.

Weber, Max, 1973 [1904]: Die «Objektivität» sozialwissenschaftlicher und sozialpolitischer Erkenntnis. In: Max Weber, *Gesammelte Aufsätze zur Wissenschaftslehre.* Edited by Johannes Winckelmann. Tübingen: Mohr, 146-214.

Wodak, Ruth, 1997: Critical discourse analysis and the study of doctor-patient interaction. In: Britt-Louise Gunnarsson/Per Linell/Bengt Nordberg (eds.), *The construction of professional discourse.* London: Longman, 173-200.

Roger Haeussling

Video analysis with a four-level interaction concept: A network-based concept of human-robot interaction

Usually, the topic of the sociological analysis of videotapes is interaction. Accordingly, social situations are documented and the way interpersonal behavior and contact evolves is recorded. Acts of emotions and social ties become reconstructable. Insofar, a methodically ambitious video analysis refers to a sociological interaction concept. In the following I would like to introduce such a concept and demonstrate its empirical realization. Initially, I will illustrate my relationalistic-hermeneutical position and perspective which particularly relies on Harrison C. White's network theory. His theory argues for a new perspective on social processes and constellations: Instead of assuming the existence of actors or social norms, he focuses on social relations and the processes these relations generate. In this sense, networks of social interaction have always been previous to interactors, so that one may speak of the *individual previousness of the network*. Within a new network they join, and they must at first take their positions before they intervene. The environment determines more or less comprehensively which positions may be taken. In a second step I will discuss my own interaction concept which takes the relational conditions and processes as a starting point. It tries to take a middle and mediating position with regard to established concepts of interaction. Thirdly, I will present one out of several case studies on the basis of which the concept was empirically tested. It concerns human-robot cooperations, in other words, a border case of social interaction. For in the field of robotics such cooperations come along with the expectation that technological laymen will interact with a robotic system without much previous experience and that interpersonal situations can be created. Therefore, the sociologically thrilling question is: How intuitively does the robotic system really work? Precisely because the approach presented here assumes processes and positional structures instead of social actors, it is possible to deal with this borderline case of social interaction without getting entangled in leveling out man and technology and their respective specific features, such as e.g. in the concept of action. This study is a non-natural setting. In a fourth step the approach concerning the video analysis will be discussed in detail. In this context I will refer to Müller-Doohm's hermeneutical analysis scheme. In a fifth step I will compare these results with those of the interviews.

The relationalistic-hermeneutical position and perspective

I will now come to the first step, namely to the short explanation of my position and perspective on interaction. As Harrison C. White puts it, it is about the formulation of a middle position (cp. also Azarian 2000: 13-14). Such a position emanates neither from the individual as a quasi isolated actor, like for example in classic action theory, nor does this position aim at postulating a structural determinism, meaning that action and communication are largely determined by norms, institutions, organizational structures, cultural values, etc. A relational solution emphasizes the intermediate, in other words, the world of social relations and interdependencies. Because of them, individual actors and their behavior on the one hand and social structural patterns on the other hand become understandable in the first place. The newborn child is already embedded in the concrete network of its family, and it takes a specific position within it (e.g. of being the pampered planned child), according to which specific relationships are organized. The latter depend on the way the parents and other members of the family influence its «anthropogenesis», to have it in Elias's words (1978). The same applies to later phases of family life, to school, to professional life, to marriage, and to leisure time. Granovetter (1985) speaks of the «embeddedness» of individuals in principal. Relatively stable social entities emerge in the process, in which expectations are answered with accordant behavior, which again stabilize expectations recursively. The reciprocity of expectations makes sure that everybody plays his part in a conventional situation.

Furthermore, structural statements need to be generated with regard to the location of interactors, too: they take positions in certain places within the network. They do not only enable interaction. They also restrict it: first, they always provide a sector-like perspective on the relational close vicinity and not a topological view of the network as a whole. Second, they are influenced by a very specific set of influences on, and expectations of the respective concrete environment. Third, there are only restricted possibilities to interfere with the network process beyond the predominant or linkable relations in the close vicinity, since the latter are the interactor's only links to his/her environment.

The four-level interaction concept

According to sociological definitions an interaction is understood as an «interrelation between actions», inasmuch as ego, under the condition of the co-presence of alter, orientates its interactive contribution towards the expectations of alter and to the appraisal of the situation in common (cp. Hillmann 1994: 381-382). Viewed in such a way, the sociological conceptualization of interaction always proceeds relationally and process-relatedly. In general, the interaction concept which is to be discussed here follows this relational perspective. It particularly aims at combining individual actors' views with the results of the change towards the level of interaction. The latter has its own dynamics and structural pattern. To fulfill this intention, four levels need to be distinguished analytically (cp. Figure 1): the level of the interaction network (a)[1], the level of interventions (b), the level of expressing emotions (c), and the level of the semantic context (d). These levels are connected to each other in a variety of ways. This connection will be dealt with in the context of explaining the level of the interaction network. They are supposed to render possible the analysis of social interaction in its multi-dimensionality. The operationalization of this concept then provides for four accordant levels of investigation. Each case requires specific research instruments. The video analysis can contribute to every level. In the following I would like to introduce these four levels individually and present initial empirical methods for their analysis at every level.

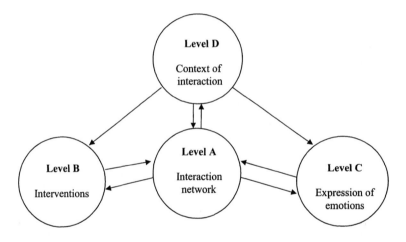

Figure 1: The four-level interaction concept and the interdependence of the levels

The level of interventions

I will undertake a selective differentiation between interactions and interventions in this four-level concept. Interventions result from micropolitical calculations of individual actors. They are therefore an expression of the effort to play a part in the ongoing interaction sequence via a contribution of one's own. If one asks for the impulse for such interventions, one is referred to motives, needs and goals of the particular actor.

---

[1] For didactic reasons this level which is the middle one in Figure 1 will be the last one to be introduced.

Insofar, it is not about a mere allocation of a specific network identity or a network position, respectively. Rather, the actors' positions are adopted individually and charged motivationally.

In principle, one can distinguish between two forms of human interventions in interactive events (cp. also Alexander 1988: 312-316): on the one hand, the kinetic initiation is an active intervention, for instance in the form of a statement, of an action as well as of non-verbal communication. On the other hand, human actors intervene by interpreting events and by drawing conclusions from the interactive event, not least because these interpretations then lead action and communication. I follow Berger and Luckmann's social constructivism here according to which the most important experience of others takes place in face-to-face situations (cp. Berger/Luckmann 1967: 28). A contribution only appears at the level of interaction when both of the two forms of human interventions merge. Both of them are thus just as constitutive for the accomplishment of an interaction. However, interventions are distributed among different actors. For example, ego acts, whereas alter interprets this as an intentional act and this narration causes him/her to act in a certain way on his/her part, and so forth (cp. Figure 2).

Even in seemingly straightforward social formations social coherences are normally notedly complex, since all participants continuously perform specific interventions which can only to a certain calculable degree be converted to contributions at the level of networks, and yielding taxable subsequent processes and backlashes proves even more difficult. Thus, the specific assimilational and converting restrictions, and most notably limitations, which are conditioned upon a position only allow the actor to view a particular part of his/her environment. Consequently, parts of the environment in which the actor is imbedded (and which influence him/her) remain neglected.

There is only a slight probability that the actor can foresee the result of his/her intervention, which interacts with the contexts in which he/she is embedded. The same certainly applies to its interpretations: they depend on the position, they only capture a section of ongoing events, and they are conditional upon the specific set of control of his/her environment (cp. also White 1992: 9-14). Actions and communications are not up for grabs independently of interpretations. However, depending on the situation, those who appear as agents or communicators are an interpretative product of the other participants of the interaction. In this sense a combination of the two forms of intervention can be comprehended as the root of a social relation.

Acts of speaking always offer a flanking aspect, too, which can be interpreted as action. And conversely, physical interventions can be interpreted by inter-actors as symbols and can, therefore, always be related to the contents of the information and communication (cp. also Geser 1996, chapter 2.2: 15-16). That something appears to be an action or a kind of communication is therefore basically a question of interpretation. Human interventions lie between intentions and interactions, and they are still sociologically and empirically approachable.

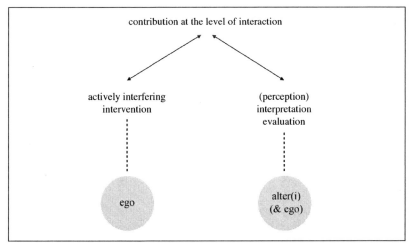

Figure 2: The two forms of intervention and their relation to the level of interaction

And what about interventions of so-called «interactive technologies» which Werner Rammert (2003: 296) understands to be situational coordinating and socially intervening systems? Basically the same applies to them as does with human interventions, with the exception that they rest on other non-social aspects. Their operation results from actuating elements and «embodied cognition» (cp. Brocks 1991). In order to appear as contributions they have to be interpreted by an individual as attempts to engage with the ongoing events (cp. Figure 3, left side). Conversely, «interactive technologies» have to analyze and determine human action (cp. Figure 3, right side). The interpretations are based on sensor technology and algorithms of so-called «shared intelligence» (SI) (cp. Bhatia/Uchiyama/Nakazato 1992).[2]

Technical interventions then lie in-between environment-sensitive «shared cognition» and interaction, and they can be approached sociologically and empirically, too. These interventions can be evaluated by way of video analysis. This is the only kind of analysis which provides the opportunity to adequately capture situative interventions and their significant contents in relation to the ongoing processes.

---

[2] «Shared intelligence» means that a technology disposes of a perception of the environment, a procedure to its situation-appropriate analysis («situated action», cp. Lobin 1993) and matched sensitive actuating elements. This is the case with human–robot cooperation.

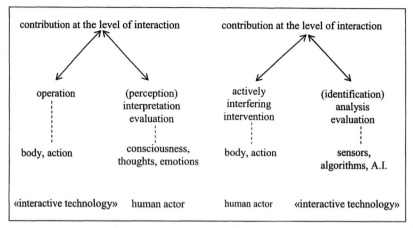

Figure 3: The interactive connection of human and robot interventions

The level of the expression of emotions

The expression of emotions is discussed as a special form of intervention at level C. They in the first place render a contact a binding social relation. They express individual actors' personal relations and relevant patterns. This level contains firstly the affiliation to groups and contexts, secondly comments on ongoing processes, thirdly the designation of own contributions and fourthly affective statements.

To the observer and with regard to social relations, the expression of emotions is always a demonstration of «closeness» or «distance», respectively. Relations which are built on this foundation, such as for example a friendship, can be interpreted as stories that are created by the participating actors for themselves and for each other (cp. White 1992: 66-70). Following Kahn and Antonucci (1980), the use of the so-called emotional network card is a suitable means to survey these stories empirically.

The expression of emotions themselves can be recorded with cameras and is available for scientific interpretation (cp. Katz 1999). During human-robot cooperation they can be interpreted as moods and sometimes as a test person's warning signal. Naturally, they do not have an effect, since the robotic system does not have adequate sensors to capture these sublime signals. Also, the robot lacks instruments for mimical and physical comprehension. Only their absence renders clear how essential nonverbal signals carry out crucial underhand corrections during ordinary interaction. Goffman and Garfinkel convincingly elaborate on this (cp. also Garfinkel 1967; Goffman 1988). (cp. also Garfinkel 1967; Goffman 1988). These insights are taken up here.

The level of the semantic context

Every interaction happens within a context and is only open to interpretation through this context. Analytically, two types of imprinting factors can be distinguished: the first type contains terms according to the specific context that must be assumed for the accomplishment of a certain interaction. Among them there are, for example, a specific role pattern and specific behavioral rituals for every single interaction. The second type contains determining factors which significantly affect the interaction from the outside, such as for example, legal, moral, and normative standards towards individual actors. To identify these heterogeneous context sizes, Niklas Luhmann's concept of semantics is applied (Luhmann 1980): based on a relatively fixed factural, temporal and social context, his concept describes the entirety of the forms of meaning. The semantic context of an interaction includes cultural symbols, terms, common language, and urban jargon, norms as well as the set of already established roles. A mix of methods can be used in order to analyze the interaction context, for example, analyses of documents, interview analyses, and the evaluation of open questions in a questionnaire.

The level of the interaction network

The level of interaction can be analytically differentiated in two ways: firstly, in terms of its structural dimensions, and secondly in terms of its dynamic aspects. According to White (1992) every member is assigned his network position or respective identity through network dynamics and network constellations. Therefore, actors take up network-specific positions which are basically designed socially and in particular semantically. Social relations and their definition are accordingly contingent due to a network of other relations. This means on the other hand: the network constellation and focal processes substantially form singular interactions as well as the actors' self- and external perception. During the focal processes »path dependency»[3] and interaction dynamics can establish themselves because of the relational constellations which give these interactions a direction. Individual actors can hardly be influenced by the latter. Video analysis can widely analyze interaction.[4]

These four levels are locked together in many ways: nonverbal acts of emotion, for example, have to revert to semantics by way of which one can express joy, approval or other forms of emotion. In this four level concept the network level takes on a key position. Their effects on the development of the in-

---

[3] «A path dependent sequence [...] is one of which important influences upon the eventual outcome can be exerted by temporally remote events, including happenings dominated by chance elements rather than systematic forces. Stochastic processes like that do not converge automatically to a fixed point distribution of outcomes, and are called non-ergodic.» (David 1985: 332).

[4] More on this in chapter 4.

teraction interaction as well as the transformation and adoption of the semantic specifications can be observed. Therefore, micropolitical interventions become visible. So much for the theoretical setting in necessary brevity. The following case study will exemplarily demonstrate its operationalization.

The case study: human-robot cooperation

The case study refers to «human-robot cooperation» (cp. Prassler et al. 2005). I carried out several test series on the University of Karlsruhe's service-robot «AMAR 3»[5]. According to the vision of robotics the future will see service robots which interact with humans in several parts of human everyday life: robots act as tour guides or receptionists, bar keepers, and household aids. There will be assisting robotic devices for elderly people, and many more. These types of service robots are usually intended to interact with people who are not robot experts: intuitive handling and natural communication are important requirements for human-robot interfaces. A major requirement for these types of intelligent systems is, on the one hand, that they should be able to act autonomously. On the other hand, they have to interact with humans and therefore know a person's ways and habits. As human behavior is comprised of a large variety of intentions, actions, emotions, and verbal and non-verbal communication, the way a human being acts is hard to foresee. This often leads to a normal person's confusion, frustration, and annoyance when interacting with a robot, since the system designer cannot anticipate all types of human behavior. Different international research teams assessed the people's reactions and feelings when they interact with robots.[6]

---

[5] AMAR 3 is the basic prototype of the Collaborative Research Center 588 «Humanoid Robots - Learning and Cooperating Multimodal Robots», which the German Research Foundation (Deutsche Forschungsgemeinschaft; DFG) established on July 1, 2001.

[6] First of all, Kerstin Dautenhahn's team analyzed the way people felt when they were approached by a service robot while they were handling a remote control from different sides (cp. Dautenhahn et al. 2006). Additionally, the spatial distance between human and robot that people describe as comfortable has been examined in large studies with adults and children (cp. Walters et al. 2007). These studies inspired a consideration of proximity: a service robot moving in an appartment respects distances people usually keep from each other in normal interaction and everyday life. In this way people feel more comfortable when being approached by a robot (cp. Alami et al. 2006). For several weeks Kanda et al. (2004) examined children's behavior at an elementary school in which a humanoid robot was used in a classroom. The children were allowed to interact with the English-speaking robot during playtime. All children had to wear specific name tags which the robot was able to identify. In order to maintain interaction with the children, the robot pursued various interacting schemes, such as, starting to have special secrets with selected children. Kanda studied the children's acceptance of the robot and its attraction. As long as the robot was new, several children wanted to talk to, and play with the robot. They even queued up and patiently waited for their turn. The number of children who played with the robot decreased steadily, especially during a period of fine weather. When the robot's departure was announced, the number of interacting children increased again. Infanoid is a humanoid torso which is learning social behavior and in-

Figure 4: The household-robot «AMAR 3»

The test series with «AMAR 3» focused on the following research question: how intuitively does the robotic system really work? A specific scene was engineered for the interaction scenario. The robot stood behind a table set with dishes. The test person stood in front of the table. There was a white wall in the background. The robot was able to detect every item on the table, the test person, and pointing gestures of the test person. The robot acted as a bartender, and the test person named an item on a table in front of the robot he or she wanted to

teraction with people (cp. Kozima/Nakagawa 2007). Using joint attention, Infanoid can focus on the object a person is looking at and can learn the name of the object from the person. Using human-like behavior and mimics, Infanoid can easily signal its internal state to the interacting person. The research team also performed studies with children who interacted with the robot. Here they found out that the children observed the robot without doing anything for a certain time. As soon as the children's mother started to interact with the robot, the children lost their shyness and started to play with the robot. Breazeal also found out that interaction with a robot becomes easier and is more accepted, if the robot is equipped with additional means of non-verbal communication and signalling (cp. Breazeal et al. 2004). In a field study with people who taught the robot Leonardo to press a specific button, Breazeal could show that the group of people who received non-verbal signals about the robot's state (the action to be performed had been understood) was more successful than a group without likewise feedback from the robot. The same could be shown by Burghart/Häußling (2005) in their study which evaluated different methods to cooperatively carry a wooden bar by a human and a robot. Usually, the actions of the robot were not transparent to the interacting person. All subjects tried to use several non-verbal communication channels like posture or mimics. Some even talked to the robot, although the sole sensing input to the robot control was a force-torque sensor.

be served with. The robot then tried to identify the selected item among others on the table by asking clarification and confirmation questions about the desired object, or to confirm its choice. The robot used the means of spoken interaction and multimodal reference. The robot's task was to understand what the person wants, to ask questions in order to obtain missing information or to clarify ambiguous information and to finally select the right object to serve the test person.

Bottles with orange juice, cups and plates could be found on the table. There was a variety of blue, red and yellow cups and plates. All items were equipped with a number, which could not be recognized by the robot. However, every test person could read the number on the item. At the beginning of the experiment the robot was taught the association between an item, i.e. a blue plate and its number. In this way the robot could ask for a confirmation of a selected item on the basis of the detection or the deduction of the position. Additionally, the robotic system was able to utter a hypothesis on the basis of the type or the colour of the item, watch out for the reaction of the test person, and then deduce the correct item. Thereby the test persons were without any further instructions and in accordance with the intuitive operation of service robots sent into cooperation. Initially they only knew how to speak to the robot, and they knew that the robot was able to recognize pointing gestures. The latter constitutes an advance in the field of nonverbal communication.[7] The robot's active word pool is limited to a few sentences only which he can somewhat vary. They are designed in such a way that the robot can handle a conversation with them.

The passive word pool of the robot is in itself capacious. The recognition of speech, however, works with an error rate not to be underestimated. (The same applies to the recognition of gestures.) The outstanding fact from the robotical point of view lies in the fact that the envisaged strategy of the robot is not, as one might expect, programmed but generated by a self-analysis of abortive and successful cooperations. Furthermore, the robot indeed knows the objects which are lying on the table. However, it is not familiar with their arrangement. In this case the robot is a «non-trivial machine» (Foerster 1997: 357ff.) that does not operate according to rules but rather learns from examples, and it optimizes itself.

One hundred eighty one-to-one cooperations were examined. In the process two groups of test persons were observed on three consecutive days each with five cooperations per test person. The first group consisted of computer science students, the other one of social science students. This way I tried to ensure that in

---

[7] The sensors of the robotic system include microphones for speech recognition: distant-speech microphones which are mounted on the head, and close-speech microphones (headset) which can be used by the subject in addition (only the latter was used for speech recognition in the experiment), a pan-tilt unit to move the head, and a stereo camera for 3D vision. During all interactions the system stores audio data as they are perceived by the system, and logging information about what has been recognized. These log-data include speech recognition results, gesture recognition results, and the interpretation of events and system output.

each case these groups would have different pre-knowledge and different expectations. This procedure guaranteed that each group stayed inside its own net work, to use my favored terminology.[8]

Figure 5: The lab setting of the recorded human-robot cooperations

A video analysis with the four-level interaction concept

The experiments were recorded by several video camera systems[9] and protocols were taken of every interaction. The test persons were interviewed[10] on a daily basis after the experiment in order to find out about their narrations about the cooperation and about the robotic system. A first review of the videos already revealed that the individual cooperations were extremely different. Some lasted

---

[8] Every day the test persons arrived one after the other. They were not allowed to watch the other test persons perform their experiments. Additionally, they were not permitted to talk to each other about the experiments or the robot. The research team enforced these measures in order to keep low external influences on the test persons which would affect the outcome of the experiments.
[9] One camera was used for the overall perspective of the set-up, the second recorded a frontal view of the test person in order to better analyze mimics, posture and gestures. The third video camera was the stereo camera head which was integrated into the robotic system. The latter was mainly used to identify the test persons' pointing gestures.
[10] The understanding of the narrations which the test persons developed with regard to the robotic systems and the situation were most important for the interviews. In Chapter 5 the way in which computer science students answered is contrasted to that of social science students.

for a few seconds only, others for several minutes. Some actors achieved a downright virtuosity on their part in the roleplay on the third day, others became frustrated. In addition, a great difference existed between the computer science and social science test persons.[11]

I will now discuss a cooperation with a computer science student which did not lead the robot to serve the requested object. However, it served something else. Especially the interactions and interventions can be examined via video analysis. The transcript (Figure 6) presents the last 12 seconds of the cooperation. They are presented here.[12]

The transcript configuration followed the four level-arrangement that I introduced. At the top I inserted a time bar. The immediate context of the interaction is located underneath. Only abnormal interventions of the environment, such as, disruptions or unauthorized support are stated there. Since the immediate context of the laboratory situation remained constant throughout the test series as described above, it is therefore not mentioned in the transcript. Dimensions of the social context were captured in interviews with the test persons afterwards.

The level of focal interactions particularly includes the verbal conversation between the test person and the robot as well as human pointing gestures, which also provide information for the robot. The protagonists' particular interventions were recorded underneath, whereas for the robot only the turning of his head was observed. On the side of the human actors especially the whole range of nonverbal statements was documented. These are the crucial indicators of what kind of sensitivities are predominant. The human actor's nonverbal signals are captured in a differentiated way by using Robert Harper`s analytical classification, which takes into consideration nonverbal aspects of speaking, motion in space, gesture, facial expression, posture, and line of sight (cp. Harper 1985).

My way of presenting the data takes the distinctiveness of the audiovisual meaning into account, because especially visual information differs fundamentally from textual information. They are not offhand translatable in a textual context, either. Visually, things are expressed which, as Boehm (1978) says, constitute themselves «as an open field of relationships and contrasts in between boundaries». Thereby non-conceptual and respective aspects, too, that cannot be

---

[11] When contemplating the aspect of success, that is, when the robot picked the right or the wrong item on the table-cooperation, the respective success rate turns out as follows: while a social science student on average realized 3.75 unsuccessful dialogs (out of a total of 15 dialogs), the corresponding number was 7.35 for computer science students. This is at first surprising, because it was assumed that computer science students would have better prior knowledge. But as is still to show, this had an especially blocking effect on the realization of the assignment.

[12] It was developed through the repeated play-back of the cooperation. In the process no slow-motion or fixed image was used, because of the problems that would have evolved. This would have meant to eventually alter the impact of the audiovisual material itself as Felicitas English (1991: 141-142) states. After all, the slow-motion elements that surface are inaccessible in a direct experience.

Video analysis with a four-level interaction concept 119

expressed are crucial, such as emotions, dispositions, etc. Visual perception grasps multifaceted, heterogeneous information simultaneously.

	11:48	11:58		12:00
Interaction context				
disruptions				
aids				
Focal interaction				
Robot	Sorry, I've to ask you again ! Of what type ist the item ?		Sorry, I've to ask you again ! Of what type ist the item ?	
Test person - verbal:		It's circular ???? Ah! Top.It's a cup.		It's a cup... to drink off!
- active intervention		unintentional double gesture of indication		
Interventions of robot				
Special aspects of speech				
Line of sight				
Interventions of test person				
Nonverbal aspects of speech		insecure hushed	hushed insecure stammers	articulate
Motion in the room				
Gesture		raises right forearm; lets hand circle	raises & drops both hands in front of stomach	stretches arms in justifying manner	leads hand to mouth; tilting motion with hand
Posture			slightly tense	
Facial expression		raises eyebrow		raises eyebrow
Line of sight		looks down on table		briefly closes eyes

Figure 6: Transcript of a short human-robot interaction sequence, analytically differentiated by the four-level interaction concept[13]

Simultaneity and the latency of meaning are the two basic differences between visual and textual perception (cp. also Wagner-Willi 2004: 50-53). Accordingly, a transcript cannot just ignore this difference. Due to this score-like editing of audiovisual events, the multi-informational purpose is maintained as well as the latency of meaning. Only by viewing the score, coherences between levels are «created» horizontally and vertically. And I deliberately say «created» in order to emphasize the creative and the constructive aspect, respectively, of the scientific interpretation of video material.[14] Insofar every new look at the score can provide details previously unperceived of, coherences and new perceptions. The interpretation remains inconclusive to a certain degree. Nevertheless, it claims to be scientific.

---

[13] The original English conversation is presented in the transcript. It contains grammatical errors.
[14] A basic reason is that videos are not reality. This is already suggested by reducing the three dimensions to two dimensions. In addition, the camera perspective is excluded (cp. also Müller-Doohm 1997: 85).

According to Stefan Mueller–Doohm's (1997: 98-100) image analysis, three steps are necessary to analyze the video material:[15]
(1) The notation of all audiovisual message elements of an interaction: at first, all individual active interventions have to be pooled in as much detail as possible. Erwin Panofsky (1970) calls this procedure a pre-iconographic description. They are listed in the score-like transcript at the particular level.
(2) The analysis of «adjacency pairs» in order to capture the relevance of expressive elements in interactive reference to each other:
According to a relational understanding of «adjacency pairs» (Sacks 1992), expressions are observed according to their interactive reference to each other. They have an indicatory iconic character. Thus, this analysis level corresponds with the iconographic degree of Panofsky's interpretation (cp. Panofsky 1970). An interaction, for example, is related to the reaction of the counterpart and regenerated, respectively, to a previous interaction. Thereby, a sequential approach of the conversation analysis is connected with a simultaneous analysis beyond the levels. The relational cross-reference between the individual elements of the message that are simultaneously and directly available to the eye and the ear, have to be reestablished.
(3) The coherence analysis in order to create a story of the course and coordination of the individual situations:
here, it is a matter of covering the entire structure of a longer course of interaction. The aim is to create a preferably coherent analysis of individual situations and the story of the development. This explicitly includes the diagnosis of disruptions and the modification of behavior.
I will now go through each of these three analytical steps of Müller-Doohm's three-step analysis scheme. Concerning the first step, the issue compilation of the transcript, I have already named the important things. However, how must the transcript be read? The chosen excerpt contains the situation of crisis during the cooperation. In this case it is especially striking how many nonverbal signals come from the test person. For example: During his comment «It's circular...», his voice changes. He becomes insecure and silent; he interrupts himself. At the same time his hands make circular motions (cp. Figure 7).

Figure 7: «It's circular...»

---

[15] I will turn to the transcript later on.

And during his following statement «It's a cup...», the test person stretches both of his arms sideways (cp. Figure 8). His posture is tense.

Figure 8: «It's a cup...»

He also remains in this posture while the robot asks again about the type of object. The following repetition of the test person's statement, «It's a cup...» is in fact at first clearly articulated. But he interrupts himself again and adds after a short pause, «...to drink out of...». In doing so he raises his left hand to his mouth. His thumb points to his mouth, and his remaining fingers face upwards. They are slightly bent. His wrist performs a tilting motion (cp. Figure 9). At the end of his gesture he closes his eyes.

Figure 9: «...to drink out of...»

The second step of Müller-Doohm's analysis scheme generates a process-related interpretation. This refers to the particular pair-sequence of an interaction. A specific protocol for video analysis based on the transcripts called Interaction Analysis Tool (IAT) (cp. Figure 10) was generated for this step. Here, a series of criteria for evaluation come into effect which capture in a systematic way the robot's action and that of the test person. In the first lines where again the IAT contains the verbal and nonverbal actions in short form, they are however already arranged as intervention pairs.

For example turn one: the robot's particular action is noted as the first part after which an expression of the test person follows. This occurs, despite the fact that the test person opens the interaction by stepping in front of the robot. This is noted in the first column of the IAT.

As will be mentioned below (cp. Figure 10), a relational evaluation of the interventions (level B of the four-level interaction concept, cp. Figure 1) follows (cp. the layers of denotation in the second building block of the IAT): if one considers the interventions as an information for the counter-part, the question will come up to what the information refers to. It may refer to the desire to open up an interaction or to end it, respectively; but it might also refer to a specific content, to the role occupied in the interaction, to the way in which the interaction takes place and how the interaction should be carried out (meta-information). It might also refer to the context of the interaction or to earlier events in the interaction. Thereby, it is not taken into account, whether the counter-part, for instance the robot, is able to understand the things that have just been said.[16] For example, «Welcome», the opening phrase of the robot in, «Welcome, I'm your bartender robot. Which item may I serve you?» includes the desire to start an interaction, «bartender» a definition of his role, «which item» a content, and «serve you» refers to the context of the interaction.

By using the system of attributes underneath (cp. the third building block of the IAT, Figure 10), relational–interactive constellations can be captured (level A of the four-level interaction concept, cp. Figure 1). Only those attributes are applied in the process which are suitable both for the actions of the robot and of the test person. In doing so, a symmetrical treatment of the human actor and the robot is indeed possible; however here the actor network theory by Callon (1986) and Latour (1987) is not followed, because the actor network theory is interested in the allocation of the activity and not in the interactive dynamics and the specific interlocking of human and technical actions in socio-technological constellations. The attribute «initiative» distinguishes between an active part which leads the conversation and a passive, reacting part. Except for the opening, the robot conducts the interaction as intended. The attribute «coherence» estimates whether actions refer to the counterpart's immediate previous actions or not. «Redundancy» indicates whether information was given or requested several times, respectively, for instance verbally and nonverbally. Thereby, the levels of reference the redundant information refers to are noted down in brackets. The degree of «complexity» results from the amount of layers of denotation to which an actor's contribution is cross-referred to, i.e. the sum of the layers of denotation. The attribute «information strategy» defines the way in which information is given and asked for. Here, strategies of the partial, singular, and entire information in order to control the hypotheses, its response and the answer out of context can be differentiated. The attribute of «transparency» indicates whether

---

[16] During the experiment there was also a reverse case, in which the robot was speaking about a blue object, and the test person was colour-blind.

However, as early as after the second turn an incoherency emerges: while the robot asks the test person only verbally indicates that the object is located on the left side without giving any information to the point of reference of this indicated direction. He then carries out a delayed, half-hearted and briefly performed pointing gesture with his forearm. The robot cannot identify such a motion as a pointing gesture. Due to his programming the robot remembers all requests for indication gestures. When the identification of the given gesture fails he tries to find out the right object by using indication gestures himself during the third term.[18]

In turn four the robot starts to assure himself of the given information and to point to this behavior. Interestingly, the test person takes on this behavior and starts to refer to previous statements himself. The robot once more changes his information strategy during turn eight. After a longer, uninterrupted period of hypothetical questions he now starts, as indicated by the category of information, to ask easy questions concerning the characteristics of the requested object.

After the robot asked the same question for a second time, the otherwise cool-headed test person becomes choked up and tries to describe the desired object, a red cup, as a geometrical figure. However, he pauses during the description, which he tries to underline with gestures (cp. Figure 7). He apparently does so, because he realizes the pointlessness of his undertaking to describe the object to the robot in this way (as if the robot would know what a «circular structure» means). He fails to do so and tries to name the main category of the item. But in doing so he makes an explaining gesture in the form of two outstretched arms (cp. Figure 8). This gesture is identified by the robot as a double pointing gesture, thus as relevant but antithetic information.

This way one encounters a basic problem of the technological actor: he absolutely cannot tell the difference between an attachment and neccessary information (cp. also Baecker 2002: 24-25). And this is not only true for the recognition of pointing gestures. It applies to the recognition of speech, too. Because of this the robot tries to solve the problem with the help of incremental steps. This again irritates the test person, so that they no longer deliver the necessary information in the optimal way. This is one of the crucial factors for the failure to find the solution for the cooperation assignment asked for. But back to the coherence analysis!

Immediately after the discussed sequence, the robot inquires about the type of object for a third time. In this instance the test person gets into explanation difficulties. Indeed, he at first states that the type of object is a cup. However, he believes that he has to complement his answer with a gesture and thus shows that it is an object from which one can drink (cp. Figure 9).

---

[18] This modification of the behavior only becomes visible, if one analyzes other transcripts for the nonverbal attribute «pointing gesture». One can then observe that the robot asks for pointing gestures more often in other interactions.

The test persons' involuntary actions express the implied stories that they created about their counterpart and about the cooperation.[19] They cause certain interventions by the robot that again lead to misinterpretations by the test persons. Since this apparent implicitness as an anthropocentric requirement is not recognized by the test persons, they are surprised that the robot does not react, or simply reacts in a wrong way to their interventions. The test person discussed in the previous section indicated in the interview that he wanted to interact without pointing gestures in order to test the system. This could be the reason why he did not point toward the item in turn two. As a result the robot stopped asking for pointing gestures due to its dialog strategy. Without an indication of the position, the task became more difficult. The robot tried to adjust itself to this disadvantage by using hypothetical questions but had to refer to the index now.

The results of the interviews interpreted according to the four-level interaction concept

As suggested by the results of the previous chapter, it is precisely the different narrations of the test persons which produced the different results of cooperation. This is in accordance with statements by other computer science students concerning the interactions and their counterpart. These students have a rather technical perception, which is focused on control-cycles of the robot. By method of elimination (for instance, to show no pointing gestures, even if the robot asked for them), they tried to find out what kind of information the robot needs. They wanted to understand, as they described, how the robotical system functions internally, which is a hopeless undertaking with a «non-trivial machine» (Foerster). Basically, they view the robot as a causal mechanism and get into difficulties because of the robot's degrees of freedom. After the third day, i.e. after 15 individual cooperations were performed, three out of four computer science students stated that only the robot is responsible for the failure of the cooperation. Two of them were convinced that the robot does not have any envisaged specifics, that the whole thing was a «fake», and that the robot was in reality guided by a real-time programmer. Such an assumption can only be made, if one is familiar with robotics and knows that so-called «wizard-of-oz-experiments» are often used. In those experiments a whole staff of software engineers insinuates the necessary instructions to the robot in real-time to accomplish the tasks. This is a particular extreme case in which prior knowledge has a downright blocking effect. And indeed, this particular test person tried to provoke the robot

---

[19] During other cooperations similar narrations could be derived from the behavior: the subjects assumed that the robot had a short-term memory when they used phrases such as, «like I just said». In addition, the distinction between left and right is anything but without presupposition, not only because it is dependent on the perspective. Moreover, it was presumed that the robotic system knew what «orange juice» or «coke» was. Also, one test person believed that the robot was able to identify the transparency of a plastic bottle.

during the third day, or maybe, the computer scientist he assumed to be operating in the background.

In contrast, there was only one out of eight social science students who put the entire blame on the robot. This group of test persons paid more attention to the conversation and the interaction itself. They wanted to find out, as they described it, in what way one has to speak (for instance slowly and clearly) so that the robot could react in the right way, or that in order to speak one had to use pointing gestures as well, or for how long one had to show the object to the robot. Accordingly, the adabtable configuration of the cooperation act in which they engaged in the robot's incremental approach is seen as the essential dimension of success. By contrast, the computer science students focused on the kind of logics the robot was following, and in doing so they exhibited an actor-centered perspective.

Conclusion

On the basis of this videoanalysis I wanted to introduce the three-step interpretation scheme according to Müller-Doohm's hermeneutical analysis strategy. As a sociological method it theoretically resorts to an interaction concept. Here, an argument is made for the shift of the scientific perspective away from the individual actor to that what lies between them, namely interactions and relations, as has been postulated by Harrison C. White. If one understands the interaction level as a level plaited out of dynamic relations, one has to make a difference between the ongoing processes that take place there and the involved persons' interventions. Thereby the nonverbal field is taken as the crucial factor. By signalling emotional ties the persons involved get into a closeness-distance relation. With that, indifference is excluded. On the nonverbal level a lot of sublime corrections are carried out. This becomes a problem in socio-technological interactions, because these misguided interactions lead to failure. Via the fine-grained differentiation of interventions and interactions as well as within interventions by way of the four-level interaction concept, it is possible to open up exactly these interaction-guiding aspects, both in comparable precision and by way of relevant micro-sociological approaches. At the same time the influence of superior contexts (such as the influence of other social networks) can be included into the analysis. Since a relationalistic approach, as emphasized by White, too, explains actors through relational and positional constellations, questions of the ability to act or of who acts are defused with regard to «interactive techniques». For this is only a question of attributing the participating humans and the way in which their expectations are met by technological interventions. In this sense we can also distance ourselves from dealing with man and technology in a radically symmetrical way, as does the actor network theory.

The multi-level categorization system (cp. Figure 10) is general enough to serve as an evaluation scheme for all human-robot interactions. Other interaction scenarios might require additional categories, which take into account different capabilities and the growing «intelligence» of the robot. Other evaluation purposes might require additional categories, too. The overall goal, however, is to detect critical phases in specific forms of interaction and to detect interaction sequences and «path dependencies». By analyzing multiple single interactions within a specific scenario, one can reveal critical states in the interaction. By analyzing the context of these states, strategies can be developed to get the person back on track or to completely avoid such situations.[20]

The type of transcript (cp. Figure 6) is seen here as especially suitable. It is supposed to take the impact latency and the simultaneity of audiovisual objects into account. It does not constitute contents with audiovisual significance hastily as do text-shaped transcripts and text, respectively. And ultimately it was important to me not to evaluate socio-technological constellations anthropocentrically. The actor-centering was completely abandoned. Instead, the focus was on the effect of technological and human actions on a socio-technological level of cooperation.

References

Abbott, Andrew, 1995: Things of boundaries – Defining the boundaries of social inquiry. In: *Social Research* 62, 857-882.
Abbott, Andrew, 2001: *Time matters. On theory and method.* Chicago et al.: Chicago University Press.
Alami, Rachid/Raja Chatila/Aurelie Clodic/Sara Fleury/Matthieu Herrb/Vincent Montreuil/Emrah Akin Sisbot, 2006: Towards human-aware cognitive robots. In: Proceedings of the *AAAI-06 Workshop on Cognitive Robotics* (Boston, Massachusetts, USA, July 2006).
Alexander, Jeffrey C., 1988: *Action and its environments. Toward a new synthesis.* New York: Columbia University Press.
Azarian, Reza, 2000: *The basic framework in the general sociology of Harrison C. White.*
<http://www.mot.chalmers.se/dept/idy/home/azarian.pdf> (17.12.2007)
Baecker, Dirk, 2002: *Wozu Systeme.* Berlin: Kadmos.
Berger, Peter L./Thomas Luckmann, 1967: *The Social construction of reality. A treatise in the sociology of knowledge.* London: The Penguin Press.
Bhatia, Praveen/Masaru Uchiyama/Hiroyuki Nakazato, 1992: Shared intelligence in path planning for telerobots with time delay. In: Conference Proceedings, *Robotic Society of Japan.* Tokyo (Japan), 453-456.
Blumer, Herbert, 1969: *Symbolic interactionism. Perspective and method.* Englewood Cliffs et al.: Prentice-Hall.
Boehm, Gottfried, 1978: Zu einer Hermeneutik des Bildes. In: Hans-Georg Gadamer/Gottfried Boehm (eds.), *Die Hermeneutik und die Wissenschaften.* Frankfurt a.M.: Suhrkamp.

---

[20] This necessitates further evaluation of different scenarios for human-robot interaction.

Breazeal, Cynthia/Andrew Brooks/Jesse Gray/Guy Hoffman/Cory D. Kidd/Hans Lee/Jeff Lieberman/Andrea Lockerd/David Chilongo, 2004: Tutelage and collaboration for humanoid robots. In: *International Journal of Humanoid Robotics* 1, 2, 315-348.
Brooks, Rodney A., 1991: Intelligence without representation. In: *Artificial Intelligence* 47, 139-160.
Burghart, Catherina R./Roger Häußling, 2005: Evaluation criteria for human robot interaction. In: Society for the Study of Artificial Intelligence and the Simulation of Behavior (ed.), *Hard problems and open challenges in robot-human interaction.* Hartfield (UK), 23-31.
Callon, Michel, 1986: Some Elements of a sociology of translation. Domestication of the scallops and the fishermen of St. Brieuc Bay. In: Law, John (ed.), *Power, action and belief. A new sociology of knowledge.* London et al.: Routledge & Kegan Paul, 196-229.
Christaller, Thomas, 1996: Kognitive Robotik. In: Christa Maar/Ernst Pöppel/Thomas Christaller (eds.), *Die Technik auf dem Weg zur Seele.* Reinbek bei Hamburg: Rowohlt Taschenbuch Verlag, 321-326.
Christaller, Thomas/Josef Wehner (eds.), 2003: *Autonome Maschinen.* Wiesbaden: Westdeutscher Verlag.
Dautenhahn Kerstin/Michael L. Walters/Sarah Woods/Kheng Lee Koay/ Chrystopher L. Nehaniv/Emrah Akin Sisbot/Rachid Alami/Thierry Siméon, 2006: How may I serve you? A robot companion approaching a seated person in a helping context. In: Proceedings of the *ACM International Conference on Human Robot Interaction HRI 06* (Salt Lake City, Utah, USA, March 2006).
David, Paul A., 1985: Clio and the economics of QWERTY. In: *Economic History,* 75, 227-332.
Elias, Norbert, 1978: *What is sociology?* London: Hutchinson.
Emirbayer, Mustafa/Jeff Goodwin, 1994: Network analysis, culture, and the problem of agency. In: *American Journal of Sociology,* 99, 6, 1411-1454.
Englisch, Felicitas, 1991: Bildanalyse in strukturalhermeneutischer Einstellung. Methodische Überlegungen und Analysebeispiele. In: Detlef Graz/Klaus Kraimer (eds.), *Qualitativ-empirische Sozialforschung.* Opladen: Westdeutscher Verlag, 133-176.
Foerster, Heinz von/Siegfried J. Schmidt, 1997: *Wissen und Gewissen. Versuch einer Brücke. Eine Festschrift mit den wichtigsten Aufsätzen von Förster.* Frankfurt a.M.: Suhrkamp.
Garfinkel, Harold, 1967: *Studies in ethnomethodology.* Englewood Cliffs: Prentice-Hall.
Geser, Hans, 1996: Die komplexe Mehrebenenstruktur kollokaler Interaktionen. In: Hans Geser (ed.), *Elementare soziale Wahrnehmungen und Interaktionen. Ein theoretischer Integrationsversuch.* <http://geser.net/elin/2_2.htm> (24.9.2007)

Gibson, David R., 2005: Taking turns and talking ties: Networks and conversational interaction. In: *American Journal of Sociology*, 110, 6, 1561-1597.
Goffman, Erving, 1988: *Exploring the interaction order.* Edited by Paul Drew/ Anthony Wootton. Cambridge: Polity.
Goodwin, Marjorie H./Charles Goodwin, 2000: Emotion within situated activity. In: Nancy Budwig/Ina C. Uzgris/James V. Wertsch (eds.), *Communication: An arena of development.* Stamfort CT, 33-54.
Granovetter, Marc, 1985: Economic action and social structure: the problem of embeddedness. In: *American Journal of Sociology*, 91, 481-510.
Harper, Richard/John Hughes, 1993: What a f-ing system. Send 'em all to the same place and then expect us to stop 'em hitting. Making technology work in air traffic control. In: Graham Button (ed.), *Technology in working order. Studies of work, interaction, and technology.* London et al.: Routledge & Kegan Paul, 127-144.
Harper, Robert G., 1985: Power, dominance, and nonverbal behavior: An overview. In: Steve L. Ellyson/John F. Dovidio (eds.), *Power, dominance, and nonverbal behavior.* New York: Springer-Verlag, 29-48.
Hillmann, Karl-Heinz (ed.), 1994: *Wörterbuch der Soziologie.* Stuttgart: Kröner, 4th edition.
Hochschild, Arlie Russel, 1979: Emotion work, feeling rules and social structure. In: *American Journal of Sociology* 85, 551-575.
Holzapfel, Hartwig/Alex Waibel, 2000: A multilingual expectations model for contextual utterances in mixed-initiative spoken sialogue. In: Proceedings of the *International Conference Interspeech 2006 – ICSLP* (Pittsburgh PA, USA, 2006).
Holzapfel, Hartwig/Kai Nickel/Rainer Stiefelhagen, 2004: Implementation and evaluation of a constraint-based multimodal fusion system for speech and 3D ointing gestures. In: Proceedings of the *International Conference on Multimodal Interfaces (ICMI)* (State College, 2004).
Kahn, Robert L./Toni C. Antonucci, 1980: Convoys over the life course: Attachment, roles and social support. In: Paul B. Baltes/Orville G. Brim (eds.), *Life-span development and behaviour.* Vol. III. New York: Academic Press, 383-405.
Kanda, Takayuki/Rumi Sato/Naoki Saiwaki/Hiroshi Ishiguro, 2004: Friendly social robot that understands human's friendly relationships. In: Proceedings of *IEEE/RSJ International Conference on Intelligent Robots and Systems (IROS2004)*, 2215-2222.
Katz, Jack, 1999: *How emotions work?* Chicago: The University of Chicago Press.
Kawamura, Kazuhiko/Robert T. Pack/Magued Bishay/Moenes Iskarous, 1996: Design philosophy for service robots. In: *Robotics and Autonomous Systems* 18: 109-116.
Kozima, Hideki/Cocoro Nakagawa, 2007: *Interactive robots as facilitators of children's social development.* In: Aleksandar Lazinica (ed.), *Mobile*

robots: Towards new applications. Vienna: Advanced Robotic Systems, 269-286.
Latour, Bruno, 1987: *Science in action: How to follow scientists and engineers through society.* Milton Keynes: Open University Press.
Luhmann, Niklas, 1980: *Gesellschaftsstruktur und Semantik. Studien zur Wissenssoziologie der modernen Gesellschaft.* Vol. 1. Frankfurt a.M.: Suhrkamp.
Mandel, Christian/Kai Huebner/Tilman Vierhuff, 2005: Towards an autonomous wheelchair: Cognitive aspects in service robotics. In: Proceedings of the International Conference *Towards Autonomous Robotic Systems (TAROS 2005),* 165–172.
Müller-Doohm, Stefan, 1997: Bildinterpretation als struktural-hermeneutische Symbolanalyse. In: Ronald Hitzler/Anne Hitzler (eds.), *Sozialwissenschaftliche Hermeneutik. Eine Einführung.* Opladen: Leske + Budrich, 81-108.
Otero, Nuno/Chrystopher L. Nehaniv/Kerstin Dautenhahn/Joe Saunders/Aris Alissandrakis, 2006: Naturally occuring gestures in a human robot interaction. In: Proceedings of the *15th IEEE International Symposium on Robot and Human Interactive Communication (ROMAN 06)* (Hartfield, GB, 2006).
Panofsky, Erwin, 1970: *Meaning in the visual arts.* Harmondsworth: Penguin.
Prassler, Erwin/Gisbert Lawitzky/Andreas Stopp/Gerhard Grunwald/Martin Hägele/Rüdiger Dillmann/Ioannis Iossifidis (eds.), 2005: *Advances in human-robot interaction.* Berlin et al.: Springer.
Rammert, Werner, 2003: Technik in Aktion: Verteiltes Handeln in soziotechnischen Konstellationen. In: Thomas Christaller/Josef Wehner (eds.), *Autonome Maschinen.* Wiesbaden: Westdeutscher Verlag, 289-315.
Rammert, Werner/Cornelius Schubert (eds.), 2006: *Technographie. Zur Mikrosoziologie der Technik.* Frankfurt a.M. et al.: Campus.
Rammert, Werner/Ingo Schulz-Schaeffer (eds.), 2002: *Können Maschinen handeln? Soziologische Beiträge zum Verhältnis von Mensch und Technik.* Frankfurt a.M. et al.: Campus.
Sacks, Harvey, 1992 [1964]: Doing «being ordinary». In: Jefferson Gail/Emanuel A. Schegloff (eds.), *Lectures on conversation.* Oxford: Blackwell.
Wagner-Willi, Monika, 2004: Videointerpretation als mehrdimensionale Mikroanalyse am Beispiel schulischer Alltagsszenen. In: *Zeitschrift für Qualitative Bildungs-, Beratungs- und Sozialforschung* 1, 182–193.
Walters, Michael L./Kerstin Dautenhahn/Sarah N. Woods/Kheng Lee Koay, 2007: Robotic etiquette: results from user studies involving a fetch and carry task. In: Proceedings of the *2nd ACM/IEEE International Conference on Human-Robot Interaction (Washington DC, USA, March 2007).*
White, Harrison C., 1992: *Identity and control. A structural theory of social action.* Princeton et al.: Princeton University Press.

Ethnography and Phenomenology

Larissa Schindler

The production of «vis-ability»: An ethnographic video analysis of a martial arts class

The technical support of data collection has long been one of the major themes in the discussion of qualitative empirical research. The advantages of video recordings for the study of interactions have been discussed extensively (cp. e.g. Heath 1997, Bergmann 1985, Knoblauch et al 2006). Limitations of this research tool, such as, the reduction of social processes to an audio-visual, two-dimensional reproduction are obvious (cp. e.g. Schnettler/Knoblauch 2008). Thus, the task of my paper is not primarily to tackle methodological issues, nor does it only present an ethnographic video analysis. Rather, it aims at describing the field of martial arts classes and the ethnographic research process and its use of video recordings at the same time. It focuses on «vis-ability», the ability to see what is being displayed, be it the members of the martial arts class or the sociological data session of a video recording of the martial arts class.

The reason for this focus is that in the course of presentations of video recordings of martial arts classes an interesting phenomenon occurred: most of my colleagues had severe problems to recognize martial arts movements in these videos, even though they could easily see that the instructor was displaying something. This matches the problem most martial arts beginners face: they have difficulties to see and understand the martial arts movements the instructor displays to them. Those who are familiar with martial arts, however, see martial arts movements in the video as well as in the instructor's performances. Therefore, I pose the following question: what is visible in the video and what is seen in it? How is the vis-ability of a martial arts movement fabricated?

I will suggest that we are not just seeing what is visible in the videoclip. Rather, vis-ability has to be fabricated by taking into consideration ethnographic knowledge. The crucial assumption that underlies this argument is that not only the reconstruction of what can be seen, but seeing itself is already a highly complex and situated activity.

The argument that seeing is a situated activity was made by Charles and Marjorie Goodwin (1996) in a study of the work of airport personnel. They point out that seeing is not a single perceptional event. Rather, it is located within a framework of different activities concerning planes, flights, tables, displays, gates. Furthermore, they suggest that «the work-relevant perceptual act [...] doesn't exist apart from the heterogeneous work involved in assembling a set of relevant perspectives for viewing it» (Goodwin/Goodwin 1996: 77). Seeing is therefore a situated activity that needs to be accomplished.

Applied to video analysis this indicates that we do not «preserve» a situation only by reproducing the visual impression of a situation. What is seen to be happening in a certain situation depends heavily upon members' background knowledge, and this background knowledge makes them see the situation properly. A camera «catches» what is visible as a perceptual act. However, it doesn't reproduce what is seen and isn't understood by the different participants of the situation. As ethnomethodologists argue, it is the practices that make themselves observable (Garfinkel 1967). The practices furthermore integrate members inter alia by rendering them visible.[1]

I use empirical data of a martial arts training to explore the process of manufacturing vis-ability for two reasons:

1. Martial arts training is concerned with the transfer of «tacit knowledge» (Polanyi 1985). Such situations contain an internal paradox: in order to transfer knowledge one must explicate it. However, this process of explication is opposed to the tacit character of the knowledge that is to be transferred. This paradoxical situation provides an extraordinary opportunity for insights into processes of explication.
2. In the course of a martial arts class students practice fighting movements. Before practicing, the instructor performs these movements in front of the students. These sequences of performing will be analyzed in the following text. They can be identified as «demonstrations» in the sense Goffman used the term (1974: 79ff.).

In order to perform such a demonstration, the instructor picks one of the students. Together they produce a visible and audible performance of a fighting movement while the other students sit quietly and watch them. This way demonstrations explicate knowledge on fighting by displaying a possible fighting episode. The instructor guides the visual explication as he comments on what the two bodies are displaying. Demonstrations are characterized by a specific order of space that enables the students physically to see: the students gather around the instructor and his partner while those two are performing the demonstration. Therefore we can say that two interactions are happening instantaneously, one being the corporeal and verbal interaction between the instructor and his partner, the other being the visual and verbal interaction with the audience.

These demonstrations place an extraordinary emphasis on visibility as they aim to display the tacit knowledge of fighting by displaying what could be a fighting movement. They are furthermore recorded by a video camera, a research tool that produces visual documents of the events. It could therefore be easy even for someone unfamiliar with the setting to see and understand the epi-

---

[1] The active work of making the audience see and understand what is being displayed is obvious in many products of the cultural industry: see Barmeyer (2006) on the production of talk-shows and Goffman (1979) on the analysis of commercial photography.

sodes by watching the footage. In the course of sociological data sessions, however, severe difficulties of vis-ability emerged: most of my colleagues are not familiar with martial arts. They expressed that they did not learn anything about martial arts when they were watching these videos. These data sessions are therefore discussed in the second section of this paper. I propose that they can be described as a specific cultural practice, namely the practice of sociologically analyzing video clips of martial arts classes. I will focus on these demonstrations in section three in order to locate how vis-ability of martial arts is produced in martial arts trainings. This part aims to reconstruct how competent field members understand what is being displayed in the demonstration. Finally, section four is concerned with the situational accomplishment of the demonstration. It focuses on the interaction between the instructor and his partner in order to delineate the work on the visibility of the fighting movements. However, before I start the discussion of empirical data, I will deal with some methodological considerations on video recording in ethnography.

Video recordings as sociological data

Ethnography which means to verbally describe cultures, is not understood as a method, but as a set of methods. As Hammersley and Atkinson put it:

«In its most characteristic form it involves the ethnographer participating, overtly or covertly, in people's daily lives for an extended period of time, watching what happens, listening to what is said, asking questions - in fact, collecting whatever data are available to throw light on issues that are the focus of the research» (Hammersley/Atkinson 1995: 1).

Although participant observation is widely understood as the core of an ethnographic investigation, much emphasis is placed on the fact that all data available should be collected (e.g. Emerson et al. 2001: 352, Lüders 2000: 384ff., Amann/Hirschauer 1997: 21ff). This research attitude is linked to the aim of sociological ethnography to describe the own culture: the anthropologist Stanislaw Malinowski initially introduced ethnography as a method in the 1920ies. He turned against conventional anthropologist ways of investigation that were in those days mostly based on reports by missionaries and travelers. Malinowski demanded a new practice of investigation as opposed to this «armchair anthropology» that should be grounded in on-site participant observation of the investigated cultures (Malinowski [1922] 1984).

The «Chicago School» first adopted the approach for sociological research. In this tradition important empirical studies, such as «The Polish Peasant» (Thomas/Znaniecky 1927) or «Street Corner Society» (Whyte 1964) emerged. The focus of these studies were unknown cultures within the own culture. Later on a second focus of studies «on the own culture» emerged, the sociological investigation of everyday life practices, in particular by Erving Goffman and by authors who were influenced by ethnomethodology.

Due to the open attitude to different data, film and photography were used for ethnographic research as soon as it became technically possible (Schändlinger 2006: 350). Until the mid 1980ies video based research was done occasionally (e.g. Ryave/Schenkein 1974); in the last two decades, however, video recording became one of the standard tools of qualitative research and an important topic of methodological debates.

Although videos are used in many ethnographic investigations, they do not substitute participant observation. Rather, they are seen as yet another research tool that – like all other research tools - provides certain insights into social processes and at the same time debars the ethnographer from other insights on the same process.

Ethnographers gather different forms of knowledge about the field by using different research tools. They reconstruct what has happened by producing jottings and later on fieldnotes.[2] By conserving events they keep an ex post view on the visible and audible, and by participating in the events they retain happenings in the corporeal and sensual memory.[3]

The aim of such multifaceted knowledge production is to gain comprehensive insights into the culture and the relevant dynamics of the investigated field. The ethnographic researcher is challenged to build «rapport» in the field in order to investigate the culture from within. This leads to a research situation in which the ethnographer must be able to integrate himself into the field and keep a certain distance at the same time. For only this distance enables him to produce sociological knowledge on the field. Introductions to ethnography discuss this problem as the challenge to avoid «going native», i.e. to avoid «over-rapport» (Hammersley/Atkinson 1995: 110ff.).

In addition to this question of research strategies, the use of different research tools provides a methodological chance: when the results of different research tools on the same phenomenon are contrasted, they indicate the potentials and limitations of the different research tools. In accordance with this consideration, the following paper does not only deal with demonstrations of martial arts classes. It also focuses on data sessions on the video footage of these martial arts classes as a kind of empirical data by asking what we are doing while we are doing sociological (ethnographic) video analysis within a data session and by classifying the data produced by video recordings.

The ability to preserve data that has so far not been interpreted can be seen as a main advantage of technically recorded data.[4] This interest in data that

---

[2] A detailed discussion of the process of ethnographic writing is provided by Emerson/Fretz/Shaw 1995, for a discussion on ethnographic research tools see Kalthoff 2003).
[3] A specific challenge in the course of the research process is to verbalize the often «silent» dimension of social phenomena (Hirschauer 2006).
[4] In particular transcripts of audio taped conversations have been considered to be «raw» data for a long time. This consideration was convincingly challenged by Psathas and Anderson

has not been interpreted is tied to the consideration that social processes are «ephemeral» (Bergmann 1985). By means of video recording these ephemeral processes are fixed in detail before they disappear the very moment they unfolded. Usually members of the situation produce reconstructions anyway, that is, they remember and sometimes reflect on what has happened. However, these reconstructions are considered to belong to field-specific habits of perception since they mainly follow field-specific relevance. Further, human observers do not completely «record» the details of the usually very complex events. By contrast, audio tapes of the situations simply record what has been expressed without any consideration of the relevance of a single utterance. Therefore, the advantage of the preservation of data that has not yet been interpreted is that technical recordings are neither tied to field-specific habits of perception, nor do they miss any details of the complexity of social processes. Instead, they provide the researcher with the chance of dissociating the «registration» of social processes from the interpretation (cf Bergmann 1985).

With some restrictions this is adaptable to visual recordings. One of these restrictions can be found in that the «raw» visual registration of social events is limited to a perspective on the event. Like a human observer, the camera only records what is visible from a certain position in the room with a certain angle and focus.[5] Still, with this perspective the camera records all details of the event. With some limitations one can therefore say that visual recordings preserve the social event and produce empirically «hard» data.

Consequently, video recordings provide the interpreter with important tools for the reconstruction of these processes. Repetition and slow-motion are mainly used as technical resources for the analysis of the recorded social processes. Undoubtedly, these tools grant access to important details of the social events (see below in sections three and four of this text). In addition to these advantages of visually recorded data, there are however structural limitations, such as the fact that odor, corporeal and other sensual impressions are not reproduced. Another limitation, namely the problem of seeing the order of unfamiliar practices, will be discussed in the following section on sociological data sessions.

Analyzing videos of a martial arts class

In the course of an ethnographic research process sociological colleagues meet for so-called «data sessions», events during which empirical data are discussed with a peer community. The following section reports on one of these data sessions in order to outline processes of fabricating vis-ability within a sociological

---

(1990) who pointed out that even word-by-word transcripts are already an interpretation. In line with this argument Watson states that not the transcript but the «transcript-as-read» has to be seen as sociological data (Watson 1995: 309, footnote 5).

[5] Consequently, moving cameras often fail to «catch» the beginning of the event of interest (cf. Luff 2003, cited in Laurier 2006: 182). See Liegl (2008) for further limitations of this approach.

peer community. The background of this report is my own ethnographic work on the transfer of martial arts knowledge. I started an ethnographic study in a martial arts club with the aim of studying the transfer of knowledge on fighting (in martial arts classes). I attended classes for half a year, I wrote fieldnotes, made some interviews, and took a few hours of video footage to be able to analyze the subject matter in detail and to illustrate my analysis by showing short video clips.

I was confronted with a fundamental problem I had not expected to exist as early as in the first presentation of some video analysis in a data session with a group of colleagues. I had chosen a unit in the footage in which the instructor performs a basic fighting movement to the pupils, i.e. a demonstration. This unit is easy to find in the footage, since a demonstration has a clear beginning and a clear end. It is framed by sequences in which students themselves practice fighting movements in pairs. The instructor interrupts these practicing sequences by verbally and visually announcing the upcoming demonstration (see below). The pupils gather around him. Then he demonstrates a certain fighting movement or further details of a movement that he had demonstrated earlier on. He ends the demonstration, and the pupils go back to practice in pairs what they have just seen in the demonstration. Practicing in pairs is easily distinguishable from demonstrations since the order of space changes notably. Pairs of students are dispersed in the room while they are practicing. When it comes to a demonstration, however, they gather around the instructor. Thus, demonstrations and practicing are easily identifiable units for a sociological analysis.

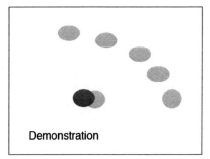
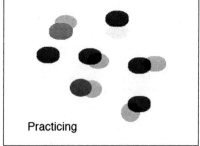

Figure 1

The analysis of the whole footage seemed quite clear to me, but when I presented video clips of these units of analysis to my colleagues there were severe differences in what they actually saw in the videos. Only one of my colleagues (he had background-knowledge in martial arts) seemed to watch and analyze easily. He saw what I saw in the video: the demonstration of some details of a martial arts movement. However, most of the other colleagues could not gather any information about martial arts from the video. Even though they could easily recognize that the video showed a demonstration, they claimed that they did not see *what* had actually been demonstrated. Even after repeating the video clip several times they only saw two people rolling around on the floor. In addition to this problem of visibility a problem of relation emerged: although they assumed, based on their background knowledge on demonstrations in general, that the instructor's verbal utterances were a commentary for the demonstration, they could not see any connection between verbal and visual impression. Rather, they perceived two people rolling on the floor of which one of them was commenting something incomprehensible to an audience.

In order to get closer to my colleagues' perception, I made an experiment which aimed at working on my own perception of the footage: I turned the volume off while I analyzed the footage in order to be able to see more clearly what was to be seen in the video clip. This procedure of concentrating purely on the visual enabled me to see two people rolling on the floor instead of a fighting movement.
As a result one could consider that the essential information of the demonstration was transferred verbally as it happens in other cultural practices, such as story-telling or phone calls[6]. In this case a word-by-word transcript of a demonstration would provide the essential information. However, without a deep analysis of the following transcript[7], one can conclude that verbal information alone does not give sufficient information on the matter.

```
Alright, next one. Another thing about what we just did - ah I
forgot what we just did - oh right: we are on his back. He
does it wrong once again. (2) Alright now: we are still pri-
marily focusing on movement, you understand? (1) I'll show it
from here: he comes up. Now: secure him from here, get inside,
get inside. Now from here we let go of him, make it easier for
him. Then from here, he does, to get up easier, get up - once
again! - I'm not making myself heavy yet, he has to - head be-
low! - because: if he wants to get up now, like (grabbing a
table) yes, he makes it easier for me and harder for himself.
```

The text is mostly indexical and fragmentary. Standing by itself there is hardly any information about fighting or the demonstrated fighting movement in it.[8] Not even a very skilled martial arts student could guess what exactly is demonstrated here, if he only had the audio track.

---

[6] Not even in story-telling or in phone calls **all** relevant information is transferred verbally. In contrast to martial arts demonstrations (and many other cultural practices), however, most stories and phone calls are understandable even when we have to rely on a verbal transcript.
[7] See transcription rules at the end of this paper.
[8] The transcript is used here to demonstrate that the demonstration is not understandable only via the verbal utterance. In section three, however, I will discuss how martial arts students do understand these utterances as a verbal guiding within the visual explications of the demonstration.

Martial arts demonstrations in my data are neither understandable when they are based on exclusively verbal information, nor when they are based on exclusively visual information. Rather, a demonstration seems to be a whole practice or, using Erving Goffman's (1974) concept, a «frame» based on what Charles Goodwin (2003) calls a «symbiotic gesture». These gestures, Goodwin states, are «built through the conjunction of quite different kinds of entities which are instantiated in diverse media: first, talk; second, gesture; and third, material and graphic structure in the environment» (Goodwin 2003: 23). Therefore, they are not comprehensible anymore as soon as they are reduced to one of these media.

A video recording could transfer these different kinds of entities to the audience. It transfers to an audience what is visible and audible in the demonstration. However, the martial arts movements were not visible for colleagues who are not familiar with martial arts. To find out more about that matter, I reread my fieldnotes. There I found what I had classified before as a typical problem at the beginning of a participant observation: when I started attending martial arts classes, I had severe problems with observing the demonstrations. I watched them, but later on I was not able to remember in detail what had been shown. Thus, it was impossible for me to repeat actively what I had seen. Hence what I had classified as a typical starting problem with little relevance for my study turned out to be one of the main challenges to martial arts beginners: the ability to see what is being demonstrated.

Members of the field are aware of this challenge. One of them told me that it took him three months to be able to understand demonstrations. Another one advised me on how to watch demonstrations. He recommended that I should focus on observable units: how does the demonstrated movement start and end, what is the main point of the instruction? Does the right or the left hand strike? What comes next? How does the partner react? Such advice helps new students to learn to see what the demonstration aims to display.

This conforms to Michael Polanyi's investigations of «tacit knowledge». He claims that the understanding of a demonstration requires the students' intellectual support (Polanyi 1985:15). This means that a demonstration cannot point at everything one needs to know in order to understand what is being displayed. Instead, the demonstration only highlights important details, and the audience must be able to understand the rest by themselves. The knowledge that is necessary to see what is being shown in the martial arts demonstration grows with the time students spend at it. After a while they recognize the situations they have seen for what they are. Step by step they learn to see fighting practices in these situations that initially seemed to consist of nothing more than two people rolling around on the floor.

At this point of the learning process the view of the situation changes. While novices had difficulties to see fighting movements before, they will only see fighting movements in these situations from now on. Once we have learnt a certain way of seeing things, we loose the capability to see as we did before. Just as we do not remember what writing looked like when we didn't know how to read, when we didn't know that reading meant to distinguish words and a page of a book looked like a black-and-white picture.

When it comes to the analysis of video footage of the martial arts training, these differences in seeing the situations emerge. Sociologists who have never been to a martial arts club before watch the recorded demonstrations in roughly the same way as someone who is in the martial arts club for the first time. By contrast, the ethnographer perceives the video as a (more or less) competent member of the situation. The analysis of video footage requires bridging the gap between the different forms of perceiving what the video actually displays. This matches a basic challenge, which «old school» ethnographies were already exposed to, namely the challenge that can be called «Coming home» (Amann/Hirschauer 1997: 28). It is seen as a remedy for the problem of «going native». «Coming home» then means to see the footage like a sociologist, not like a field member. Thus, the video is a tool that is able to create a distance to the ethnographer's background knowledge in order to enable him to transfer ethnographic knowledge to the sociological community.

To sum up more generally: In the course of an ethnographic project we accumulate knowledge about the field we investigate and about the topic we study. However, in this process of accumulating knowledge we forget the problems of understanding we had in the beginning, as Alfred Schütz describes it in «The stranger» (1944) and in «The Homecomer» (1945). This is a very useful process for members of the field, but not for the sociologist who aims to reconstruct the knowledge that is specific to the field.

In this process a video recording is able to fix an ephemeral phenomenon. The fixed phenomenon, however, is not the knowledge that is specific to the field, and it is not fixed in the pictures themselves. Rather, it consists of the different views of the same video clip. These different perspectives are tied to a different background knowledge. Discussing the video uncovers the difference of perceiving of something and gives rise to the reconstruction of the background knowledge that is essential to understanding the investigated practice, in this case the practice of seeing fighting movements.

Video recordings therefore provide an important perspective on the study, but they do not reproduce what has happened.[9] The footage grants the opportunity to see what members as well as unfamiliar observers see. However, it does not enable the unfamiliar observer to see what members see. It displays details

---

[9] Hirschauer (2006) argues that the recording and the transcript of a conversation produce the notion of a coherent event that does not exist in the perception of the members in the situation. He mentions a marital dispute to depict that conversations are continuously reinterpreted based on their members reconstructions of what happened (Hirschauer 2006: 420). He states that «the issue is not so much that recordings should be the truest copies of what the participants have indeed done, but that from the start (i.e., before beginning with the data analysis) they outdo what participants could have known about the situation» (Hirschauer 2006: 420).

of situations that neither a participant observer nor other members of the situation notice. In this sense it contains more information than a participant observation, but in another sense it lacks important information a participant observer is able to impart: the background knowledge about how to understand the recorded pictures of social processes.

What has been said now mirrors the relation of two types of knowledge that are produced in an ethnographic research process, of which one is sociological knowledge on the field and the other the members' background knowledge. The difference between those two types is considered to be crucial to what is seen in video recordings. The following sections concentrate on the production of field-specific seeing in the martial arts classes. The particularities of demonstrations as an empirical matter become relevant here. Just as the sociological research process consists of a transfer of knowledge, demonstrations aim to impart knowledge to their audience. Therefore, working on visibility is central to the accomplishment of demonstrations. For this reason investigating demonstrations provides us with explicit empirical opportunities for the study of the producing of vis-ability.

How to see a single movement within a demonstration

As illustrated before, the first skill a martial arts student has to develop is to see what is being demonstrated. Thus, the question arises how seeing as a situated activity is produced in the martial arts training classes. In this case an ethnographically informed analysis of the footage gives important insights into the situation. Questions such as the following are raised here:

What do members see when they watch a martial arts demonstration? How does the demonstration attract attention to itself?

How do martial arts students come to see what is being demonstrated, i.e. how do they learn to focus on the relevant aspects of the demonstration?

Demonstrations, as Erving Goffman points out, are «performances of a task like activity out of its usual functional context» (Goffman 1974: 79). The aim of these performances is to introduce the audience to a certain course of action. In order to make fighting principles observable, the martial arts demonstration presents 'fighting episodes'. These consist of chains of movements that simulate what could be a moment within a fight. Different reactions of a combatant are assumed in those fighting episodes. This applies to the combatant's fighting strategies as well as to his bodily reactions.

In order to give such insights into the principles of fighting, a certain order of space is produced. One can see pairs of martial arts students who are practicing a fighting movement before a demonstration starts. Sometimes the instructor makes a loud comment, such as, «Once again ... » or, «Listen ...». He moves to the center of the room, he passes by a student (mostly an experienced one) and nods at him to join in. Those two then stand in the middle of the room for a moment, while the students one by one start to pay attention. The students look to the center of the room and see the instructor there together with another student. Pairs turn into individuals again. These individuals gather around the instructor and his partner. The two of them become the focus of the situation. As soon as all the students watch them, they start to simulate a fighting episode. This actually means that the instructor displays a movement using his partner's body as a means to demonstrate an episode. The spatial order of those two men in the center of an audience facilitates the visual order and substantiates the functional difference between the instructor and the audience.

There is a clearly visible difference between the two groups who engage in different activities.[10]

Figure 2

If we entered the room while the students were practicing, we would have to look around for a while to find the instructor. While he is demonstrating a technique, the instructor can be identified easily though, because he is the focus of the situation. One stable element of the transfer-situation is the functional difference. The instructor and his partner are moving, and the instructor is talking. Meanwhile the audience hardly moves. It watches attentively instead. This order of glances and of moving is typical for demonstrations, be it the security instructions in an airplane or the demonstration of a vacuum cleaner. But compared to security instructions in an airplane or to a chemistry-class at school, it is noticeable that all of the martial arts students are concentrating on what is happening.

---

[10] The video will be published soon.

The visual order is not only tied to the spatial order but to the instructor's work of guiding the view of the audience, too. This work on the visibility of what is shown involves:
- the reduction of speed: fighting movements are shown in slow-motion, while in a real fight speed is a central strategy.
- fragmentation: the instructor intends to display movements step by step. That means movements are transferred into chains of movement, and the links of the chain can be seen and memorized.
- repetition: fragments as well as full-blown movements are repeated.
- commentary: not only does the instructor display a certain movement, he comments on his actions at the same time.

These elements that guide the spectator's view work together. In one line of the transcript the instructor says, «I'll show it from here: he comes up. Now: secure him from here». Standing by itself, his utterance is, as I argued before, hardly comprehensible. While watching the demonstration a skilled student would however relate the words, «I'll show it from here» to the corporeal and thus visible position the instructor and his partner hold at this moment. Most of the time the instructor interrupts his movements at this very moment. Thus, the utterance goes along with a kind of freeze-frame, which a skilled audience is able to notice and keep in mind. «He comes up» is related to a movement of the instructor's partner. This movement is thus marked as a combatant's assumed reaction. «Now» is understood as a marker to attract attention to the next movement. The utterance works like a «verbal pointing» at an important moment to follow. The crucial point of this demonstration is how to fix, that is, how to «secure» the possible combatant's body in this moment in order to make sure he cannot attack «me» (that is, the experienced member of the audience) any longer.

The use of the grammatical third person singular seems to describe the partner's or a combatant's reaction to what the instructor is demonstrating. By using the third person singular instead of addressing the partner, the instructor makes clear that the utterance is directed to the watching audience. Its function is to relate the instructor's movements to his partner's movements. As a result the impression of a chain of movement emerges. Visually almost coinstantaneous movements are verbally transferred into a sequence of movements. This way the movements become understandable as: the instructor does this, the partner reacts that way, now he is secured in this form, and so on. In this respect the structure of the comments is similar to a television commentary on a sports channel. It resembles very much the way a reporter of e.g. a soccer match relates single movements to one another in order to delineate the game's course of action.

As a second result, the use of the third person singular functions to guide the spectators' perspective to the instructor's side. In a further comment on a demonstration the instructor even uses the first person plural instead of the singular. At the beginning of the demonstration the instructor for instance says, «We are on the back». This is used to make the audience focus on his, that is, the instructor's perspective in the demonstration, because later on they are supposed to repeat what he is doing now. However, at the time of the utterance nobody is on anybody's back, and later on it is only the instructor who is on the back while the audience watches.

From the perspective of the audience the martial arts demonstrations conduct their views on the situation by a combination of visual and verbal pointing. In this manner the demonstrations also teach the audience to observe the display of fighting movements. This also indicates that an understanding of what is being displayed in the demonstration is accomplished through a concerted action (Garfinkel 1967: 76) between the demonstrating and the watching members.

So far the question was considered how students become able to see what is being displayed in the demonstration. Such an analysis handles the problem of how competent members understand the same visual impression in a different way than (unfamiliar) sociologists and novices. However, in order to understand how the demonstration is accomplished as a social phenomenon, a further analysis of the demonstration process and its interactions are required.

How to conduct a demonstration

Demonstrations in a martial arts club are hardly ever arranged beforehand. The instructor watches the students while they practice what they have seen before. He picks up basic or frequent problems and makes up a demonstration based on his observations. He seems to generate the demonstration while he is demonstrating. Therefore, his partner cannot know in advance what is going to be displayed, although the partner's cooperation is required. How do the partners in the demonstration accomplish this cooperation?

A more detailed viewing of both the video and the transcript unfolds a second conversational structure, which is important to the interaction between the instructor and his partner. Even though the commentary for the audience outnumbers everything, one finds instructions to the partner in between. The latter are necessary because the partner usually does not know what exactly is going to be demonstrated. After all, he is one of the students, mainly a good and experienced student, but sometimes it is just someone who happens to be at hand. As the partner does not know what is going to be demonstrated, the instructor gives him instructions every now and then. In the following transcript of a demonstration these instructions to the partner are marked with italic letters.

```
I'll show it from here: he comes up. Now: secure him from
here, get inside, get inside. Now from here we let go of him,
make it easier for him. Then from here, he does, to get up
easier, get up - once again! - I'm not making myself heavy
yet, he has to - head down! - because: if he wants to get up
```

now, like (grabbing a table) yes, he makes it easier for me
and harder for himself.

Instructions to the partner appear in two forms. One is obviously an order, such as, «head down!» or «once again!» as it is outlined in the transcript. The other one is to be found in sections that seem to be a description for the audience of what is going on. Again, these utterances are marked with italic letters.

I'll show it from here: *he comes up*. Now: secure him from here, get inside, get inside. Now from here we let go of him, make it easier for him. Then from here, he does, to get up easier, get up - once again! - I'm not making myself heavy yet, he has to - head down! - because: if he wants to get up now, like (grabbing a table) yes, he makes it easier for me and harder for himself.

That means: he keeps his head down. *He can even have his head on the floor*, alright, now he has another support, then *he raises his butt*. Now it's harder for me. Alright? And now he goes there, I'm making it easy for him. *And he crawls on his hands step by step. And then goes with his le(-) walks backward*. Right. Okay. That would be his movement.

These sequences seem to be descriptions. The form of a description in, e.g., «And then [he] [...] walks backward» suggests that the movement happens and is subsequently described. Analyzing the details of the video however unfolds a different structure: the instructor e.g. says, «And then [he] [...] walks backward» and the partner moves afterwards.

This sequential organization suggests that the utterance is, furthermore, to be understood as an instruction to the partner: the instructor says, «And then ...» and thus indicates to his partner that he should walk backwards. Consequently these utterances fulfill two tasks at the same time: they serve as a commentary to the audience and as an instruction to the partner.

In this sequence the instructor adds a gesture to his utterance: his fingers crawl backwards over the floor to signify that the partner should walk back. This gesture addresses the audience as well as the partner. The matter of the utterance is illustrated for both of them as the instructor's finger crawl backwards. Other movements of the instructor also address both the audience and the partner, but they instruct in a different manner: the body of the partner is moved by the instructor's movements. For the partner the matter of the demonstration is indicated corporally as he can feel how the instructor moves his body. For the audience the information is basically visual: they can only observe how a body is moved by the instructor's movements.

As I mentioned before the demonstration contains a visual part of demonstrating bodies and a verbal part of the instructor commenting on his actions. However, the interaction between the instructor and his partner consists of a verbal and a corporeal part to handle the problem of cooperation.

Conclusion

The analysis revealed that seeing what the demonstrations display is a complex and situated activity. When we put the last two sections together we can reconstruct how the situation is accomplished. During the demonstration the students' job is to watch. This action is close to what the camera does. The main difference between them is that the human observer relates the visual impressions to principles of fighting and to former impressions, while the camera relates them by way of a technical recording of visually perceptible sequences (cf. Amann/Hirschauer 1997).

Meanwhile the instructor's partner works on the cooperation with the instructor, that is, he reacts to the instructor's movements and tries to anticipate what is going to come next. The instructor does a double job of conducting his partner's body as well as his audience's attention. His body engages in a concerted movement with the partner. This action aims to display how a certain fighting movement has to be accomplished. Therefore the instructor points out his movements corporally and verbally to the students. In addition, he conducts his partner with his own movements and instructs him with verbal utterances, if necessary.

Producing the vis-ability of fighting movements therefore consists of two instantaneously occurring interactions, of which one is the interaction of the instructor and the audience and the other the interaction of the instructor and his partner. The former requires that the students see what is being displayed, while the instructor points visually and audibly at important aspects of the demonstration. The latter consists of a corporeal and sometimes verbal interaction between the instructor and his partner which requires of the partner not only to be attentive but also to anticipate up to a certain point what is going to happen next. Both interactions need to be accomplished in concert by all members. Both interactions are necessary to fabricate vis-ability in the training.

The problem of understanding a video clip that emerged in the data sessions can be applied to any video analysis of cultures that are unfamiliar to the audience. Quite often showing a video clip does not suffice to transfer the ethnographic knowledge to a sociological audience. Rather, it is an important challenge to the ethnographer to bridge the sociological, but unfamiliar view of his peers with the background knowledge that results from participant observation.

The study of demonstrations points out that learning to see what is being demonstrated by watching the video correlates to a certain point with learning to see what is being demonstrated within the martial arts class. Here, video analysis conforms remarkably with the practices to accomplish vis-ability that one can observe in the training lessons. Note that the observation strategies which competent martial arts students recommended to me (see section two) correspond to central strategies of video analysis, that is, identifying units of analysis, finding out what is central in the identified unit, and analyzing sequential organizations. Likewise, visualization strategies of demonstrations (section three) conform to central technical tools that are provided by a video: repetition, reduction of speed, and fragmentation.

Hence we can draw the following conclusion: at first glance video recordings seem to provide «hard» visual data that might solve the problem of the ephemerality of social processes. However, as I have shown, fixing social processes in moving pictures is only one step on the way to describe them in detail. In order to allow for a sociological analysis, several types of transfers of knowledge need to be accomplished. In the case of martial arts classes three types of transfers of knowledge are at stake:

1. The transfer of knowledge within the martial arts classes is the focus of the investigation. This transfer of knowledge is based on the challenge to see what is being displayed in the demonstration. It is accomplished by two instantaneously occurring interactions, of which one is to display what is to be seen and the other to see what is being displayed.
2. During the transfer of knowledge from the ethnographer «back home» to the sociological audience the ethnographer is challenged to render visual impressions visible by transferring background knowledge from ethnography. This is mostly done by comments on the footage. As the sociological audience lacks vis-ability of the situations, this transfer cannot be accomplished simply by presenting a video clip to the audience.
3. In between those two processes there is the transfer of knowledge from the field to the ethnographer. The obtained background knowledge must be outlined additionally in order to enable the sociological audience to see what can be seen in the video.

Many other empirical studies will not focus on the explicit transfer of knowledge as it can be investigated in demonstrations. Nevertheless, any social practice makes itself observable, be it more or less explicitly. Hence, any video analysis is challenged by the problem of producing vis-ability of the video footage for the peer audience.

Transcription

As the situations were recorded in Germany, all utterances were made in German and were translated into English for this paper. The «transcript» contains all utterances that were recorded, but does not cite specificities of any dialect. They hardly exist in the instructor's diction and, in addition, they are not relevant for the proposed analysis.

(grabbing a table) Utterances that could not definitely be understood are put in parentheses.
le(-) An uncompleted word within an utterance.
(2) A break of two seconds.
- once again! - Inserted utterances that are clearly addressed to the partner; the dash therefore marks the changing of the addressed audience.

Punctuation marks are used according to the literal conventions, such as a full stop at the end of a sentence, etc.

References

Amann, Klaus/Stefan Hirschauer, 1997: Die Befremdung der eigenen Kultur. Ein Programm. In: Klaus Amann/Stefan Hirschauer (eds), *Die Befremdung der eigenen Kultur. Zur ethnographischen Herausforderung soziologischer Empirie*. Frankfurt a.M.: Suhrkamp, 7-52.
Barmeyer, Mareike, 2006: *The endogenous orderliness of talk shows: an ethnomethodological investigation*. PhD dissertation Manchester Metropolitan University.
Bergmann, Jörg, 1985: Flüchtigkeit und methodische Fixierung sozialer Wirklichkeit: Aufzeichnungen als Daten der interpretativen Soziologie. In: *Soziale Welt*. Sonderband 3, edited by Wolfgang Bonß/Heinz Hartmann, *Entzauberte Wissenschaft. Zur Relativität und Geltung soziologischer Forschung*, 299-320.
Emerson, Robert M./Rachel I. Fretz/Linda L. Shaw, 1995: *Writing ethnographic fieldnotes*. Chicago: The University of Chicago Press
Emerson, Robert M. et al, 2001: Participant observation and fieldnotes. In: Paul Atkinson et al. (eds), *Handbook of ethnography*. London et al.: Sage, 352-368.
Garfinkel, Harold, 1967: *Studies in ethnomethodology*. Englewood Cliffs: Prentice Hall.
Goffman, Erving, 1974: *Frame analysis. An essay on the organization of experience*. New York: Harper and Row.
Goffman, Erving, 1979: *Gender advertisements*. New York: Harper and Row.
Goodwin, Charles/Marjorie Harness Goodwin, 1996: Seeing as a situated activity: Formulating planes. In: Yrjö Engeström/David Middleton (eds), *Cognition and communication at work*. Cambridge: Cambridge University Press, 61-95.
Goodwin, Charles, 2003: The body in action. In: Justin Coupland/Richard Gwyn: *Discourse, the body and identity*. Palgrave Macmillan, 19-42.

Hammersley, Martyn/Paul Atkinson, 1995: *Ethnography. Principles in practice.* London et al.: Routledge, 2nd edition.
Heath, Christian, 1997: The analysis of activities in face to face interaction using video. In: David Silverman, *Qualitative research. Theory, method and practice.* London: Sage, 183-200.
Hirschauer, Stefan, 2006: Putting things into words. Ethnographic description and the silence of the social. In: *Human Studies* 29, 413-441.
Kalthoff, Herbert, 2003: Beobachtende Differenz. Instrumente der ethnografisch-soziologischen Forschung. In: *Zeitschrift für Soziologie* 32: 70-90.
Knoblauch, Hubert/Jürgen Raab/Hans-Georg Soeffner/Bernt Schnettler (eds.), 2006: *Video-Analysis, methodology and methods. Qualitative audiovisual data analysis in sociology.* Frankfurt a.M.: Peter Lang.
Laurier, Eric, 2006: Natural problems of naturalistic video data. In: Hubert Knoblauch/Jürgen Raab/Hans-Georg Soeffner/Bernt Schnettler (eds.), *Video-Analysis, methodology and methods. Qualitative audiovisual data analysis in sociology.* Frankfurt a.M.: Peter Lang, 183-192.
Liegl, Michael, 2008: *Performing technology. Das postmoderne Kreativsubjekt in technischer und musikalischer Vergemeinschaftung.* PHD Dissertation Johannes-Gutenberg-Universität Mainz.
Lüders, Christian, 2000: Beobachten im Feld und Ethnographie. In: Uwe Flick/Ernst von Kardoff/Ines Steinke (eds.), *Qualitative Sozialforschung. Ein Handbuch.* Reinbeck bei Hamburg: Rowohlt, 384-401.
Malinowski, Bronisław, 1984 [1922]: *Argonauts of the western pacific: An account of native enterprise and adventure in the Archipelagoes of Melanesian New Guinea.* London: Waveland Press.
Miner, Horace, 1956: Body ritual among the nacirema. In: *The American Anthropologist* 58, 503-507.
Polanyi, Michael, 1985: *Implizites Wissen.* Frankfurt a.M.: Suhrkamp. (Originally published as *The tacit dimension,* 1966)
Psathas, George/Timothy Anderson, 1990: The «practices» of transcription in conversation analysis. In: *Semiotica* 78, 75-99.
Ryave, A. Lincoln/Schenkein, James N., 1974: Notes on the art of walking. In: Roy Turner (ed.), *Ethnomethodology. Selected readings.* Harmondsworth: Penguin Education, 265-275.
Schändlinger, Robert: Visuelle Ethnographie. In: Ruth Ayaß/Jörg Bergmann (eds.), *Qualitative Methoden in der Medienforschung.* Reinbeck bei Hamburg: Rowohlt Taschenbuch Verlag, 350-388.
Schnettler, Bernt/Hubert Knoblauch, 2008: Videoanalyse. In: Stefan Kühl/Petra Strodtholz (eds.), *Methoden der Organisationsforschung. Ein Handbuch.* Reinbeck bei Hamburg: Rowohlt Taschenbuch Verlag, in print.
Schütz, Alfred, 1944: The stranger: An essay in social psychology. In: *American Journal of Sociology* 49, 499-507.
Schütz, Alfred, 1945: The homecomer. In: *American Journal of Sociology* 50, 369-376.

Watson, Rod, 1995: Some potentialities and pitfalls in the analysis of process and personal change in counselling and therapeutic interaction. In: Jurg Siegfried (ed.), *Therapeutic and everyday discourse as behavior change: Towards a micro-analysis in psychotherapy process research*. Norwood et al.: Ablex, 301–339.

White, William F., 1964: *Street corner society*. Chicago et al.: University of Chicago Press.

Thomas, William Isaac/Florian Znaniecky, 1927: *The polish peasant in europe and america*. New York: Knopf.

Lars Frers

Video research in the open – Encounters involving the researcher-camera

Filming is an encounter. The person wielding the camera, the camera itself, and the people and things around them enter a dynamic relationship. This relationship unfolds itself according to the rules set by the social, spatial, and material features and practices that constitute it. These features and practices constitute it, but they do not determine it in a linear way – too many contingencies enter the interaction process, disrupting, changing, or reorienting it.

When I quickly unpack my camera, alerted by some action that I want to record, my perception changes. I focus my attention on viewing angles, light conditions, obstacles, and on the reactions displayed by others who are witnessing me. I become someone who is videotaping them and their surroundings. Before I start recording, I can never be totally sure of what is going to happen. How will people react? Will I record something that can be used for my research? Am I encroaching on anybody's privacy? Where should I point my camera, which part of my surroundings seems to be most interesting, which part looks less promising?

In this essay, I will focus on the surprising, unplanned side of doing video research, pointing out both the risks and the opportunities that are part and parcel of filming non-staged everyday life in public settings. I would not claim that public settings are quantitatively more or less structured than private settings. Since I have not performed any video research in private settings, I cannot compare the two. Instead, I want to pay full attention to the peculiarities of the publicly accessible settings I encountered. The use of an approach inspired but not constricted by ethnomethodology[1] allows me to investigate the encounters or interactions in a way that is open to small details, disruptions, and to the interpretations offered by the members of the settings themselves. Most of the recordings and experiences on which this essay is based were collected during my research on railway and ferry terminals.[2] These places are – even when they are owned by private companies – accessible to, and used by a highly diverse public. Accordingly, I had the opportunity to record a host of different situations and encounters. Working in the midst of this diversity made me aware of the

---

[1] See Garfinkel, 1984; Garfinkel and Sacks, 1986, for the basic theoretical and methodological assumptions of ethnomethodology and Maynard and Clayman, 1991, for a discussion of the diversity of ethnomethodology.

[2] See for example Frers, 2007a; Frers, 2007b. In addition, I did some videotaping for a long-term research project about a blossoming cherry tree in Berlin and for my new project on the perceptions of the materiality of islands in a time of climate change.

great variety of situations with which a video researcher is faced. It is these experiences, the challenges one may face while being out in the open, equipped with a video camera, that I want to ponder here.

Where, what, who

While investigating issues of social control and generally examining the relations between the social and the material, I used a handheld DV camcorder to record what is happening in railway and ferry terminals. I covered almost all times of the day and the night but recorded mostly during the day. I filmed many different locations in the terminals: main entrances, ticket selling machines, passages, niches and corners, plazas in front of the terminal, waiting areas on the platforms, and so on. I mainly filmed in German cities, but also in a few other places in Norway, Denmark, and the United States.

In a way this information could be interpreted as providing an answer to the question about «where» with regard to my research. The researcher has been positioned in terms of geographical location. But there is much more to be said about the whereabouts – when it is asking for her or his position in the social and material field. In this section, I will only provide a brief theoretical reflection on this question, the actual answering will be done by analyzing what happened when I performed my recordings. Thinking about one's location in the *social field*, it is, of course, Bourdieu (for example Bourdieu and Wacquant, 1992: 15-19, 26-35) who pops into mind. My economical, cultural, and to a degree also my social capital put me into a position in which I dress, talk, move, and perceive of things in a way that is closely related to the way I have been raised in my family and in academia, to the amount of money that I have at my disposal, and to the taste and style that I developed in exchange with my peers and with the things that I witness in the media and in everyday life. Thus equipped, I establish distances towards others who are co-present in the place of my investigation. Some may appear inferior, others superior, others both or difficult to judge. I watch others, judging their appearance and actions, while they are doing the same, both being aware of the other one's awareness.

But what about the position in the *material field*? Is that not the same thing as the geographical location? In the way that materiality is conceptualized for this essay, there is more to this position than physical location. Drawing both on Merleau-Ponty's phenomenology of the body (Merleau-Ponty, 1962; Merleau-Ponty and Lefort, 1968) and on works published in the wide field of science and technology studies (Garfinkel et al., 1981; Latour, 1987; Pickering, 1995), I want to propose that the position I take as a bodily actor in the material field at least temporarily becomes that of a hybrid of man and machine: a camera-researcher. The way I position myself is guided by the way *I observe with and as the camera*, by the way *the camera observes with and as me*. I am not a disembodied subject that perceives of its surroundings, analyzes its perceptions, then decides on what to do next, step by step, one after the other in a logical sequence. Instead, I am oriented towards the world, always perceiving something and acting at the same time, seamlessly going into alliances and oppositions with the things around me (Merleau-Ponty, 1962: 143). Things and others which/who become parts of the horizon of possibilities that I enter and constitute at the same time.

At this point in the essay this reference to the body in action as something that acts beside the subject–object or human–thing/technology divide is mostly a programmatic statement. The same proves true for the claim that the researcher and the camera form a unit of perception. We will see what kinds of analytical and self-reflective insights are possible by taking this perspective in the following sections.

Hierarchies of the gaze

Since this volume focuses on video and video analysis, I will first pay particular attention to the gaze, how it is used, how it is put into interaction with the surroundings, and how it is modified by becoming the gaze of a camera. Gazing at others, filming them and putting them into the camera's focus establishes a specific set of hierarchies, one that is being produced by the actant-bundle[3] researcher and camera.

Camera & film

Video research produces recordings. Usually, it is the researcher who is *controlling the camera*, thus *controlling the field of vision* that is covered and recorded. When working in public settings, one cannot or does not want to direct what is happening as a director of a movie would do. Instead, the directing is mostly limited to deciding how things are recorded. Accordingly, it is the actual camera-work, turning the lens into a particular direction, or carrying the camera around, by which the researcher exerts his particular kind of power. He or she decides whom or what to follow, to leave in peace, to ignore, or to sneak upon. The others who are co-present have to live with the visual regime that is being established. As we will see later on, that does not mean that they are powerless. However, it means that the hierarchy is set by the researcher. The hierarchy can be challenged or not, but it is present.

It is present even if those who are being filmed do not realize that this is the case. Depending on the way the filming is set up, it is more or less discernible to others. The range of possibilities extends from hidden (surveillance) cameras to cameras operated by a staff of people using tripods, lights, and microphones, attracting the attention of everybody around. Since for ethical and practical reasons most academic social research in public settings will probably not be conducted in one of those extreme ways, it makes sense to pay some more

---

[3] «Actant» is used by Latour (2005) to refer to the agency of both things and people.

attention to the range in-between these extremes. Using a handheld DV camcorder, I was able to use different tactics to position me-the-camera. Most of the tactics I employed in the field served to limit my impact on the setting. For ethical reasons, I did not want to conceal my operations completely, but I still wanted to limit the effect that I had on the field.[4]

To conceal my filming would have felt as if I had become one with the system of surveillance that sweeps through the terminals – I would become part of the panoptic system that makes everyone feel observed by an entity that cannot be seen and that might look anywhere at any time. (See Foucault, 1995: 200-209.) Since one of my objectives was to engage myself critically with surveillance technology, I needed to keep a distance between my way of filming and the filming that is being done by surveillance cameras. However, when the German federal police was hunting two men who had planted bombs in trains (the bombs did not explode), they made some surveillance material public showing their suspects. When watching the material, I was struck by the similarities between their recordings and mine. Although the intention and some technical aspects were quite different, there was an eerie overlap in the content, in what could actually be seen on the recordings: mundane activity, people walking, talking, and waiting. Just like in my recordings. But these recordings were not about everyday life, they were about the big specter of our time: terrorism. (See Frers, 2007b: 205-207.)

It was obvious to me that people would feel observed when I put the camera's eye-piece to my eyes, practically aiming my full attention at them in a way that is hard to overlook. This feeling was so strong that I even had difficulties trying this out just to judge its effect. It felt highly uncomfortable to put people into such a position of being obviously scrutinized. In this way, the fact that I produced a visual hierarchy became tangible for me. This kind of taking into the gaze is so obvious that it exerts a strong pressure, pushing those who are affected by the camera-researcher's gaze to openly acknowledge the presence of the observation. Both parties know who is being filmed, and the one who is subjected to the gaze has to react, knowing that his or her reaction will be recorded. It is this double discomfort (being subjected and knowing that the researcher-camera knows this and still keeps on doing it) that I did not want to evoke. Accordingly, making precautions to keep the directedness of the gaze of the researcher-camera unclear or at least unobtrusive was one of the tactics I employed while I was recording in the field. This was accomplished best by holding the camera in front of my belly, either looking at the camera's display, which was flipped out to allow me to watch it from above, or by placing the camera on some kind of even surface close to me, for example on a flat handrail. The direction of my gaze compared to the direction of the camera's gaze was

---

[4] There is a wealth of studies on participant observation and its relation to what is going on in the observed setting. The following titles might hint at of the breadth of this field: Bondi, 2005; Girtler, 2001; Heath and Hindmarsh, 2002; Kanstrup, 2002; Lofland and Lofland, 1995.

important for those who were co-present. That is, neither my gaze for itself, nor the camera's gaze for itself were relevant, instead it was the gaze as it was performed by myself and the camera together. As long as I gazed directly at the people who were in the eye of the camera, I seemed to evoke discomfort or irritation. When I looked at the display or, even more so, in a direction completely unrelated to their position, they did not show the same amount of discomfort and usually did not show any kind of acknowledgement of the camera-researcher's presence at all. Thus I tried to keep low both the discomfort that I caused by doing my research and the general impact on the field, which I wanted to study in its «normal», researcher-camera-free configuration.

Depending on the way the camera-researcher is oriented, people are compelled to or are enabled to their behavior. They have at least potential access to seeing and reconstructing what is going on, and they can act accordingly. This fragile balance is undermined by one aspect of filming (and taking photographs) that should not be underestimated in its effect. By *controlling the zoom* one is able to creep or *sneak into the intimate*. It is practically impossible for those who are being filmed to judge or recognize how close the observer moves toward them with the zoom. Therefore, they cannot adequately react and change or modify their behavior in a way that would help them to protect their intimacy. Going into full zoom, I could have observed people who were using the ticket machine as if I had been standing right next to them, staring unblinkingly at their fingers, their faces, and their bodily posture – perhaps even at the PIN code which they are typing into the money transfer interface.

The zoom is a powerful tool. Using it is very tempting, because using the zoom allows me to discern the small details of people's interactions, and it is exactly those small details that I was interested in. On the other hand, it is a sneaky affair that robs those whom I am studying of parts of their dignity. They feel unobserved and disclose things which they probably would want to keep to themselves. Using the zoom, I become a voyeur more than with any other function that is offered by the camera. Because of this highly problematic and ambivalent aspect of the zoom, I tried to avoid it most of the time. One exception to this rule were cases in which I would not have been able to get access to information that I thought was highly valuable. At the same time, though, I had the impression that the situation was not particularly delicate, nor the people involved particularly vulnerable. (Another exception will be discussed in the section «double-challenge».)

The final aspect of the hierarchy of the gaze that I want to discuss in this section is related to the concrete product of the recording activity in the field. By *keeping the recording* the researcher can exert his or her real power. She or he can decide when to watch a scene - again and again, forwards and backwards, slowly, frame by frame, or quickly skim through the recording. What is even more problematic: he or she can also show the recording to anybody, e.g., the participants of a conference, the readers of a book who can look at video-stills or watch the accompanying DVD, or even to everyone who has access to the internet and a computer able to play video files. When the researcher keeps the recording, those who were filmed *lose control of their self-presentation*. This puts a lot of responsibility into the researcher's hands. One never knows whether one's recordings contain compromising information that might get someone into trouble. One way to deal with this is to anonymize those who have been recorded. Anonymizing someone in a video track, however, does not only require an uncommon amount of technical know-how and sophisticated software. When looking at it in detail, it becomes apparent that it is very hard to decide what degree of anonymization is actually required. Does it suffice to pixelate the eyes, or the whole face? What about clothes? People one knows closely are easily recognized by their gait, which will be very difficult to get rid of without losing everything one needs in the recording. It should be obvious that an adequate handling of the problem of losing control of one's self-presentation cannot be accomplished by adhering to a recipe-like practice of anonymization. Depending on the setting, the situation, and the vulnerability of those involved, one should decide on appropriate measures. Maybe it is even possible to think about this while one is still in the field, i.e. when the question is if one should continue to record or not. One minimal requirement is, of course, to make sure that access to the material is limited by securely erasing hard drives and USB sticks before selling or giving them away, by keeping potentially sensitive material locked or encrypted or both, and by employing other standard measures for privacy protection.

In the introduction I wrote that researcher and the camera become hybridized because they observe together and relate themselves to the world. That is, they constitute a unit with a shared perspective and agency. However, in the first part of this section, I also demonstrated that the researcher and the camera are treated as a unit by those who are interacting with them. Depending on the way the camera-researcher distributes attention, on the way they are configured with regard to each other and thus with their surroundings, they are treated differently by those who encounter them. Since the researcher-camera is both acting as a hybrid and being treated as such, I would argue that it makes sense to treat them as a unit on an analytical level. Therefore, when I am speaking of my recordings or my attention in the following text, this usually includes a reference to the camera as being part of me, too.[5]

Being an academic

In this section, I will approach the establishment of a hierarchy of the gaze from another perspective. Looking at the researcher's position in the social field, I want to map a set of distinctions that should help to problematize the power effects that accompany field work in public settings.

---

[5] Of course, that does not mean that a camera has the same epistemological status as a self-reflective human being.

The first aspect that I want to inspect is the particular location that an academic takes in relation to the *power–knowledge* complex (see Foucault, 1978, vol. 1: 92-102; Foucault, 1980). In the Foucauldian sense, the academic can speak the truth, that is he or she can position him- or herself in a discourse that produces the truth, or he or she can even create this discourse together with others. The knowledge claimed by the researcher grants him a very specific kind of power, i.e. the power to name and to define. Vested with this power–knowledge, the researcher can arrange others and their statements, which either discredits them, or lifts them into a higher position, or the researcher can be cryptic and esoteric in different kinds of ways and just baffle and confuse them. Thus, the researcher not only acquires an advantage in long-term negotiations of his or her social position but also gains additional opportunities in short-term, situational negotiations. However, this power–knowledge complex does not only grant superiority in discourse in the more delimited sense of talk and writing. It also grants a better position in terms of the gaze. What the researcher sees and what she or he looks at gains particular attention. It is not only looked at, but it is scrutinized by science. Science will decide if it is right or wrong, will count, measure and explicate it, tear it out of its own context, connect it with unforeseen and uncontrollable other entities and finally present it in its own framework. Seen from this perspective, it becomes obvious that to be investigated by the gaze of science can cause a considerable amount of unease.

The second aspect is somewhat related to the first, but the focus moves from knowledge and discourse to the habitus of the researcher. The researcher always uses *practices of distinction* (see Bourdieu, 1984, chapters three and five) and distances himself from others who are co-present in the field. I mentioned Bourdieu's framework as the evident point of reference earlier in the text. At this point I only want to provide some more details with regard to how the researcher maintains a distance. Since my personal capital is pretty much distributed accurately as it has been outlined by Bourdieu for average academics (that is little economic capital, some social capital in the form of good connections to others who might potentially become relevant in talk or negotiations, and a much higher than average cultural capital), I do have to struggle in relation to those who have more financial capital. Depending on the way they dress or the newspapers and books they read, the kind of electronic gadgets they use, etc., I can try to see them as unrefined, show-offs, nouveau-riche, etc. or I have to acknowledge their obvious superiority in the social field and live with it. In relation to those whom I perceive to be in a similar position, I can either try to positively identify with them (from my male perspective this might go along the lines of, «he has a nice style», «she is quite attractive», «I always wanted to read that, too», etc.) or I can try to look out for clues that might offer opportunities for a positive distinction from their position («who wears this much makeup?», «sneakers with these kinds of pants? It seems he is trying to pretend he's still twenty-five»). With those below my position, I can also either sympathize and tell myself that they probably earned to be in a better position, or I can see them as just having bad taste, slow wits, rude behavior, etc. It is certainly not easy, and probably impossible to rid oneself of all of these preconceptions and the many subtle practices of distinction that go along with them while one is in the field. One tactic that I employed to raise my awareness of these issues was to try to put on different kinds of clothes while I was filming. Sometimes I would film in a punkrock-style black leather jacket with a red hooded sweater and a pair of washed out jeans, sometimes I would wear a functional all-weather jacket and sensible clothes, and at other times corduroy pants with an upscale brand shirt and Budapest-style shoes. I was not able to quantify or measure the effect these changes of outfit had on my observation practices in the field. However, I certainly felt different: sometimes more uneasy towards the lower strata of the social scale, sometimes more uneasy towards the upper strata, and I certainly had the impression that both genders looked at me or treated me differently, depending on my appearance (see Frers, 2007b: 236-242).

The final aspect that I want to focus upon in this section are positional advantages that stem from *having a legitimization*. When I was in the field, both in the railway and in the ferry terminals, I usually had acquired prior permission for filming and photographing. In the case of the ferry terminals, this was handled informally by talking to some representative of the shipping company who would usually not be particularly interested and who would just grant me permission in a wave-me-through gesture. I was obviously not seen as a threat in any way, more as a minor nuisance or as a strange but harmless person. In contrast, I had to acquire permission to film from a higher-up (a press representative) in the Deutsche Bahn company, for which I needed to file an application, provide information about myself, my research, the concrete way in which I wanted to film (what kind of equipment, alone or with a team, etc.), the time period, and the different locations that I wanted to cover. After handing these things in the permission (which was valid for one year) was granted without much further ado. However, I had to present my permission at every terminal in which I wanted to film. This way, most of the personnel was informed about my activities. There were significant local variations in the way my presence was handled. Sometimes it was quite relaxed, that is, a glance at the permission was deemed sufficient. However, in other places, such as at Leipzig Hauptbahnhof, my permission was copied and my presence announced to the security staff of the terminal. Thus, my presence was officially legitimate and proven by an official sheet of paper. This gave me a somewhat secure position, although I was sometimes treated with a distanced but pronounced suspicion. The security staff would keep an eye on me from a distance, from outside of the perceived viewing angle of my camera, demonstrating to me that I am being observed, too. Nonetheless, equipped with this kind of legitimization, I was in a safe and sound position when compared to others in the terminal. Everyone's presence is open to suspicion: are they legitimate travellers or shoppers, or are they loitering, perhaps even begging or otherwise breaching the rules of the house? In contrast to the average other, I was not alone. By carrying a sheet of paper, by having communicated with someone from the Deutsche Bahn management, by coming from a university, by having an official mission, and by having an academic title I was different from them, i.e. I was connected to a large network of more or less powerful or symbolically important people and institutions.

Taken together, the camera-researcher has many features that constitute a locally specific and multi-dimensional hierarchy of the gaze. By controlling the recording of the action and by being equipped with formal and informal resources, skills, and legitimizations, the researcher-camera has several responsibilities in his relation to the field and the people she or he is recording or observing, because their privacy and their social position is often more vulnerable. Negotiating the relations between researcher-camera and those who are being filmed is a delicate and contingent process.

In the open

Because of the open-endedness and the delicate character of doing video research in public settings, I chose to label this kind of research as being «in the open». It is open to modifications, surprises, and challenges from many different sources. In the following sections I want to present evidence which supports this statement and that supports the emphasis that I put on using the term encounter, a term that is intended to stress the indeterminacy of interactions.[6] I will demonstrate how the people in the field reacted to my presence, how they interacted with me-the-camera, thus putting their mark on my research, and implicitly or explicitly questioning my position.

Invisible evasions

The first set of interactions that I want to discuss is both obvious and hidden. When people detect the presence of me and my camera in time or from the right location, they will often have the opportunity to evade the camera-researcher. By taking a different route, perhaps by passing me from behind or by using another entrance/exit, they can avoid being recorded at all. Since my vision was not restricted to what the camera recorded (as I wrote earlier, I often looked into a direction that was different from the direction the camera was pointed at), I could sometimes see people who did not enter the area covered by the camera. By following them in my peripheral vision, I could see how they moved past me and perhaps even threw one or two suspicious glances in my direction. More often than not, people who would choose to evade being recorded were those who spent a substantial amount of time in the terminal, who had enough time to observe me, and who make up their mind about what I am doing. Service and security staff, people who waited for extended periods of time, and people who

---

[6] Helen Liggett uses the term encounter in a very similar way, see the introduction in Liggett, 2003.

did not have a clear mission sometimes scrutinized me from a distance, keeping clear of the camera. To evade being recorded is an obvious tactic to protect oneself, even if the process cannot be seen on my recordings. Most people, however, would just pass through the camera's field of recording. They were either unaware or aloof of my presence.

Keeping a distance

The second set of interactions encompasses encounters between others and the camera-researcher in which the others preserve a distance. My argument is that by keeping a distance, they maintain the order of the setting, that is they do not challenge the hierarchy of the gaze that is being established.

Figure 1: throwing a passing glance while walking by

The video-still printed here shows a woman (in company of a man who is walking to her left) who passes by while I am recording. I am holding the camera in front of my belly. The couple was coming all the way down the main hall, and passed by on their way to the exit of the railway terminal. They were engaged in conversation and did not pay particularly noticeable attention to me while they approached. However, in the few steps which took them past me, both of them threw one or two short glances towards me-the-camera. They only did this when they were almost out of the field of vision of the camera. They did not turn their heads in an obvious way, either. They just shot their gaze towards me and the camera for a moment, and took their gaze back to the field in front of them immediately afterwards.

This kind of *passing glance* is a very common behavior. People displayed these short glances in practically all locations where they had to pass somewhat close to me-the-camera. Some of them maintained their gaze for a longer time, some only very briefly.[7] Some of them made an interested impression (this was most often the case with children, adolescents, and some men), some of them appeared to be skeptic (mostly adult men), but most people did not display a change of expression when they threw a glance towards me-the-camera.

Another reaction that I could track on my recordings is *checking* behavior. Some people who realize that they or their surroundings are being filmed will then look around and usually scrutinize the area which they believe is being filmed. In one case in which I filmed in the same location where I took the «passing glance» video-still I had two adolescents approach me up to the area between the two standing signs at the entrance to the ticket selling area (in the left half of the video-still). At that point one of them stops, while the other one continues to walk on until he passes me and then disappears out of the recording. The other one, however, remains standing right in the middle of the area which I am filming. He looks in my direction and after a bit more than a second he turns his head around twice. The second time he includes his upper body in the turning movement and gazes over his shoulder for a longer period of time. After that, he remains standing where he is and looks in my general direction without making the impression that he is feeling uneasy or that he is watching me. A few seconds later his companion reappears from behind me and walks back to his waiting counterpart. They meet, the one who waited says something to the one who returned, and while they both walk into the ticket selling area, the one who came back looks into my direction twice, turning his whole upper body around each time and regulating his steps in a way that allows him to look back into my direction while he is moving on.

In this case the two young men acknowledge the existence of the-camera-me in the way they throw looks into my direction, and they also display an exchange that is highly likely to concern me-the-camera. The one who waited used his time and attention to examine the situation with which he was faced by checking the field of vision that was covered by the camera. Of course, I do not have any solid basis for guessing what he was thinking about my activity or what he was telling his companion about me filming them and their surroundings. I can only demonstrate that when they encountered the-camera-me, they displayed their awareness of my presence in a distinct but distanced way. They looked at me, and probably talked about me, but they did not approach me in

---

[7] I did not try to quantify this, but the range does probably extend from maintaining the gaze for three full steps to a brief flick of the eye.

any direct way.[8] I was surprised how rarely those who do realize that they are being filmed *move away*.

Figure 2: entering the field of recording and leaving it again (13 seconds)

The woman shown on the sequence of video-stills is entering and leaving the area that is being recorded in the course of a bit more than 13 seconds. She comes into view from the right (first video-still). She stops after one further step and now stands right in the middle of the area that is covered by the DV camcorder. As usual, I am holding the camcorder in front of my belly, looking at the display. While she stops, she turns around and pulls her trolley towards herself, so that it is standing on its own. While she is turning, however, she also lets her gaze rest on me for a prolonged period of time. Looking at the recording frame by frame, it becomes apparent that she is moving her pupils into my direction well before her head actually faces me (it takes about 0.6 seconds from the first eye movement to full face-to-face). When the turning movement is almost completed and while she is pulling the trolley closer, she looks into the direction of the trolley. Half a second later, however, she is looking into me-the-camera's direction again (second video-still), this time for about 0.8 seconds. As far as I can discern on the recording, she uses the first observation to look at the camera and the second to look at my head (my gaze is directed downwards to the cam-

---

[8] This is a case where just writing about an event is very much different than actually seeing or witnessing it, even if it is only on a recording. When I wrote this paragraph, I had to re-edit it several times, in order to try to avoid raising the suspicion that I might inadequately over-interpret the situation. However, when I am showing the actual video sequence to others, thus presenting the action as it unfolds itself, the (mostly visual) evidence seems to be so convincing that I never heard any objections with regard to my interpretation of the situation. I see this as a strong argument for including the performative aspect of social action not only in the analysis but also in the representation of data. Text, or academic writing, is a limited medium for evoking both the full complexity and the intelligibility of social life. Thrift and Dewsbury, 2000; Jones, 2005; Rose, 2006; Spinney, 2006, discuss related issues of representation and performativity.

era's display). Then she turns a bit more to her left, keeping one hand on the handle of the trolley, and using the other hand to fidget around with her coat (third video-still) for five seconds. During that time I pull the zoom out as far as I can[9], hence getting some distance between me-the-camera and the woman on my display/in front of me. After sucking in her lips for a moment the woman lifts her left hand to her mouth for two seconds (fourth video-still). When she ends this gesture she leans forward and starts to move out of the picture (final video-still) while she is throwing a glance at the trolley which she is pulling along.

When I recorded this sequence I felt uneasy about being too close to the woman. I was not sure what I was to do, and I quickly had to decide whether I wanted to try to keep going as I was, hoping to demonstrate to the woman that she is not disturbing me and that she might not be recorded, or whether I should make an obvious break, either by shutting down the camera and moving away or by turning it into a different direction. I decided in favor of the former, because in the situation this seemed to be causing the smallest amount of disturbance both for me and for her.

By only throwing passing glances, by checking the covered area from a distance, and by moving out of the covered area, people keep a distance between themselves and me-the-camera. They do not get too close, or if they are close, they keep the contact as distanced as possible without causing a disturbance. The passers-by only flick their eyes into my direction for a moment, the checking does not result in a confrontation or in a question about what I am recording, and when she is standing right in front of the lens the woman only displays some minor signs of unease before she leaves the area. Although a distance is maintained in all of these instances (and many others that were similar), they still caused a slight amount of confusion, surprise, or even irritation, both for me and for the others who were involved.

Getting close

The third set of interactions shows what happens when the usual divide between researcher-camera and others is crossed. The hierarchy of the gaze is transformed in different ways. In the first case that I want to discuss a man approaches me from behind and asks me for some money.

Transcript 1: bumming[10]

```
[him] [speaking with a local accent] sorry
[I]   yes
```

---

[9] I slightly zoomed in (perhaps x1.3) to have a better view of the entrance area of the terminal, which is visible in the back of the recording. I used the zoom because during that recording session I was trying to get a grip on how people orient themselves when entering the terminal.
[10] The transcription rules are explained at the end of this chapter.

[him] one question
       (0.5)
       over there I've just
       (0.5)
[him] at the Luisenplatz left my car |and the key
[I] |yes
       (0.5)
[him] would you just have 50 cents so that I could call the
       ADAC [German Automobile Club] please?
       (0.5)
[I]   yes
       (0.5)
[him] super
       (3.0) [camera display makes a noise while being closed]
       well till I get at it there
       (0.5)
[I]   yes
[him] they would've perhaps already towed the car |(.) eh
[I] |yaya eheh
       (0.5)
       fiffy cent?
[him] (right)
       (9.0)
[I]   (wait a sec)
       (0.5)
       (erm)
       (0.5)
       fifty cent coin isn't necessary or what?
       (1.0) [his mobile phone rings]
[him] yes, I put in five |Euro
[I] |or what?
       (1.5)
[him] (moment)
       (1.0) [mobile rings]
[I]   okay
       (1.5)
[him] (many thanks)
       (2.5) [he leaves, I take up the camera] (2.0)
[I]   Well: that was bad luck (3.0) the ladies took off (.)
       I did not observe what how they continued

After I acknowledge the presence of the man talking to me with a «yes», he starts to formulate his request, pausing several times in his talk. I do not make use of these pauses to provide any further acknowledgement. Instead I wait for more information to pour in and only offer another single «yes» that overlaps with his talk, in which he tells me about his problem. When he finally closes his question adding a «please» I again wait for a short time before I tell him that I will help him out with fifty cents. While I am taking my time to look for the money, he further elaborates on his problem. Several seconds later (I have to get rid of the running camcorder and fumble for my wallet), while rummaging through the contents of my wallet, I ask him if he needs a fifty cent coin, closing the question with a somewhat rude and informal «or what», which I repeat during his answer, again in overlap with his talk and in addition to the first ring of his mobile phone. The ringing phone causes some additional delays and confusion until I finally give him the coin, and he leaves, taking the call on the mobile and thanking me. After I have finally taken up the camcorder again, I comment on my bad luck, which sabotaged the recording of two ladies who seemed to have problems using the ticket selling machine.

This sequence shows how both parties feel bad about the interaction and about the disruption of my-the-camera's activity. The man who bums me for fifty cents justifies himself, while I express a certain annoyance via my reluctance and the informality of addressing him (in the original sequence he is using the formal third person to address me, while I am addressing him informally using the second person). The distance is not being kept, but since the interaction is asymmetric with him being in a weaker position than me, the hierarchy of this interaction parallels the hierarchy of the gaze that is established through me-the-camera's position in the field.

The following sequence is the only instance in which I was directly approached and challenged by someone who was not an employee working in the terminal. The sequence happened while I was recording commuters leaving an evening express train. The man who approached me was probably in his forties. He wore a business suit and carried a briefcase. As I was able to discern when I screened my recording later on, he walked through the area which I was recording and threw a glance in my direction before he approached me. He walked past me and then must have turned around and approached me from the side. I did not notice him until he started talking to me.

Transcript 2: challenge

```
[him]  I have a question why are you filming here in the first
       place?
[I]    Sorry?
[him]  May I ask why you are filming?
[I]    Erm, I make- this is a research project of the
       Technische Universität Darmstadt (.) abou:t erm:
       (0.5)
[I]    m: orientation in railway and ferry terminals in harbors
[him]  I see |because
[I]          |I also have a license to film and one for the
       railway
[him]  ok, yes, I am only wondering because
[I]    no no, it's often (.) completely (understandable) yes
       |it's=
[him]  |mhm
[I]    =no problem yes | (hn)
[him]                  |is something different
[I]    few people wonder (.) am surprised myself
```

```
        (1.0)
[him]   yes, because
        (0.5)
        usually I do not like to be on films |but=
[I]                                          |yes, yes
[him]   =this is okay
[I]     he he
```

He is asking me to justify myself. He is not asking what I am filming, but «why» – even stronger, «why at all». When I fail to answer his initial question he rephrases the question in a very formal way. For me this decided politeness, together with his clothes and his general demeanor, generated the impression of interacting with somebody who claims to have a higher status than mine. I only answer him with difficulty, inserting several pauses and extending the duration of the «erms» that I utter. However, I finally manage to present my main legitimization assets: first, that I am doing research for an academic institution, and, after a short delay (overlapping and thus interrupting his turn), secondly, that I have a license for my activity. He acknowledges this information twice («I see» and, after the overlap, «ok, yes»), and then goes on to provide information that legitimizes his challenge to my activity («I am only wondering»). Before he can tell me why he feels legitimized to approach me, I display to him that I understood his claim and that I think it is «completely understandable yes no problem yes». He in turn also reinforces his acknowledgement of my legitimacy by stating that this «is something different». The interaction was almost finished at that turn, and he proceeds to leave the scene. However, while he turns away, I raise my voice and try to elicit more information from him, telling him that I am wondering why so few people wonder about my activity. It takes him a moment to return to the conversation and to provide an answer: «usually I do not like to be on films». However, he affirms my legitimacy once more by repeating that he thinks that «this is okay». I provide an agreement token for both of his statements, and the conversation is over without any further utterances that mark its ending.

This sequence does not only show how quickly difficult claims to legitimacy can be negotiated, hence reaching a shared interpretation of the situation. It also displays how both participants in the interaction provide justifications for their respective position as soon as the legitimacy of the other's claim has been acknowledged. It thus becomes apparent that, while the hierarchy of the gaze can be challenged actively, those who challenge it might maneuver themselves into a position where they have to provide reasons for their challenge. Taken together, this very brief sequence demonstrates how the habitus, the different kinds of symbolic capital, and the hierarchy of the gaze appear in his and in my performance and how we both negotiate our status or position in the field.

In the last sequence that I want to discuss in this section it is not necessarily the-camera-me that is challenged. Instead, I-the-camera am challenging those who have more authority than I have in the terminal, namely the security personnel.

Figure 3: direct gaze exchange

After panning through the terminal building as a whole, I move the focus of the camcorder to the service point, where two security employees, both currently on duty, are standing.

Transcript 3: double challenge

```
[I] mhm (.) that (is now) kind of interesting
    [zooming in on security personnel and ServicePoint]
    (49.0)
    (4.0) [man raises walkie-talkie and fixes his hair]
    whats curious now↓ usually I always feel a bit uneasy:↓
    (1.0) affected, when so (.) the security personell pays
    attention to me (1.0) in this case: I've got a somewhat
    more offensive stance (1.0) because I have just seen'im
    sending-off [a homeless person] and erm (4.0) this is why
    I feel the other way round
```

While I am looking at the display of the camcorder when the employees get into focus, I make a comment for the recording, saying «that is interesting now». Then I do a full zoom, closing in on the employees. Two seconds later, the employee to the right turns his head in my direction and keeps his gaze steady for two seconds. During this time, the other employee also turns her gaze into my direction (this is the moment displayed in the video-still). At that time, I start to pan a bit to the right, so that both of them move out of the center of the recording and into the periphery. After having kept them in the periphery for about seven seconds, I zoom out almost fully, only to zoom back in about a second later. However, I do not zoom in as close as I did the first time. I keep zoom and focus set on them for almost a minute. During this time both of them repeatedly turn their gaze into my direction. At one point the man raises his walkie-talkie, looks intently at its display and then makes a movement with his other hand, apparently fixing his hair. After he finishes this move I start making the rest of the transcribed commentary, elaborating on what is interesting about this situation. I say that I usually feel uncomfortable about staff watching me. However, «in *this* case» I feel otherwise because I witnessed how the man sent off someone who was «loitering» at one of the entrances and who made the impression on me of being homeless. This makes me feel «the other way round» (in German «anders gepolt», translated literally as «with the pole in the other direction»), that is, I do not feel uneasy and like a victim of his attention. To the contrary, I am in an offensive, aggressive «watching-back» mood, trying to produce the same feeling of discomfort or unease in those who usually evoke it. When it appears to me that I am successful in this endeavor, I keep the gaze of me-the-camera steady for another fifteen seconds before a woman carrying luggage enters the area of focus, when I finally zoom out as far as I can, keeping her and her luggage in view until she passes me.

As I stated in the section «Camera & film», I usually tried not to use the zoom in order to protect the intimacy of others and not to subject them to my gaze more than I think is necessary for my research. In this case, however, I am making an exception, an exception that I explicitly comment, trying to justify it while I am recording. While I am aware of the disquieting power of the hierarchy of the gaze, which is being established by me-the-camera, I am trying to exert this power in order to switch or at least to destabilize the hierarchy between security personnel and non-employees in the terminal. Although I feel somewhat uneasy while I am doing this, I keep going for a while until several factors come together. I have the impression that I achieved my goal. I feel that if I keep recording for too long, I might cause too much provocation or an illegitimate amount of unease (after all, I can say to myself that he just did his job). In addition, someone else enters the field of recording and provides a new opportunity to do video research and to follow the objectives of my study.

In all of the three cases discussed in this section, the hierarchy of the gaze is being mangled.[11] Me-the-camera and others encounter each other, all of us have different interests and feel different constraints. In the encounter, however, the hierarchy of the gaze becomes unsteady. It falls prey to the contingencies of the situation and to the processes of mutual negotiation. Everyone involved in the encounter employs certain practices, which relate to each other's position in the social (and material) field. At the same time the whole interaction is embedded in a general flow of events and intentions. I want to return to my recording, the businessman wants to be at home, the security staff wants to avoid disturbances of the order, someone enters the field of view and attracts my interest,

---

[11] I borrowed this term from Pickering, 1995, who uses it in his analysis of the entanglement of human and non-human agency.

etc. The encounters which destabilize the hierarchy of the gaze only last for a brief period of time.

Conclusion

Video research in the open is a process full of contingencies and challenges, full of unplanned encounters between researcher-camera and others in the field. I argue that in spite of the potentially problematic impact of the researcher on the field, this kind of video research offers many opportunities for analysis exactly because of its contingent nature. Interruptions and irritations should not be regarded as research-induced artifacts that have to be cut out of the analysis. To the contrary, they offer a wealth of material for study and throw a spotlight on several important aspects of video research in publicly accessible places. Since it will usually be practically impossible to get explicit consent for filming in these kinds of places, the presence of the researcher-camera has to be negotiated in the field, in the encounter. This is one of the reasons why it is so important to study the relation of the camera-researcher to the field. It helps to assess the way the researcher-camera's presence changes the social-spatial-material constellation that she or he enters together with the camera.

First, I want to re-visit the decision to use the notion of the «researcher-camera» that I introduced in this essay. Are the researcher and the camera a unit? Do they act together? The answer is decidedly ‹yes and no›. They do act together in two ways. Together, they constitute a field of perception (see Merleau-Ponty 1962, chapter five). Without the camera, the researcher would see the world differently. He or she would not be able to zoom into it, to keep a steady and unflickering eye on one region for long periods of time, and to rip it out of the flow of time while keeping it available as a recording for future uses. Without the researcher, the camera would not be able to pan around and follow those people and events that might be interesting for analysis, that is, it would lose an aspect of perception which is perhaps its important feature: its innate connection to intentionality (Merleau-Ponty, 1962: 130-139). Together, the camera-researcher can do things they cannot do on their own. They can create ambivalences for the others who are present, because they can easily display ambiguous orientations. Thus, they make it difficult for others to perceive what is going on, to see whether they are the subject of the camera-researcher's gaze or not.

These examples should suffice to demonstrate that it makes sense for the analysis to treat the researcher and the camera as a unit, a bundle of actants, or a hybrid that constitutes a distinctive relation to the world around it that is different from the relation created by each of them alone. Nonetheless, it is also quite obvious that they are separate entities. The camera can be put aside, it can stop working but the researcher will still be able to continue her or his observations and even record them, for example by logging them into a notebook. The camera can, of course, be put somewhere and it can continue to record even without the researcher's presence. Treating the researcher and the camera as a unit for analytical purposes does not mean to sell one's soul to some kind of hype about hybrids and the dissolution of the subject-object divide (although it should make you think about how much sense this divide actually makes). However, it should enable oneself to treat events, things, and people in an analytically open way, thus helping to avoid blind spots in the research and to acknowledge the multidimensionality of social processes.

Strategies & tactics

To provide some analytical depth to the discussion of the researcher-camera's relation to the field, I want to employ Michel de Certeau's distinction between strategy and tactics (Certeau, 1984: xix-xxx). *Strategies* are those aspects of social practice that relate to temporally and spatially stable entities. Like the strategical positions and the equipment that place an army in a good or bad position for a battle, they set the frame, they determine the positions people take in the field, and determine advantages as well as disadvantages. Similarly, there are strategical aspects to doing video research in the open. The researcher-camera takes a distinct position in the field. She or he is equipped with certain amounts of capital, with certificates, and connected to a wider network that provides resources that the camera-researcher can use. Equipped this way and entering the field with a certain habitus, specific intentions, and modern technology, the camera-researcher establishes a hierarchy of the gaze. As has been shown in particular in the sections «invisible evasions» and «keeping the distance», this puts him or her in a relatively advantaged position, particularly when compared to everyday people passing through his or her area of observation.[12]

Strategies or strategic positions are highly influential. They shape the specific normality of a place or a general setting. However, they do not determine what is happening. Specifically, they might exert a great influence on the outcome of events, but they do not necessarily shape the way an outcome is achieved. It is this particular aspect, the way normality, social control, and practices of everyday life work that is at the heart of de Certeau's interest. In his words, it is the *tactics* that are the subject of interest. In a way this whole essay can be read as an inquiry into the role of tactics in video research. The strategic positions and advantages are distributed. We read and understood Bourdieu, we know of the importance of the habitus, and we learned about the importance of being in control of technological augmentations such as the camera. But this is not all that happens. When one looks at the details, it becomes apparent that the rules are used, undermined, and challenged in multiple ways. People can comply to the rules by embracing them, by only following them hesitatingly, by playing contradicting or conflicting sets of rules against each other. Thus, the setting and

---

[12] Of course, this is not the only strategic component of the setting. Other factors such as the gender of those involved, and the social, spatial, and material setup of the place itself also participate in distributing strategical positions in the field.

the processes and practices that constitute the setting become open to variation. I can make use of the power of the camera and my certificates to turn around the hierarchy of the gaze with regard to the security personnel. The inquisitive questions of a businessman reveal how I actually make use of my claims to legitimacy. They also display how a stranger can make use of his position in the social field to destabilize my position in the local hierarchy of the gaze. The fact that I have to remain in one place for a prolonged period of time to produce a recording makes me vulnerable to become the target of requests for assistance. Taken together, all the individuals co-present in the field have a range of tactical moves at their disposition for dealing with the constraints, and for making use of sudden opportunities. This is what tactics are about. They usually cannot change strategic distributions, they have no control over the place, they cannot fortify positions. But they take control over the time in which they are performed. They can create holes in a defense, make a surprise move and use the non-determined to their advantage.

I hope to have demonstrated that both the strategic and the tactical aspects of the dynamic setting are relevant to doing video research in the open. They show how the setting is created structurally and in action. As might have become apparent by now, taking an ethnomethodologically inspired approach to the analysis is an excellent way of creating awareness for both the tactical and the strategic aspect. Since ethnomethodology studies how practices *make and are* the rules that govern social settings (Garfinkel and Rawls, 2002: 99, 272), it offers a perspective on the small and large features of social action, which together generate the dynamic stability of places and of social-spatial-material constellations. The recorded events which are transcribed and analyzed in this essay display how both the researcher-camera and the others employ their own, localized methods, their ethno-methods, in dealing with the setting that they encounter and constitute.

Acknowledgements

I wish to thank both the German Research Foundation (DFG) and the Center for Teknologi, Innovasjon og Kultur (TIK) for providing me with money and an office that allowed me to write this article during my stay as a guest researcher at Oslo University, Norway in the fall of 2007. Further thanks go to Ulrike Kissmann and her team for providing a friendly and professional setting during the conference on video analysis that she hosted in May 2007.

Transcription

The transcripts are all translated from German. For the originals, see Frers, 2007b: 148-149, 149, 153.

[ ]   is used for remarks about the situation and other explanations

| is used to mark the beginning of overlapping talk
=   is used to mark talk that continues without pause over several lines in the transcript
(.)   is used to mark a <0.5 sec pause
↓   is used to mark a fall in accentuation
italics are used to mark louder speech.

References

Bondi, Liz, 2005: The place of emotions in research: From partitioning emotion and reason to the emotional dynamics of research relationships. In: Liz Bondi Joyce Davidson/Mick Smith (eds.), *Emotional geographies*. Aldershot: Ashgate, 231-246.

Bourdieu, Pierre, 1984: *Distinction: A social critique of the judgement of taste*. Translated by Richard Nice. Cambridge et al.: Harvard University Press.

Bourdieu, Pierre/Loïc J. D. Wacquant, 1992: *An invitation into reflexive sociology*. Chicago: University of Chicago Press.

Certeau, Michel de, 1984: *The practice of everyday life*. Translated by Steven Rendall. Berkeley: University of California Press.

Foucault, Michel, 1978: *The history of sexuality*. Translated by Robert Hurley. Vol. 3. New York: Pantheon Books.

Foucault, Michel, 1980: *Power/Knowledge: Selected interviews and other writings, 1972-1977*. Translated by Colin Gordon. New York: Pantheon Books.

Foucault, Michel, 1995: *Discipline and punish: The birth of the prison*. Translated by Alan Sheridan. New York: Vintage Books.

Frers, Lars, 2007a: Perception, aesthetics, and envelopment: Encountering space and materiality. In: Lars Frers/Lars Meier (eds.), *Encountering urban places: Visual and material performances in the city*. Aldershot: Ashgate, 25-45.

Frers, Lars, 2007b: *Einhüllende Materialitäten: Eine Phänomenologie des Wahrnehmens und Handelns an Bahnhöfen und Fährterminals*. Bielefeld: transcript.

Garfinkel, Harold/Eric Livingston/Michael Lynch, 1981: The work of a discovering science construed with materials from the optically discovered pulsar. In: *Philosophy of the Social Sciences* 11, 2, 131-158.

Garfinkel, Harold, 1984: Studies of the routine grounds of everyday activities. In: Harold Garfinkel (ed.), *Studies in ethnomethodology*. Malden et al.: Polity Press/Blackwell Publishing, 35-75.

Garfinkel, Harold/Harvey Sacks, 1986: On formal structures of practical actions. In: Harold Garfinkel (ed.), *Ethnomethodological studies of work*. Routledge & Kegan Paul, 160-193.

Garfinkel, Harold/Anne Warfield Rawls, 2002: *Ethnomethodology's program: Working out durkheim's aphorism*. Lanham et al.: Rowman & Littlefield.

Girtler, Roland, 2001: *Methoden der Feldforschung*. Wien: UTB, 4th edition.
Heath, Christian/Jon Hindmarsh, 2002: Analysing interaction: Video, ethnography and situated conduct. In: Tim May (ed.), *Qualitative research in practice*. London: SAGE, 99-121.
Jones, Owain, 2005: An ecology of emotion, memory, self and landscape. In: Liz Bondi Joyce Davidson/Mick Smith (eds.), *Emotional geographies*. Aldershot: Ashgate, 205-218.
Kanstrup, Anne Marie, 2002: Picture the practice: Using photography to explore use of technology within teacher's work practices. In: *Forum Qualitative Research* 3, 2. <http://www.qualitative-research.net/fqs-texte/2-02/2-02kanstrup-e.pdf>
Latour, Bruno, 1987: Science in action: *How to follow engineers and scientists through society*. Cambridge et al.: Harvard University Press.
Latour, Bruno, 2005: Reassembling the social: *An introduction to actor-network-theory*. Oxford: Oxford University Press.
Liggett, Helen, 2003: *Urban encounters*. Minneapolis: University of Minnesota Press.
Lofland, John/Lyn H. Lofland, 1995: *Analyzing social settings: A guide to qualitative observation and analysis*. Belmont et al.: Wadsworth, 3rd edition.
Maynard, Douglas/Steven E. Clayman, 1991: The diversity of ethnomethodology. In: *Annual Review of Sociology* 17, 385-418.
Merleau-Ponty, Maurice, 1962: *Phenomenology of perception*. Translated by Colin Smith. London: Routledge & Kegan Paul Humanities Press.
Merleau-Ponty, Maurice/Claude Lefort, 1968: *The visible and the invisible: Followed by working notes*. Translated by Alphonso Lingis. Evanston et al.: Northwestern University Press.
Pickering, Andrew, 1995: *The mangle of practice: Time, agency & science*. Chicago: University of Chicago Press.
Rose, Mitch, 2006: Gathering «dreams of presence»: A project for the cultural landscape. In: *Environment and Planning D: Society and Space* 24, 4: 537-554.
Spinney, Justin, 2006: A place of sense: A kinaesthetic ethnography of cyclists on mont ventoux. In: *Environment and Planning D: Society and Space* 24, 5, 709-732.
Thrift, Nigel/John-David Dewsbury, 2000: Dead geographies: And how to make them live. In: *Environment and Planning D: Society and Space* 18, 4, 411-423.

Focussed Ethnography

Hubert Knoblauch

Social constructivism and the three levels of video analysis[1]

Introduction

The interpretive analysis of video is a new branch of qualitative research that is for various reasons rapidly becoming part of the established canon of methods in the social sciences. On the one hand, the sheer availability of video allows more and more researchers to use the technology; secondly, more and more actors are using the video medium itself so that their practices and products are becoming part of the cultures that we are studying. And finally and not least importantly, there is a range of studies that have established ways and methods how to approach video data in the social sciences. Across various disciplines ranging from linguistics to anthropology and from education to sociology, a number of researchers are using videos in a way that is based on conversation analysis. As conversation analysis is based empirically on tape recordings of naturally occurring conversations, video analysis in this tradition focuses on videos of naturally occurring interactions, i.e. interactions that would have occurred even if the researchers had not taped them.[2] This way, it needs to be distinguished from the huge number of studies particularly in psychology and social psychology that record experimental interaction. In addition, it also differs from those interpretive approaches that try to reconstruct social action and interaction from indirect data, such as interviews. As the title indicates, video analysis performed along the lines referred to here has another distinctive feature that will be highlighted here: it is interpretive. By interpretive we mean that what can be observed by video tapes is action that is meaningful to the actors themselves. That is to say an analysis has to focus on the actors' meaning that is being expressed in their visual conduct. The axiom that socio-scientific action studies are pre-interpreted by the actors themselves and that these pre-interpretations should be considered as the starting point of any analysis of action has been coined as «first order constructs» by Alfred Schütz (1962), one of the major founders of interpretive social science. Building on this insight, conversation analysis tried to exploit the fact that speakers render their actions understandable and interpretable to themselves as one of the major resources in order to analyze spoken conversation (Sacks/Schegloff/Jefferson 1974). Whereas early conversation analysis restricted the analysis to spoken discourse collected via tape recorder, some turned to video recordings as early as the late 1970s. Thus, Goodwin (1986) started to

---

[1] An earlier version of this paper is being published in Norwegian; parts of the contribution are based on Knoblauch (2005a).
[2] This is not to understate the problem of «reactivity» (cf. Knoblauch/Schnettler/Raab 2006).

analyze the interplay between the visual and the spoken in naturally occurring interactions, and Heath (1986) focused on the role of visual and spoken aspects of interaction in medical encounters. Video and its interpretive analysis slowly became part of ethnographies in the analysis of various work settings (Heath/Knoblauch/Luff 2001) and other settings. Thus, one can consider the field-informed video analysis as one particular genre in the field of qualitative methods, i.e. videography (cf. Knoblauch 2006).

There is no doubt that videography is based primarily on video recordings of social interaction. In this respect, it may be apt to talk about video-interaction-analysis (Knoblauch 2005b) as the core of videography. Work done so far in this field has shown that the methodology of conversation analysis has been a most useful tool for the analysis of video data, given that it needed and needs to be adapted to this particular kind of data. Although a systematic overview of the methods of analysis of this kind of data is still missing at the moment, we already have a number of methodological texts that indicate as to how to proceed (cf. Heath 1997; Heath/Hindmarsh 2002; Ten Have 1999; Knoblauch/Schnettler/Raab/Soeffner 2006).

As important as it may be to develop the methods of video analysis of interaction further, one should be aware that video is but one means to collect data. Taking a constructivist stance, one could say that data are the products of the researchers' actions. Researchers are not only «collecting» data, they are producing data by way of their actions, and one can distinguish types of data according to the ways and methods of collection: whereas interviews are co-produced in their very content by the researchers (who are subtracted in the interpretation in order to produce the «subjects'» voices), tape and video recordings are constructed by technical means. Whereas researchers attempt to remain «passive» in attempts to record naturally occurring situations, hence only «recording» what is going on, there are other video data sorts that are produced more actively, such as video diaries (produced by the subjects themselves). Data are, at any rate, produced by the researchers' and the subjects' actions.

In those cases in which video can become a «natural» part of the situation, it can allow to access interaction processes in such detail that they might not be available even to the actors themselves. It is under the circumstances when interaction seems to produce the meanings in toto that analysts claim a situationalist approach to the data: the meaning of actions seems to lie only within the actions themselves, actions that can be accessed via video or participant observation (Suchman 1987). Indeed, much of the ethnomethodologically informed research with video seems to share the view that meanings are situational and that even institutions are somehow «reflected» in situations. As helpful as this view may be in order to interpret situational actions, this view does not only ignore the institutional prerequisites of its own research; it follows an in-explicated radical constructivist assumption that considers reality as something that is continually constructed in action. If one is aware of the fact that the data means we are using are themselves not only subject-matters of our research but also our ways of action, we might want to take a more reflected stance towards our own research. This stance, I want to argue, parallels the basic approach of the social construction of reality as suggested by Peter Berger and Thomas Luckmann. This theoretical approach allows us to regard video analysis as part of a more encompassing enterprise that not only relates video interaction analysis empirically to the context of interaction – institutions and agents. (In order to stress the importance of context I have suggested to use video as part of a focused ethnography, i.e. as «videography» (Knoblauch 2006). Social constructivism does not only account for the process of interaction represented by the activities on the video. Social constructivism, furthermore, demands to account for the contexts of these activities. This way social constructivism provides a blue-print for qualitative methodology.

In the next part I will therefore sketch the basic dimensions of the social construction of reality and relate them to the levels of empirical analysis. Only then will I turn to sketch some of the major aspects of video (interaction) analysis in order to then turn to the additional non-situational features of videography.

Social constructivism and the three levels of analysis

Although interpretive social science consists of a large variety of different approaches, they all share the assumption that social actions are to be understood from the actor's point of view or, to state it in more general terms, from the subjective perspective. Social science, however, is not restricted to subjective meaning but allows for the possibility of «objective shared meanings» that result from the interaction of subjective meanings. There have been several theoretical attempts to reconstruct the relationship between subjective and objective meanings, such as, e.g. Pierre Bourdieu's (1979) or Anthony Giddens's (1984) widely discussed approaches. Whereas these approaches do have a rather loose relation to interpretive social sciences, it is social constructivism that originally and most pertinently addressed the relationship between subjectivity and objectivity and that at the same time had a strong impact on interpretive methods (cf. Knoblauch/Flick/Maeder 2005).

By social constructivism I mean the interpretive sociological approach based on the writings of Alfred Schütz e.g. (1967/1932), Thomas Luckmann and Peter Berger (1966). As opposed to «social constructionism» (Burr 1995), this approach is not to be reduced to «discourse» but also addresses institutions and structures. In fact, its major question is how actors succeed in constructing social order by means of social actions and institutions. The process of the «social construction of reality» is analyzed by Berger and Luckmann as dialectics of externalization and internalization. Berger and Luckmann delineated analytically abstract processes in this construction process: interactive objectivation of meaning, institutionalization, internalization that can be illustrated as a social constructivist triangle:

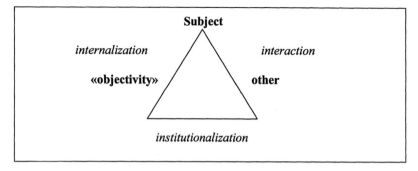

Figure 1: The dialectical triangle

Since interaction is the major dynamic process in the social construction of reality (Berger/Luckmann 1966, 19-46), the very subject matter of video analysis, i.e. interaction, is of utter importance to any social constructivist analysis. In fact, one can say that video analysis is foremost the analysis of visible social interaction. Thus, video analysis focuses on questions as to how actors objectify meaning and how they thereby coordinate their actions and the meanings of their actions. By using video instead of audio recordings (as it has been the rule in conventional conversation analysis) this kind of interaction analysis accounts for the fact that interaction cannot be reduced to spoken or linguistic exchanges only. The detailed recordings of the interaction, on the other hand, allow to access the fine-grained details of interactive coordination in a detail that is not even accessible to the actors themselves.

The fact that actors are not explicitly aware of the meaning of minute details of action although they as well as the interpreters understand their meanings, hints at the importance of «practice» as habitual forms of actions built into the ongoing process of interaction. That is to say that the meaning of action cannot be reduced to situative contexts, as e.g. ethnomethodology makes us believe (Suchman 1987). The most distinctive feature in contrast to the ethnomethodological view is that social constructivism maintains that meanings can be habitualized, routinized and institutionalized socially in various forms; they become fixed patterns that are habitualized by actors, objectified in signs or cultural and technical artifacts (and legitimized by those who want to keep them). These «situated» rather than «situational» features of interactions[3] are not easily accessed by video tapes and visual data only. Although they are often represented in visual artefacts, their meaning needs to be reconstructed by other means. It is here where ethnography comes in, the method by which the typical meanings of specific social fields are recovered. Ethnography in a way accounts for the socially constructed «objectivity» of the social world as always pre-

---

[3] The notions «situated» and «situational» go back to Goffman (1963).

existing, and assumes that actors have knowledge of the situation that enters into the situation in the video.

As objectified as the meanings might be, they are always related to someone who needs to understand them. In fact, even the analysis of video data presupposes a subjective understanding of what is being said. The very method of sequential analysis starts from a common sense or subjective understanding of what is being seen and heard on the video. The actors' and interpreters' subjective understanding of actions is a third major momentum of any interpretive methodology. This momentum is accounted for by the hermeneutic elements common to sequential analysis as well as by ethnography (cf. Luckmann 1981; Soeffner 1997). Whereas ethnography demands to take into account participants' subjective perspective (e.g. by elicitation, autoethnography or phenomenology (Van Maanen 1992), the analysis of video data (as the analysis of audio data) starts with the interpreters' subjective understandings of the data. It is only by way of the description of the data in terms of analytical categories and the comparison of data described in this way that the interpreters may claim more generalizable statements.

Thus one can see that the major aspects of videography do correspond to major theoretical aspects of, and thus to the methodology of social constructivism. That is to say that the process of research of videography interrelates the crucial aspects of the social construction of reality by way of specific methods: the actors' and interpreters' subjective perspective is accounted for by hermeneutics, phenomenology and other introspectionist methods, the interactive and situational construction of meaning by sequential analysis and the institutional context by ethnography. Since the development of video analysis is the most crucial part of this process of research, I will focus on some features of sequential analysis in the following part. In the conclusion of the chapter I will indicate the ways in which the different aspects might be integrated into this holistic three-dimensional approach. The following diagram indicates some of the methods used in qualitative research and tries to locate their most common methodological focus with respect to the social constructivist triangle. (See figure 2)

Video interaction analysis: sequentiality and visuality

Let us first turn to the core of interaction analysis, i.e. the analysis of video recordings of interactions. Video analysis builds on a number of features of the medium of video filming in general. On the one hand, the desire to record the «natural situation» is founded on the «mimesis» assumption that video recordings do indeed represent to some degree what is going on in situations that can be observed without a technological device. Despite the jeremiads on the «crisis of representation» and contrary to written documents of the situation, even the convinced post-modernist cannot deny that video recordings are accessible to other observers in ways that allow them to make new observations and interpretations and to give evidence for (and possibly against) other analyses.

186 Hubert Knoblauch

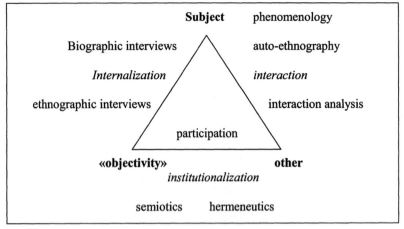

Figure 2: The dialectical triangle and corresponding methods

On the other hand, video analysis exploits another crucial feature of this medium: its temporality. Like film, video is also defined by the temporal sequence of pictures (it is the fact that this temporality is no longer built into the new digital storage medium that may cause the changes just mentioned above). As a result of their temporality, pictures are watched in consecutive *sequentiality*.[4]

Sequentiality as a feature of video analysis corresponds to the principle of sequentiality that is also prominent in most interaction analysis in the line of conversation analysis (Silverman 1998). Although we will argue later that sequentiality is one, yet not the only principle of analysis of interaction, it is this feature of sequentiality which has influenced the particular focus of much interpretive video analysis. The focus of video analysis is, as a rule, on actions and interactions. And since video as a medium preserves the time structure of these temporal processes, it allows for an analysis of interaction which is to a degree unprecedented by earlier media (except for film). As video recordings mimic audiovisual conduct in time, they serve as a perfect medium to analyze the sequencing of action and the coordination of interaction through time.

Let us briefly sketch how sequentiality can be considered the basis of interpretation and analysis of interactions. Firstly, interpretations of video recordings focus on audiovisual conduct. They assume that what is happening (and what is understood to be happening) can be only understood if one looks

---

[4] This also holds true for digital data that are no longer stored on a continuous tape: recording is still a process in time, and despite the fact that we can order various video frames at the same time on the screen, we still need to watch what is happening on one frame as a continuous moving picture in time in order to understand «what is going on».

closely at the actions, action sequences and interactions that are expressed in audiovisual conduct. Actions (as we call this basic category for the sake of convenience – without defining their boundaries) are assumed to be produced *methodically* in certain ways, and it is only by being performed in certain ways that certain things are brought about. Thus, a PowerPoint presentation (to take an example from our current research) would not be regarded as some background activity to what might be considered the core activity (e.g. «the transfer of knowledge»). Rather, the series of actions involved in doing the presentation will be considered as the very essence of this activity. The focus of analysis then, lies in *how* those actions are being performed.[5]

This is linked to an additional assumption which again places emphasis on the audiovisual: whatever is observable and understandable should not be considered as being due to external factors beyond the video recorded scene itself, such as «drives», «subconscious desires», attitudes or interests, but as being motivated by the local sequence of the action recorded. As Goodwin (1986) revealed, even alleged «adaptors» (as Ekman/Friesen 1969 call gestures such as scratching or coughing) turn out not to be simply «outbreaks of nature». Rather, they appear to be sensitively built into the sequential order of actions, and thus prove to be actions themselves. As opposed to conventional sociological lore, actions here are not seen as relating to other factors outside the specific situation in which they occur. This is at the heart of what we mean by sequential analysis where one considers any action (note: action not actors) as having been motivated by prior actions and as motivating future actions. As mentioned above, this assumption is often equated with the «situative» character of social action (Suchman 1987). However, I would consider situativeness a methodological principle applied to the data by the analyst as long as possible, and I would avoid treating it as a substantial feature of social actions. In fact, talking about the situative character precludes the observation of actions which cannot be interpreted by situative, local resources only – and in which institutional regulations, social asymmetries and power might figure.

Reflexivity is another highly important methodological concept. By reflexivity we do not mean that actions are reflected consciously. On the contrary, most studies do address what might be called routinized, implicit knowledge or social practice. Reflexivity means that actors do not only act but also «indicate», «frame» or «contextualize» how their action is to be understood and how they have interpreted a prior action to which they are responding.[6] Thus we do not simply ask a question, we demonstrate that it is a question which we are formulating. It is because of this reflexivity that co-actors can understand what is meant by an action. By «investigating the methodological resources used by par-

---

[5] I have shown this in more detail in Knoblauch (in print).
[6] This notion of reflexivity differs from notions of reflexivity that address the presentation of research (cf. Ruby 2000). Of course, reflexivity applies here, too, but this is not a feature of research only. What is meant by reflexivity is explained in more detail in Knoblauch (2001a).

ticipants themselves in the production of social actions and activities» (Heath 1997: 184), it is also the reflexivity of the action that allows for an analytic interpretation.[7]

It is at this point that the sequential method relates to the other aspects of videography, because the possibility that interpreters and analysts make use of reflexivity does not only demand that they know the culture they are studying e.g. ethnographically. It also makes hermeneutic requirements: they need to understand what is going on in subjective terms. Such an understanding means that analysts who did not participate in the event that was recorded are, in principle, able to make sense of what is going on in the actions and interactions. This understanding has very practical aspects, because words and sentences have to be understood in order to be transcribed: one has to «see» the directions of gazes on the recordings or know what actors are referring to so that all essential parts (sentence, word, movement) of a sequence make sense to the participants. It is at this basic level of everyday understanding that ethnographic knowledge figures principally.

Interpretation may be regarded, therefore, as the very first step of approaching the data, i.e. the tapes and transcripts. An interpretation that is related to the everyday understanding of what is seen and heard, needs to be distinguished from analysis. By *analysis* we do not necessarily mean the distinction of different modes of audiovisual conduct (visual, verbal, paralinguistic, etc.), although it is necessary at certain points to focus on certain aspects, e.g. pointing gestures during PowerPoint presentations. Analysis means identifying units of action and their interrelationships with one another in the sequence of their production. Whatever may appear to be a unit is to be interpreted in relation to what occurred prior to it, and whatever the interpretation will be, it will be tested for its significance in the next unit (or turn).

One should be aware that transcription, interpretation and analysis often occur simultaneously; in the course of trying to understand what is going on, one might find that certain observations ought to be transcribed more precisely than before, and finding these details again might give rise to analytical observations.[8]

Analysis, again, is the attempt to identify general patterns within detailed ongoings. In order to do so, conversation analysis has provided us with a number of categories that allow to formally identify such patterns, at least with respect to spoken language (Sacks/Schegloff/Jefferson 1974). In this respect the basic unit of the sequence is the «turn». As opposed to the «speech act» that is defined linguistically, the turn is solely defined by the actors as a stretch of talk or, with respect to video, visual conduct, that may be followed by another step. For this reason, there is no objective «boundary». Turns are no «unit acts» or

---

[7] In conversation analysis, it was assumed that reflexivity of spoken communication is framed in spoken communication only, an assumption that is not adopted by video analysis.

[8] Jefferson (1985) demonstrated this beautifully in her analysis of laughter within turns.

«basic actions».[9] The boundaries of turns can only be identified if one understands the meaning of the activity in question. It requires, as we said, interpretation. Turns must be analyzed by looking at exactly how the utterances and the transitions and boundaries are produced. In order to understand the utterances, one might first try to look for acoustic cues, such as phrase intonations, pauses, and rhythms. Scrutinizing the transcript does not only allow us to become more familiar with the transcript and the spoken words (which often leads to a continuous refinement and correction of the transcript). It is also the basis for analytical observations of the structure of the sequences studied. Moreover, the reading of the transcript serves a secondary function when the video and the visual conduct are watched in more detail. The familiarity with the words spoken makes it easier to identify the sequence of events and to «relate» the visual events to the text. The video sequence can be watched repeatedly so as to discover the order of acoustic and visual events (what is happening at what time) and to identify when things are being done or said.

Since figures more often than not talk in most of our visual conduct, we can start the interpretation by focusing on the transcriptions of texts first. The understanding of the words is, at any rate, a prerequisite for understanding other elements of the activities, too. (By activities I refer to any sequence of coordinated visual conduct, be they performed by one or several actors). Some argue that this analysis could be accomplished without the transcript. Experience however has shown that the availability of a written transcript functions as a kind of location device that guides the analyst in the video. The analysis of the consequent sequences thus moves from the (transcribed) written to the visual aspect. However, the visual is not treated merely as an addendum to the spoken. Rather, in watching the video recordings one frequently discovers additional sequences which allow oneself to make sense of prior interpretations or sequences.

In looking at both, the spoken and the visual conduct, one can then discern that the visual conduct is constructed in such a way as to support the text the speaker is producing and vice versa. Analyses of this kind aim at the sequential structure of actions, the construction of meaningful units, participation structures, the spatial organization of activities, and the role of artefacts for performing activities etc. (Jordan/Henderson 1995).

Currently, many researchers opt for analyzing interaction in terms of *multimodality*. In terms of research practices this means that they attempt to cut the forms of such visual conduct into dimensions that appear to be analyzable independently of each other. Thus gestures are analyzed independently of (and only later again related to), e.g. speech, the direction of the gaze or the posture of the body (Schmitt 2007). As popular as this approach of multimodality is in the fields of prosody or gesture, it leads to a serious problem that has been formulated by Luckmann. In an early project on the analysis of interaction by video,

---

[9] That is to be distinguished not only from Parsons's theory of action but also from analytical notions, such as the «basic actions» by Danto (1965).

Luckmann and Gross (1977) tried to produce an interaction score made up of up to ten different modes (such as body posture, prosody, speech, gaze direction etc.) As Luckmann (2006) later confessed, the attempts to re-synthesize the various dimensions or «modes» into a holistic picture of interaction proved to be too complex and so far not really successful. For this and other reasons (i.e. the hermeneutic unity of actions) it seems more promising to take a holistic approach to the analysis of action that also allows to identify the dimensions that are relevant in a given situation. What role does the gesture play now, and in what relation does it stand to the spoken or other visual cues?

How can we approach this problem? In order to facilitate the identification of relevant dimensions and the boundaries of action, there are two criteria. The first is mentioned above, it is the criterion of sequentiality. Analysis depends on what occurs audio-visually: every utterance, every gaze, every move of the body or the head is being taken into consideration if, and in which ways it forms part of a sequence. Sequences are not identified independently of the sequences prior to, or subsequent to themselves, but by their immediate local context. One does not need to consider everything on the screen, but only that which stands in a recognizable relation to what appeared before and what comes thereafter. Thus, turns of talk may not be the relevant units of sequences at all. But whatever might be considered as unit must be shown to be bound by audiovisual conduct itself.

The criterion of sequentiality is complemented by a second criterion: what is of importance in the visual must not be speculated about but be indicated by the actors themselves. Do actors look at the screen before they push a button? Does it ring before A walks away? Does A look at B before A moves towards C? Schegloff (1992) calls this the «criterion of relevance», i.e. what is relevant to the analyst must be shown to be relevant to the actors. Or, as Goodwin (2000: 1508-1509) formulates: «Rather than wandering onto field-sites as disinterested observers, attempting the impossible task of trying to catalogue everything in the setting, we can use the visible orientation of the participants as a spotlight to show us just those features of context that we have to come to terms with if we are to adequately describe the organization of their action». This task can be accomplished by an analyst who knows both the field and the video data well. In addition, it is beneficial to regularly hold data sessions in which the analytical observations of sequential orders are subjected to the critical gazes of other observers who can gradually become familiar with the data. Finally, data workshops with other researchers and students who are less familiar with the data can be organized which might provide additional perspectives and/or help in testing more encompassing observations.

Non-situational features of videography

Up to this point we have focused on the sequence of actions that is realized situationally. However, the analysis of a video cannot be reduced to the activities represented on the video. This becomes particularly visible when the events recorded are not focused interactions, when spoken words are only of minor importance and when, therefore, the visual gains importance. For the spoken might be represented in a sequential and linear order corresponding to time, that is a diachronic order. Yet the visual denotes an additional synchronous dimension of simultaneity, i.e. the visually represented courses and resources of action, features of actors, and thus the contexts may not be organized on a turn-by-turn basis.

In terms of sequential analysis one becomes aware of the role of the situated context if validation by the criterion of relevance does not yield meaningful results, i.e. it does not allow to understand the sequence of action. In order to clarify the meaning and signification of visual elements in the recorded data, therefore, one further possible procedure is elicitation, auto-confrontation or video-based interviewing in order to retrieve the subjective meanings of the actors.[10] This means that the recordings are shown to the actors involved in order to reconstruct their subjective perspective on the phenomena. Thus it might be necessary to know what actors know about other actors, about certain artefacts or about what they perceived. To give a somewhat exotic example: In one of our tapes we recorded a Marian apparition that happens to three adult women (see picture below). However, on the video Mary is not visible either to the audience present or to the analyst; since the three women are obviously focusing on something invisible that remains massively subjective, it seems pertinent in this case to gather information about these subjective perceptions. (See figure 3)

In addition to the retrieval of the subjective perspective, the understanding of visual data requires observation, interviews, and expert interviews of the situations recorded. That is, it requires ethnography in order to become familiar with, and make sense of the settings in which we produce the video recordings. For example, we may need to acquire the knowledge necessary to understand actions that may involve intricate technologies and their activities. Thus, videography still addresses the emic perspective of the natives' point of view, yet in a very specific sense: specified with respect to certain situations (situated), activities, and actions. This does not mean that one needs to reconstruct the stock of cultural knowledge (i.e., members' knowledge) necessary to act in the domain as a whole. The task of the researcher is to acquire sufficient knowledge, particularly those elements of knowledge, partly embodied and relevant to the activity on which the study focuses. When studying technological activities, for example, especially those elements of knowledge necessary and relevant to understand the practices involved in handling that technology are sought.

To give another example from our data on the Marian apparitions. Most of these apparitions did not occur «spontaneously» but were preannounced so that the seers and an interested audience would gather at the apparition site. The «vision» was not only part of a social occasion, as Goffman (1963) would call it.

---

[10] Cf. Bayart/Borzeix/Lacoste (1997). The method can, of course, be traced back to Jean Rouch, cf. Jackson (2004).

Figure 3: The Marian visionaries during the vision

```
1  crowd:         Von¹¹ dort wird er kommen zu richten die Lebenden und die Toten
2                 From thence He shall come to judge the living and the dead.
3                 (-) ich glaube an den Heiligen Geist (-) die heilige katholische
4                 I believe in the Holy Spirit (-) the holy Catholic Church
5                 Kirche (-) Gemeinschaft der Heiligen (-) Vergebung der Sünden (-)
6                 (-) the communion of saints (-) the forgiveness of sins (-)
7                 Auferstehung der Toten (-) und das ewige Leben (-) Amen
8                 The resurrection of the body (-) and life everlasting (-) Amen
9                 (7.6)
10 male speaker:  Die Mutter Gottes ist bereits hier wer kann möchte sich knien
11                The Mother of God is already here; you may kneel down if you
12                can.
```

The example shows the beginning of the Marian apparition by one of the female seers, and the announcment by a male speaker with the microphone (10-12). The vision follows a pause in which the three seers obviously change their position in the local site, moving towards the free space. This again is followed by the text of which we find a fragment just before the announcement. Readers will easily recognize that the crowd recites the Apostolic Credo prayed by the male speaker and the audience together. Given this, one may note that the announce-

---

¹¹ See transcriptions rules at the end of the paper.

ment of the apparitions follows the prayer. In the pause (9) the movement of the three visionaries occurs. Although their movements are coordinated spontaneously, there is quite a rigid frame for these situated actions: the vision is followed by other prayers, and it is embedded in a liturgical structure that only allows for the vision to appear at certain places within the liturgy. Although one of the visionaries seems to start her vision as early as during the Credo, it is only after the end of the Credo that the vision may be made public. And after the three women have taken their position in the open space (which is represented in the picture above) the crowd starts to pray the Marian Prayer. This liturgical frame of the visionaries' activities is not only situational but also situated (Goffman 1981). It is embedded in an institutional structure that is reflected in a pre-fixed sequence of activities, such as prayers. (One need only mention that the spatial behavior, too, can only be understood against the background of the institutional setting. The vision is made outside the chapel for the very fact that it is not accepted by the church, and the direction of the visionaries is oriented towards a Marian sculpture that represents a vision that happened at the same place almost one hundred years ago).

This interpretation can only be adumbrated. However, it might have become clear how important it is to take the institutional setting into account. In fact, trying to interpret the sequence of activities from e.g. lines 8 to 10 will reveal that one is not able to understand what is going on from the situational coordination only. One needs to know the role of the Credo, the coordinating role of the priest and his substitutes in the Catholic Liturgy, even the pre-history of the earlier apparition.[12]

No doubt, the question as to the point at which the background knowledge of situations might be activated remains crucial for any video analysis. As a rule one can say that one should stick to the interpretation of what can be seen in the visual conduct only. However, as a reflexive researcher one might then realize that this interpretation already relates to knowledge of the situation that is imported by the interpreter. This is what one might call the hermeneutic circle. Within videography as a multi-methodic enterprise, the circle is however not one-dimensional. Based on the distinction of methods, data and data sorts, we are able to relate understandings and references to different methodical procedures: the interpretation of the content of the apparitions is dependent on interviews with the visionaries and text analysis, the knowledge of the institutional context depends on expert interviews and documents and the performance of the apparitions itself on the video-document. Thus, videographic analysis consists of a triangulation of different data and methods.[13]

---

[12] The history of the preceding apparition has been vividly reconstructed in the classical study by Blackbourn (1993).
[13] To be sure, comparison and contextual variation is a further principle of the analysis of contextual elements that cannot be dealt with here in detail; but cf. Knoblauch (2006).

Conclusion

As can be seen from this sketch, videography is not just one specialized method to analyze video frames. It is rather designed as an integrated sociological method that accounts for the constructedness of social reality. It attempts to relate the actors' subjective meanings (and the interpreters' meanings) to the records of their interactions (and the respective communicative objectivations) and to relate these to the social context of interaction reconstructed by means of ethnography.

In order to illustrate these dimensions, we can distinguish some of the methods and sort the data mentioned accordingly:

Subjective knowledge	Interactional, practical knowledge	Institutional knowledge
Participation	Participation	Participation
Interview	Observation	Expert interviews
Elicitation	Audiovisual data	Documents and discourse

Figure 5: Three levels of analysis and corresponding methods

It should be stressed that the distinction between these dimensions is not arbitrary or inductive. It is based on the theory of the social construction of reality that serves, as we have tried to show, as a methodology to capture the very construction as well as the constructedness of social reality. This way, social constructivist methodology avoids the dangers of situationalism as well as of objectivism. To be true, this methodological background does not yet solve all problems. Thus, there is no doubt that the problem of the triangulation of the various methods, such as sequential analysis and elicitation, has still to be solved in each singular interpretive empirical study; there is no doubt, either, that the relevance of the methods depends on the research question asked. As videography reveals, the social construction of reality provides a useful background in order to realize decisive methodological questions and offers an analytical tool to tackle them.

Transcription conventions

, ?   slightly/ strongly rising intonation
: .   slightly / strongly falling intonation

(-)	short pause
(5.0)	long pause (in seconds)
dam-	unfinished utterance
=	quick link
ne:::	extended
*	stressed
°	calm
LAUT	loud
(wann)	uncertain transcription
( )	not identified utterance
<u>double lines</u>:	accompanied by pointing gestures
<u>single lines:</u>	accompanied by discursive gestures

For all proper names (people, cities, geographic identifications and scientific notions) pseudonyms have been used in the transcripts.

References

Bayart, Denis/Anni Borzeix/Michèle Lacoste (eds.), 1997: Les traversées de la gare: Filmer des activités itinerantes. In: *Champs visuels* 6, 75-90.

Berger, Peter/Thomas Luckmann, 1966: *The social construction of reality*. London: Free Press.

Blackbourne, David, 1993: *Marpingen. Apparitions of the virgin mary in bismarckian germany*. Oxford: Clarendon.

Burr, Vivien, 1995: *An introduction to social constructionism*. London: Routledge.

Bourdieu, Pierre, 1979: *La distinction. Critique sociale du jugement*. Paris: editions du minuit.

Danto, Arthur C., 1965: Basic actions. In: *American Philosophical Quarterly* 2, 141-148.

Ekman, Paul/Wallace V. Friesen, 1969a: The repertoire of nonverbal behavior: Categories, origins, usage and coding. In: *Semiotica* 1, 63-68.

Ekman, Paul/Wallace V. Friesen, 1969b: A tool for the analysis of motion picture film or videotapes. In: *American Psychologist* 24, 3, 240-243.

Goffman, Erving, 1963: *Behavior in public places. Notes on the social organization of gatherings*. New York: Free Press.

Goffman, Erving, 1981: *Forms of talk*. Philadelphia: University of Pennsylvania Press.

Goffman, Erving, 1983: The interaction order. In: *American Sociological Review* 48, 1-17.

Goodwin, Charles, 1986: Gestures as a resource for the organization of mutual orientation. In: *Semiotica* 62, 1/2, 29-49.

Goodwin, Charles, 2000: Action and embodiment within situated human interaction. In: *Journal of Pragmatics* 32, 1489-1522.

Giddens, Anthony, 1984: *The constitution of society*: London: Polity Press.

Günthner, Susanne/Hubert Knoblauch, 1995: Culturally patterned speaking practices - The analysis of communicative genres. In: *Pragmatics* 5, 1-32.
Heath, Christian, 1986: *Body movement and speech in medical interaction.* Cambridge et al.: Cambridge University Press.
Heath, Christian, 1997: The analysis of activities in face to face interaction using video. In: David Silverman (ed.), *Qualitative research theory, method and practice.* London: Sage, 183-200.
Heath, Christian/Jon Hindmarsh, 2002: Analysing interaction: Video, ethnography and situated conduct. In: Tim May (ed.), *Qualitative research in action.* London: Sage, 99-121.
Heath, Christian/Hubert Knoblauch/Paul Luff, 2000: Technology and social interaction: the emergence of ›workplace studies‹. In: *British Journal of Sociology* 51, 2, 299-320.
Jackson, John, 2004: An ethnographic flimflam: Giving gifts, doing research, and videotaping the native subject/object. In: *American Anthropologist* 106, 1, 32-42.
Jefferson, Gail, 1985: An exercise in the transcription and analysis of laughter. In: Teun Adrianus van Dijk (ed.), *Handbook of discourse analysis*, Vol. 3: *Discourse and dialogue.* London: Academic, 25-35.
Jordan, Brigitte/Austin Henderson, 1995: Interaction analysis: Foundations and practice. In: *The Journal of the Learning Sciences* 4, 1, 39-103.
Kendon, Adam, 2004: *Gesture. Visible action as utterance.* Cambridge: Cambridge University Press.
Knoblauch, Hubert, 2001: Communication, contexts and culture. A communicative constructivist approach to intercultural communication. In: Aldo di Luzio/Susanne Günthner/Franca Orletti (eds.), *Culture in communication. Analyses of intercultural situations.* Amsterdam et al.: John Benjamins, 3-33.
Knoblauch, Hubert, 2005a: Focused ethnography. In: *Forum Qualitative Sozialforschung* 6/3.
<http://www.qualitative-research.net/fqs-texte/3-05/05-3-44-e.htm>
Knoblauch, Hubert, 2005b: Video-Interaktions-Sequenzanalyse. In: Christoph Wulf/Jörg Zirfas (eds.), *Ikonologie des Performativen.* München: Wilhelm Fink, 263-278.
Knoblauch, Hubert, 2006: Videography. Focused ethnography and Video Analysis. In: Hubert Knoblauch/Bernt Schnettler/Jürgen Raab/Hans-Georg Soeffner (eds.), *Video Analysis. Methodology and methods. Qualitative audiovisual data analysis in sociology.* Frankfurt a.M. et al.: Peter Lang, 35-50.
Knoblauch, Hubert, 2008: The performance of knowledge. Pointing and knowledge in powerpoint-presentations. In: *Cultural Sociology*, in print.
Knoblauch, Hubert/Uwe Flick/Christoph Maeder, 2005: Qualitative methods in europe: The variety of social research. In: *Forum Qualitative Social Research* 6/3.

<http://www.qualitative-research.net/fqs-texte/3-05/05-3-34-e.htm>
Knoblauch, Hubert/Bernt Schnettler/Jürgen Raab, 2006: Video-Analysis. Methodological aspects of interpretive audiovisual analysis in social research. In: Hubert Knoblauch/Bernt Schnettler/Jürgen Raab/Hans-Georg Soeffner (eds.), *Video Analysis. Methodology and methods. Qualitative audiovisual data analysis in sociology.* Frankfurt a.M. et al.: Peter Lang, 9-28.

Koch, Sabine C./Jörg Zumbach, 2002: The use of Video Analysis software in behavior observation research: Interaction patterns of task-oriented small groups. In: *Forum Qualitative Social Research* 3/2. <http://www.qualitative-research.net/fqs-texte/3-05/05-3-34-e.htm>

Luckmann, Thomas, 1979: Philosophy, science and everyday life. In: Thomas Luckmann (ed.), *Phenomenology and sociology.* Harmondsworth: Penguin, 217-253.

Luckmann, Thomas, 1981: Hermeneutics as a paradigm for social science? In: Michael Brenner (ed.), *Social method and social life.* London: Academic Press, 219-230.

Luckmann, Thomas, 2006: Some remarks on scores in multimodal sequential analysis. In: Hubert Knoblauch/Bernt Schnettler/Jürgen Raab/Hans-Georg Soeffner (eds.), *Video Analysis. Methodology and methods. Qualitative audiovisual data analysis in sociology.* Frankfurt a.M. et al.: Peter Lang, 29-35.

Luckmann, Thomas/Peter Gross, 1977: Analyse unmittelbarer Kommunikation und Interaktion als Zugang zum Problem der Entstehung sozialwissenschaftlicher Daten. In: Hans-Ulrich Bielefeld (ed.): Soziolinguistik und Empirie. Beiträge zu Problemen der Corpusgewinnung und –auswertung. Wiesbaden: Athenaion, 198-207.

Mittenecker, Erich, 1987: *Video in der Psychologie. Methoden und Anwendungsbeispiele in Forschung und Praxis.* Bern: Haupt.

Peräkylä, Anssi, 1997: Reliability and validity in research based on tapes and transcripts. In: David Silverman (ed.), *Qualitative research theory, method and practice.* London: Sage, 199-220.

Ruby, Jay, 2000: *Picturing culture: Explorations of film and anthropology.* Chicago: UCP.

Sacks, Harvey/Emanuel Schegloff/Gail Jefferson, 1978: A simplest systematics for the organization of turn-taking in conversation. In: Jim Schenkein (ed.), *Studies in the organization of conversational interaction.* New York: Academic Press, 5-56.

Sacks, Harvey, 1992 [1964]: Doing «being ordinary». In: Jefferson Gail/Emanuel A. Schegloff (eds.), *Lectures on conversation.* Oxford: Blackwell.

Schegloff, Emanuel A., 1992: On talk and its institutional occasions. In: Paul Drew/John Heritage (eds.), *Talk at work. Interaction in institutional settings.* Cambridge: Cambridge University Press, 101-136.

Schmitt, Reinhold (ed.), 2007: *Koordination. Analysen zur multimodalen Interaktion*. Tübingen: Narr.
Schubert, Cornelius, 2005: Video-Analysis of practice and the practice of Video-Analysis. In: Hubert Knoblauch/Bernt Schnettler/Jürgen Raab/Hans-Georg Soeffner (eds.), *Video Analysis. Methodology and methods. Qualitative audiovisual data analysis in sociology*. Frankfurt a.M. et al.: Peter Lang, 115-126.
Schütz, Alfred, 1962: Common sense and scientific interpretation of human action. In: *Collected Papers I*. The Hague: Nijhoff, 3-47.
Schütz, Alfred, 1967 [1932]: *The phenomenology of the social world*. Evanston Ill: Northwestern University Press.
Schütz, Alfred/Thomas Luckmann, 1974: *The structures of the life world*. London: Heinemann.
Soeffner, Hans-Georg, 1997: *The order of ritual: The interpretation of everyday life*. New Brunswick: Transaction Publishers.
Suchman, Lucy A., 1987: *Plans and situated actions. The problem of human-machine communication*. Cambridge: Cambridge University Press.
Suchman, Lucy A./Randall H. Trigg, 1991: Understanding practice: Video as a medium for reflection and design. In: Joan Greenbaum/Morten Kyng (eds.), *Design at work. Cooperative design of computer systems*. Hillsdale: Lawrence Erlbaum, 65-89.
Silverman, David, 1998: *Harvey Sacks. Social science and conversation analysis*. New York: Oxford University Press.
Ten Have, Paul, 1999: *Doing conversation analysis. A practical guide*. London: Sage.
Van Maanen, Max (ed.), 2002: *Writing in the dark. Phenomenological studies in interpretive inquiry*. London: Althouse Press.

Cornelius Schubert

Videographic elicitation interviews: Exploring technologies, practices and narratives in organizations

Introduction

Work in high-tech situations may appear as alien to the ethnographer as do tribal rituals on far away islands. Therefore, mere participant observation is often not sufficient to grasp the complexities of either modern work places or ancient rituals. In anthropology, especially visual anthropology, this has long been recognized (Collier 1967), and elicitation techniques have been widely employed to generate feedback and gather detailed information from those observed (see Schensul et al. 1999). The interview as such has also been a central element of anthropological ethnographic research (Spradley 1979). In this paper I will argue that in combination, interviews and elicitation techniques provide a fruitful instrument for two general purposes in the research process. The purposes are, on the one hand, *validation*, i.e. cross-checking the researcher's interpretations with the native's point of view and, on the other hand, *exploration*, i.e. learning more about the meaning of practices and the structure of knowledge of the given field (cf. Harper 1984).

Validation and exploration are especially important if the researcher is not familiar with the field under study. This is often the case with modern workplaces, and here the field of anesthesia will be used as an example for a highly complex and highly technicized workplace. In order to analyze the practices and knowledge of anesthetists, the ethnographer will have to carefully observe their work and in addition interview them about their work. The latter aspect is especially important for the use of elicitation interviews, since the anesthetist's work in an operating room (OR) or intensive care unit (ICU) has to be analyzed with respect to the organizational (e.g. training) and biographical (e.g. experience) influences in the given situation, which may not be openly displayed in the situation. Also, because the anesthesia's work consists to a large proportion of «machine work» (Strauss et al. 1997 [1985]: 40-68), many of the characteristics of the work situation may either be invisibly buried in the routines of day-to-day activities or may be conducted in the silent, isolated activities of machine operation.

Videographic elicitation interviews are a promising way to generate accounts of such «invisible» phenomena. In addition, if the narrative aspects of medical knowledge and medical work (Fleck 1980 [1935]; Montgomery Hunter 1991; Atkinson 1995) are taken seriously, especially with respect to the anecdotes and «war stories» of high-risk and high-tech work (Orr 1996; Barley/Orr 1997; Rochlin 1999), then the elicitization of such anecdotes and war stories becomes an interesting question. The videographic elicitation interview outlined here is aimed at generating anecdotes in which knowledge of relevant (safety) issues of (machine) work is presented via short video sequences to anesthetists as a «focus» for discussion (cf. Merton/Kendall 1946). Therefore, there will be an emphasis on the explorative character of videographic elicitation interviews and how they help to create narratives as accounts of technologies and as accounts of organizational order.

The empirical material in this chapter comes from a focused ethnographic study (Knoblauch 2001) of the work of anesthetists in surgical operating rooms. The ethnographic study was focused in so far that the field and focus of the research were strongly guided, yet not determined by analytical considerations (Schubert 2006a). In the study participant observations using pen and paper were supplemented by video interaction analysis (Ruhleder/Jordan 1997; Knoblauch 2004) and videographic elicitation interviews. The main aim of the study was to analyze the cooperation and interaction between nurses and doctors as well as their interactivity with media and machines with respect to patient safety. The videographic elicitation interview can supplement the often video-based observations of high-tech worksites, commonly referred to as workplace studies (Heath et al. 2000, Heath et al. 2004), which already have an emphasis on practice (Chaiklin/Lave 1996), and cognition and communication (Engeström/Middleton 1996) with respect to technology and organization.

The study reveals how closely related working with and talking about machines are and how an organizational order can be studied through interviews. Stories about machines convey practical and undocumented knowledge necessary for machine operation as well as information about intransparent cause-effect relationships in complex socio-technical ensembles. Stories about the organizational order convey knowledge of the informal rules of organized medicine and show how day-to-day activities deviate from ideal types of bureaucratic control and standardized operating procedures.

I will first outline the methodological issues of videographic elicitation interviews and put them in the context of ethnography, workplace studies, and organization studies. I will then show how the practices of anesthesia may be elicited as narrative accounts of complex technological and organizational tasks and conclude with a brief discussion of the advantages and disadvantages of the method.

Videographic elicitation interviews

Especially in ethnographic research, participant observation may not be adequate to collect sufficient data on the complex systems or structures of meaning, relevance, and knowledge. Elicitation techniques in turn generate a deeper understanding of the field from the informants' perspective and there are manifold methods and purposes (e.g. generating information about a cultural domain, Schensul et al. 1999). The videographic elicitation interview described here serves the purposes of eliciting feedback for the exploration of work practices as well as generating communicative validation from the informants and enabling validation through data triangulation (cf. Denzin 1989 [1970]: 225-227).[1] As Denzin puts it with respect to photos: «Photography of natives at work or pictures of citizens in their community can serve as a starting point for discussion of the everyday lives of the individuals being studied» (ibid: 226).

Using visual data from the field as feedback material – be they photos (Collier 1967) or films (Krebs 1975) – helps the informants to recall similar situations and reflect routine day-to-day activities. These two aspects are especially important if the research is directed towards knowledge and practice and only partly towards social interaction, since cognitive processes and habitual procedures are often hard, if not impossible, to observe. Also, they are not always subject to reflection by the informants. The video sequences help them to talk about aspects of their work which they usually do not think about. Eliciting feedback from the field therefore supports a broader and more complex reconstruction of knowledge, especially once we encounter «tacit knowledge» (Polanyi 1983 [1966]) and «habits» (Dewey 2002 [1922]) in terms of skills or «practical consciousness» (Giddens 1984). As we will see later, these are key aspects of work in knowledge-intensive and highly technicized situations, such as, modern medical practice. Eliciting feedback concerning the cognitive, social and material practices and knowledge resources thus becomes the central feature of videographic elicitation interviews.

Generating communicative validation and enabling data triangulation with videographic elicitation interviews supplement the reconstruction of work practices. Communicative validation may be of two sorts. First, the researcher can match his or her interpretation of the data with the informant's point of view, typically somewhere along the continuum between consent, correction or rejection. Second, the same film clip can be shown to multiple informants in order to either contrast different evaluations of the same situation or to affirm shared views. Data triangulation is important because videographic elicitation interviews of work practices are hardly the only source of information. Usually they are aligned with participant observations, where classic pen and paper observations may be used to acquire a general understanding of the procedures, and context and video-based observations are then used to focus on specific details of work, e.g. selected sequences of individual machine operation or collaborative tasks. This selection is one important aspect of combining focused ethnography and video analysis in videographic research (Knoblauch 2006; Schubert 2006a).

---

[1] Unlike the «ethnographic interview» (Spradley 1979: 58-68), it is not conducted as an informal, friendly conversation with the informant, but is framed as a distinct research situation to which the informant has agreed beforehand and which takes place in a quiet setting with the appropriate audiovisual technology for playback *and* recording. The video elicitation interview thus closely resembles the «focuses interview» (Merton/Kendall 1946), with the characteristic that the film used as focus is a video sequence recorded by the researcher during the participant observation of the informant's routine work.

Workplace studies and videography

Since Lucy Suchman's seminal book *Plans and situated actions* (1987, 2nd ed. 2007) and with the subsequent formation of a whole research approach called workplace studies (Heath et al. 2000, see also the British Journal of Sociology 53, 2: 157–317) the use of audiovisual recordings for analyzing work practices in highly technicized settings has become increasingly popular (see also Knoblauch in this volume). The sites of work range from underground control rooms (Heath/Luff 1992), airport control rooms (Goodwin/Goodwin 1996; Suchman 1996), radio control rooms (Knoblauch 1998), to sites of medical practice (Hindmarsh/Pilnick 2002) and financial transactions (Heath et al. 2002), to name only a few. Videography – understood in part as video interaction analysis (Suchman/Trigg 1991; Jordan/Henderson 1995; Heath/Hindmarsh 2002; Knoblauch 2004) – focuses on the «merely situated» and «situational» aspects of situated activity (Goffman 1966 [1963]: 21-22) as well as on the immediate social interaction.

In addition to video interaction analysis, videography also draws on ethnographic methods (Corsaro 1982; Knoblauch 2006). In this respect, the afore mentioned *focused ethnography* (Knoblauch 2001) draws more on the sociological ethnographic tradition of the Chicago School than on ethnological ethnography. Instead of longsome visits, a succession of shorter periods of fieldwork is desirable. Also, the researcher is not confronted with an alien culture, but with selected aspects of her own culture and often aided by multiple recording technologies. Focused ethnography is conducted in groups, and intensive periods of observation usually overlap with those of analysis. In addition to these general characteristics, there are four issues that need to be addressed concerning the relation of ethnographic studies of work and the use of video interaction analysis with respect to videographic elicitation interviews.

First, as said before, work practices – especially in high-tech settings and however alien and strange they might appear to the observer – are the routine day-to-day activities of those doing the work. This calls for a detailed *in situ observation* of such work practices, which is a tenor in workplace studies where approved ethnographic methods, such as participant observation, are commonly used for this purpose. Also, participant observation helps to render the work practices intelligible to the researcher. Whereas we usually do have sufficient competency to judge situations of everyday public life (e.g. in a school, shop, museum or café), our understanding of the complex relations of man and machine activities in high-tech work settings is often limited if not completely absent. Under such circumstances prior ethnographic research is essential for the subsequent video analysis. Furthermore, the ethnographic fieldwork will not only get the researcher acquainted with the field but also vice versa, which is not to be underestimated with respect to video recordings. In particular this is true for restricted access and potentially risky (e.g. medical, military or financial) settings, where small mistakes may have disastrous consequences.

Therefore, becoming a credible and trustworthy participant of the social situation (not of the work practices!) is essential for conducting videographic research. Even though the ethnographic approach generates a substantial body of knowledge of the work practices, which is needed to conduct a video interaction analysis, it cannot supersede video interaction analysis itself.

Second, the *immediate technical or social interaction* in complex organizations lends relevance to videographic research for two reasons: the every day operation of technology as well as the routine coordination of humans is often conducted in a swift and silent manner (cf. Schubert 2006b). The swiftness calls for a medium that can record the subtleties of everyday work and render them available for analysis. The technical advantages of video observations compared to those with plain eye are a commonplace in the literature. The relative silence in which routine cooperation is coordinated by gestures, facial expression or bodily configurations draws our attention away from audible conversations to visual and material aspects of cooperation. Here too, these non-verbal aspects of coordination can be captured quite well with video. The focus on immediate interaction resonates well with the ethnomethodological and interactionist roots of workplace studies, where interaction is considered not a mere by-product of cooperative work, but one of its constitutive elements. This is where videography using video interaction analysis exceeds standard ethnography, not by reintroducing positivist notions of realism but by enabling new levels of detail (e.g. through playback and slow-motion) in the analysis of interaction on the basis of «raw» audiovisual data. Raw in this sense means that the data corpus is not based on post-hoc accounts of the observed, although it may (and probably should) be selective according to the videographer's research interests (Schubert 2006a).

Third, and following the notion of «theoretical sampling» (Glaser/Strauss 1967: 45), video interaction analysis can be used to *focus and compare relevant sequences* of interaction. Based on ethnographic fieldwork and the research question, the researcher can identify such instances and use video recordings to generate a corpus of comparable sequences, which are not so much discrepant as such (like the psychiatrist and the prostitute in the famous example by Hughes 1971: 316) but reveal their differences in the subtleties of interaction, e.g. of an experienced nurse working at one time with an experienced doctor and at another time with a novice, as we will see later. Likewise it is possible to record the operation of a piece of machinery by several different people or by the same people under different circumstances (cf. Schubert 2007a). Sampling and comparing video sequences for studying work practices supports the collective analysis of the practices by a team of researchers not present in the situation and is – as will be shown later – essential for conducting videographic elicitation interviews.

Fourth, workplace studies have not only pointed out that work practices are situated actions, embedded in the in-situ practices and constituted through the ongoing interactions of everyday activities, but they have always related the situated actions to the *larger organizational context*. As Heath et al. (2000: 314) point out: «Whilst preserving a commitment to the interactional accomplishment of workspace activities, workplace studies consider the ways in which the visual, the vocal, and the material, feature with talk, in the production and coordination of organizational conduct». Following the agenda of workplace studies and interactionist studies of work we can state that: «Most work goes on within or in connection with organizations» (Strauss et al. 1997 [1985]: 289). Often, the organizational context is investigated through participant observation, because it remains implicit in many routine work activities and may not be recorded in focused video sequences. While video interaction analysis has undisputed advantages regarding the analysis of the visual and material features of work, its value for studying the relation of talk and organizational conduct still can be spelled out more precisely. The latter aspect has been more prominent in the studies of computer supported cooperative work (CSCW), where distributed activities need to be coordinated via a computerized infrastructure (Bowers/Benford 1991).

Summing up the relevance of workplace studies and videography for videographic elicitation interviews, workplace studies highlight the aspects of situated action (Suchman 1987) and technology in action (Heath/Luff 2000) that are both embedded in complex organizational interaction. The ethnomethodological/interactionist research agenda of workplace studies usually focuses on immediate (face-to-face) interaction, but may also be extended to technologically mediated interaction (as in the case of CSCW). Conceptually, the in situ study of work practices calls for a fine grained video analysis of interaction as well as an ethnographic investigation of organizational contexts. Videography particularly highlights the visual and material aspects of work, and videographic elicitation interviews can be used as a means of generating validating rapports from the informants with regard to the researcher's interpretations of their work practices (cf. Schensul et al. 1999). In high risk environments the informants are also able to evaluate in how far the sequence recorded is relevant to safety issues and in how far the sequence mirrors their everyday work activities, i.e. typical routine conduct or whether it is a singular episode of exceptional interaction. Since routine conduct is not readily accessible to reflection, especially during the work itself, the recorded sequences can travel – somewhat like «immutable mobile» (Latour 1986) – from the work setting to the interview setting, where the informant and the researcher may discuss the visual, material and vocal aspects of machine operation or human cooperation at length.

In addition to the validation, the discussion of selected video sequences with the informants gives new insights into the material from the native's point of view. Therefore «theoretical saturation» (Glaser/Strauss 1967: 61) can only be achieved temporarily and videographic elicitation interviews are a fruitful instrument for generating new questions and re-focusing the research. In the process of studying a workplace, even though the interviews first of all follow the ethnographic fieldwork and the video interaction analysis, they themselves should be followed by more ethnographic fieldwork and new video recordings. The iterative composition of observation, video analysis and interviews in the research process is especially useful in order to explore the complex relations of humans and machines in high-tech work settings. In the following section I will elaborate how videographic elicitation interviews may also help to bridge the gap between the analysis of interaction and that of the organization.

Ethnography and narratives in organizational research

One possible gateway to the study of organizations through interactions is the so-called «narrative approach» in organization studies (Czarniawska 1998) and possibly also the focus on «organizational discourse» (Grant et al. 1998). However, highlighting the importance of talk, especially anecdotes, does by no means underestimate the importance of the visual and material aspects of organizations (cf. Iedema 2007). Especially ethnomethodology (Garfinkel 1967) with its focus on interaction and conversation analysis (Sacks et al. 1974), with its focus on talk – irrespective of their merits for studying talk and interaction – tend to obscure, for instance, the visual, material, and organizational aspects of work, which are of course highly relevant in high-tech work settings (cf. Lynch 1985: 8-9).

Because videographic elicitation interviews are not conversations in the workplace but dislocated in time and space from the worksite itself, the question remains how they might be used to go beyond mere communicative validation, i.e. how talk that happens outside an organization may be important for the study of talk inside organizations. In the following sections I will try to answer this question by focusing on anecdotes and their relation to work practices. Anecdotes or «war stories» have been regarded as a central element of technical work (Orr 1986: 125-143), related to safety issues within organizational culture (Weick 2001: 341) and alleged to be an indispensable feature of societal interaction per se (Goffman 1983 [1959]: 17). For the purpose of the paper I will limit myself to the relation of anecdotes to technical work and safety issues, which are of prime concern when studying workplaces such as the surgical OR. For the study of High Reliability Organizations (HROs) Weick points out:

> «Culture coordinates action at a distance by several symbolic means, and one that seems of particular importance is the use of stories. Stories remind people of key values on which they are centralized.... Stories are important, not just because they coordinate, but also because they register, summarize, and allow the reconstruction of scenarios that are too complex for logical linear summaries to preserve». (2001: 341)

In this line of research, organizational narratives are seen «as the main mode of knowing and communicating in organizations» (Czarniawska 1998: 16). The tales from the field lend themselves to the study of organizations especially when the actors have to make sense of the organization (Weick 1995). This way, stories have a twofold effect. First, they serve as a knowledge reservoir of personal experience (Labov/Waletsky 1967) as well as that of others, which can be shared and which can help to reduce the ever growing complexities of high-tech workplaces. Second, they can help to manage unexpected events by creating work and organization-specific perceptions of possible problems, sometimes including solutions to those problems, e.g. by using clinical incident reporting systems for risk management. As work and organizations become more complex, story telling can be seen as a continuous endeavour to create meaning, reduce ambiguity, and reproduce practices, e.g. in using stories to teach novices. Whether they in fact constitute the main mode of knowing in organizations and the way they relate to other forms of knowledge reservoirs, e.g. to files, reports or electronic communication systems, remain questions to be answered by empirical studies.

Especially ethnographic organizational research has drawn attention to the importance of work practices for studying organizations (Barley 1996) and stories told in the course of work (Orr 1996; Bechky 2006). Especially Orr's study of war stories as a diagnostic activity of service technicians (1996: 125-143) reveals that stories are not a mere addition to the work but an integral part of it. They have a twofold function, since «they preserve and circulate hard-won information and are used to make claims of membership or seniority within the community» (ibid.: 126). Orr distinguishes five classes of stories. (1) Some stories are used to accentuate the idiosyncratic nature of each specific situation in pointing out how they are not like others. (2) Other stories, however, are a reminder of sometimes invisible or illogical machine functions, containing knowledge not found in the manuals. (3) Then there are stories which are supposed to increase or develop diagnostic understanding. The three classes of stories above are relevant to the practice of diagnostics. They are supplemented by stories addressing two other important issues. (4) Stories are used to illustrate (to a novice) how to deal with difficult situations, to challenge or to instruct. (5) Last not least, they are told to celebrate the heroic nature of the technician's work for transforming novices into experts. The stories which were elicited in the study presented here mainly fall into category (2) and (4). They are stories about hidden interactions between machines, undocumented features as well as avoiding and dealing with breakdowns.

However, difficult situations also arise from the organizational structure of medical work, and the stories are told as guidelines for adequate instead of formally correct behavior. In this sense, war stories are brief narrative accounts of relevant incidents, and eliciting such stories is a different matter to generating larger accounts, e.g. biographical narratives (cf. Kissmann in this volume). Whereas the latter give detailed insight into the informant's perspective, the former are part of everyday work and communication and give us an insight into the narrative structure of medical knowledge.

In general, most stories have to do with the inherent uncertainty of organized modern medical practice, which is likewise true for the work of service technicians. This is mainly due to the often opaque connections of symptoms to their causes in both realms. One might even argue for medicine that it has become doubly opaque with the broad introduction of medical technologies. First, medicine is itself inherently uncertain (Parsons 1951: 428-479; Fox 1957; Wagner 1995; Schubert 2007b) and second, especially diagnostic tools may produce new uncertainties (Pasveer 1989; Yoxen 1989). From this perspective, safety in such settings cannot be understood as a permanent organizational feature, but must be considered the continuous accomplishment of the people involved. The ability to act safely is then a product of «heedful interrelating» (Weick/Roberts 1993) or «distributed knowledge» (Hutchins 1996: 287-316) and is accomplished at the same time as the work goes on itself. Work is then directly regarded as a context for learning (Lave 1993; Wenger 1998), and stories about safety are an integral part of providing high reliability in complex work environments (Rochlin 1999).

The narrative structure of medical knowledge lends itself particularly well to this kind of analysis. Although modern medical practice (or organizations) cannot be reduced to narratives, they do play an important role. I will briefly sketch two studies concerned with the relation of medical knowledge and narratives (Montgomery Hunter 1991; Atkinson 1995), so that the use of elicitation techniques becomes more distinct in the ethnographic study of professional work in organizations.

Atkinson sees the sociological question arising from this for doctor-patient consultations as in how far «the organized routines of everyday practice transmute the unique, biographically constituted troubles of the person into the appropriate classes of diagnoses and management» (Atkinson 1995: 33). When looking at the plurality of medical practices however, we must not only look at patient consultations, but also at more remote settings, such as laboratories (e.g. concerning distributed knowledge, Cicourel 1990) or operating rooms (e.g. with respect to the embodiment of action, Moreira 2004). Atkinson stresses the importance of not confining our analysis to one doctor only, but to extending it to the collaborative nature of medical work itself. Following Atkinson, the social organization of collaborative medical work cannot be dissociated from medical talk, which often takes on a liturgical form. He concludes that even in highly bureaucratized organizational settings, such as hospitals, there is enough room for ceremonial and ritualized discourse, for instance when a case is presented to others. From such a perspective clinical reasoning cannot be understood as a solitary individual act but as a culturally and materially situated practice, as the so-called laboratory studies (Latour/Woolgar 1979; Knorr Cetina 1981) have shown in the case of scientific practice.

Hunter especially analyzed the use of anecdotes in medicine which according to her are mainly due to «the imperfect fit between biological knowledge and the expression and treatment of disease in the individual» (Montgomery Hunter

1991: 69). She points out how the presentation of single cases used to be the main vehicle of medical knowledge up to the late 18th century. Although today the anecdotes are more likely to be found in informal talk rather than scientific speech, they are still carriers of relevant medical information. They serve as a pool of knowledge required to stay sensitive to the idiosyncrasies of each patient and not to overgeneralize diagnosis and treatment. I would like to highlight another aspect here. Anecdotes are an indispensable reservoir not only of medical, but also of organizational knowledge. Such anecdotes contain relevant information about the organizational procedures connected with each case (ibid: 73). Especially novice doctors build up a large corpus of knowledge about their superiors this way, and they learn when and how to get them involved and when not to.

Eliciting the practices of anesthesia

The uncertainties introduced by medical technologies are a good vantage point to enter the study of technologies, practices and narratives in complex work settings such as the OR. Unlike, for instance, in schools or other public and semi-public spaces, researchers usually do not have prior knowledge of the work in high-tech work settings, such as control centres, nuclear power plants or operating rooms. For studying practices in those settings, videographic methods do not suffice. A research agenda to explore such spaces must draw on a variety of methods to generate the necessary context knowledge for analysis.

The videographic elicitation interviews presented here were a semi-final step in an ongoing process (cf. Schubert 2006a for an extended account). The field research was started with traditional pen and paper participant observations of routine surgical operations by job shadowing anesthetists. This way, the relevant medical knowledge as well as the rules of appropriate conduct, i.e. concerning sterile equipment, was generated. The mutual acquaintance of the researcher and the operating team is an essential prerequisite not only for later video recordings, but also for ethnographic interviews with surgeons, nurses and other anesthetists to make sense of the situation. After several days in the OR a mobile video camera was used to film sequences of interest. The sequences were selected according to the research question, previous observations and situational conditions. Critical situations were not filmed. The videotaped material was then analyzed by individuals as well as in group settings, which is the central component of video interaction analysis (Jordan/Henderson 1995, Ruhleder/Jordan 1997). Particularly interesting episodes were isolated and used for the videographic elicitation interviews. At first, the episodes were used as «mere» audio-visual data for confirmation and validation by experts, but they also served as a focus for enabling a lengthy discussion between the researcher and the anesthetists with the purpose of generating further research questions. Such longer discussions cannot be conducted during the actual work itself, and the use of video recordings lends itself well as a focus for discussion in a setting that is dislocated from the work site. Eliciting the practices of anesthesia must therefore be seen as a multi-method approach which cannot be reduced to the use of visual elicitation techniques.

Stories as accounts of technology

Like many other modern medical disciplines, the practice of anesthesia is inseparably linked with its tools and artefacts (cf. Reiser 1978; Heath et al. 2003; Timmermans/Berg 2003). Think of the drugs, syringes, artificial respiration units, monitoring equipment and protocols. Working with those machines and artefacts requires a high level of skill and competence. The knowledge necessary to perform a safe narcosis thus not only concerns medical conditions, but also the adequate operation and control of the material environment. One of the interesting issues with regard to safety is how the anesthetists assert the state of the patient via the various sources of information in the OR, which range from the direct visual and tactile observation of the patient to blood pressure measurements and electroencephalograms.

During the participant observations I noted that there was often some trouble with a certain machine, namely the infusion pump or perfusor, which is used to continually administer intravenous drugs during the operation. After a full syringe is loaded into the pump and the dose is set, the motor of the pump slowly pushes the plunger of the syringe in, thus administering the medication. This is especially the case with total intravenous anesthesia (TIVA) where the hypnotic and analgesic agents are delivered intravenously instead of being inhaled. The drugs used for TIVA are both potent and short-acting, and they therefore – in theory – facilitate a precise and predictable narcosis. I then began recording the beginning of TIVA narcosis on video in order to analyze the details of the interaction. Three short episodes of different stages of machine-related problems were cut into a short video clip of roughly 2min 30sec which was then shown to three anesthetists in the course of videographic elicitation interviews. In the first episode the problem could be fixed routinely by the anesthetist, in the second episode the technological dysfunction was compensated by the anesthetist, and in the third episode the anesthetist and a nurse improvised to maintain a stable sequence of actions (see Schubert 2007a for details). Even though problems with medical technologies are commonplace in modern medical practice, they also bear the potential for critical events and are taken seriously by doctors as well as nurses. When asked to comment on the reliability and the typical malfunctions of the perfusors all anesthetists produced long narratives about their stance towards these machines.

Interestingly, all anesthetists expressed their affinity towards perfusor models they were used to in their work, just as they articulated in unison their dislike for others. This evaluation was embedded in narratives of own previous experiences as well as hearsay anecdotes of others. I observed the telling of such anecdotes in the OR most often when a machine malfunction occurred in the presence of a novice. The experienced anesthetist then set the malfunction in a broader context, commented on the cause and the solution of the problem and illustrated the possible consequences by referring to a critical episode which might arise from such problems. With respect to the use of technology the video clip sparked a broader discussion of the merits and obstacles of medical machines within the interview, and I will select two significant issues here.

First, the anesthetists did not confine themselves to reflecting on the situation in the clip but quickly pointed to the problem of complex interrelations between multiple technologies. One of them highlighted the tight coupling of bodies, drugs, and technologies in modern anesthesia as follows. With older infusion pumps the motor which pushes the plunger into the syringe and thus the drugs into the patient's body sometimes does not work evenly. As a consequence the potent anesthetic drugs are not consistently administered and this may, for instance, lead to a slight rise and fall in blood pressure or heart rate over time. These small alternations are picked up by the sensory equipment and turned into a visible wavelike pattern on the monitoring screen. Such accounts of opaque and unanticipated cause-effect relationships point to increasingly complex links between technology and knowledge in modern medical practice (Wagner 1995). In the interview the anesthetist concluded by quoting one of his former superiors who, in his mind, subsumed the essential relation of knowledge and action in anesthesia by proverbially stating that: «you have to know a lot to do nothing». Even though this account of the invisible interrelations and potential pitfalls has few anecdotal qualities, it gives valuable insights into the practices of working in complex socio-technical settings. Videographic elicitation interviews help to discuss such issues under circumstances detached from the pressures of everyday work, providing for the undivided attention from the experts. The video clips help to ground such a discussion in concrete situations.

Second, the interviewed experts often embedded anecdotes of critical events into their accounts of technologies. This mostly happened as a way of bringing to attention possible complications and warning novices of technical problems they might encounter later on. After seeing the perfusor episodes, an anesthetist commented on one of the malfunctions related to an insufficiently recharged battery. He points out that the batteries pose a serious risk when transporting patients and then inserts a story: «there we (the anesthetist and his critical patient) were in the elevator and suddenly ... snap, the adrenalin pump stops without warning. And you can't regulate adrenalin manually from those syringes. Then you really have to improvise and administer highly diluted adrenalin manually. Really, those batteries are a main concern». The drastic content of the story is a clear warning and a good reminder to check the pump's batteries before moving a patient from the OR to the ICU. Even though such stories are an integral part of everyday work, it is interesting to see how they can be elicited easily through the use of video clips.

Working with technology requires not only narratives but a great deal of expertise with the material equipment (Hoc et al. 1995). It becomes quite obvious, how closely the use of technology is connected with talking about technology. Knowledge of obscure cause-effect relationships and potential pitfalls of medical technologies is transferred and preserved in the anecdotes and stories that medical doctors tell. As said before, since most interaction with machines happens in a silent and swift routine manner, elicitation techniques help to look behind the routines of everyday work by providing a space for discussion and reflection, exploring the practices in high-tech workplaces further than possible with observation only.

Stories as accounts of organizational order

In order to elicit organizational aspects of work, a second video recording was used in the interviews. It consisted of a roughly 3min clip showing two episodes from different intubations. The first was an experienced and the second an inexperienced anesthetist. Both were working with an experienced nurse. During the intubation a plastic tube is inserted into the patient's trachea to allow for artificial respiration. In the cooperation between the nurse and the anesthetist the former usually assists the latter by handing over the necessary instruments. This cooperation is typically conducted swiftly and silently in a routine manner, and a cursory observation of the two episodes would not reveal much difference in the interaction. The repeated, slow motion analysis of the video, however, uncovered a significant difference in the order of interaction (cf. Hindmarsh/Pilnick 2002).

In contrast to the expert-expert interaction in the first episode, the nurse in the second episode did not so much assist as more than anything guide the novice doctor through the intubation procedure. She had every instrument ready in the right order and when handing over the tube she held on to it a little longer than necessary to draw the anesthetist's attention to the correct position for inserting the tube. She was not only always a step ahead of the novice doctor and engaged in the subtle structuring of the procedure by handing him the right tools at the right time, she also used the tube itself as a means of an embodied/material teaching act. She did this even though an experienced anesthetist was present at the time, who could have instructed the novice explicitly. This way, the nurse not only supported the intubation as such but also aided the novice in *maintaining face* under the eyes of a superior (cf. Goffman 1999 [1967]: 10-53). However, the novice was too concentrated on the intubation task to properly acknowledge the subtle support from the nurse and failed his first intubation attempt. His superior noticed the problem and explained to him verbally and with gestures, how to correctly insert the tube, which finally resulted in a successful intubation. After seeing this episode the interviewed anesthetists all commented at length about the importance of competent nurses, especially in the early years of their training.

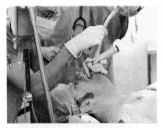

Segment 1: The nurse hands the tube over to the novice anesthetist with her left hand. He reaches for it with his right hand while holding the laryngoscope in position with his left.

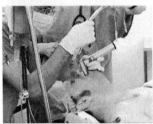

Segment 2: As the novice anesthetist pulls on the tube, the nurse does not let go, so the doctor looks away from the patient and up to the tube. Only after the tube is in a good position the nurse lets go. In real time this roughly takes 3.5 seconds.

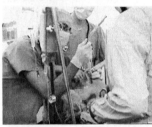

Segment 3: After the first unsuccessful attempt, the senior doctor (entering the scene from the right) moves in and the novice holds the tube up towards him. His thumb marks the point where the tube bends. On the video tape it is unintelligible what the senior says or does, but after 2 seconds the novice resumes the intubation.

Segment 4: After reinserting the tube into the patient's mouth the senior doctor makes a downward movement with his hand, indicating the correct movement for inserting the tube (see the white arrow). The novice looks at the hand movement and then successfully performs the intubation.

One anesthetist commenced a narrative about his early training and the organizational circumstances in which it happened: «Unfortunately, in the first week on my own, I had to work with a really bad nurse. She was an alcoholic. They did not fire her, because she once had an affair with a senior doctor. One of the senior doctors was an alcoholic, too. And this nurse made my life pretty much hell. A year later I had a near catastrophic event with her and then I changed my behavior towards her». Such biographical anecdotes can tell us a lot about the organization of medical work. It does not need to be as dramatic as in the case above, but every doctor had a story to tell how a competent nurse was helpful in the very early days of their practice and how a baneful nurse made their life difficult. The message such anecdotes convey is twofold. On the one hand: «seek and respect the knowledge and competence of experienced nurses», on the other hand «be aware of untrustworthy ones». Also, the story above strongly suggests that there might be informal alliances within the staff of a hospital, thus do not blindly count on your superiors to help you. Thus, these anecdotes are an integral part of learning how medical work is actually done in organizational settings and how it diverges from the idealized conceptions of university training and bureaucratic control.

The daily routines and talk of medical work are of course best studied by conducting ethnographic fieldwork. However, the video elicitation interviews can supplement the research process by providing – if I may borrow a medical term here – a minimally invasive, keyhole perspective of the organization. Especially in the case of doctor-nurse interactions, the anesthetists delivered rich biographical accounts of their experiences of working in hospitals. Using video sequences of everyday routine work as a focus, the anesthetists could immediately relate to the recorded scene. They were not only able to give detailed assessments of the situations, pointing out aspects not picked up by the researcher, but they also produced anecdotes, such as those mentioned above, and with those stories we can elicit interesting details about the practice of anesthesia.

Even though there still exists a gap between saying and doing something (cf. LaPierre 1934), and the keyhole ethnography using video elicitation interviews should not be mistaken for fieldwork ethnography, the narrative approach in organization studies informs us that while narratives may not be the only aspect of organizational life, they do play an important role with regard to the understanding of how (high-tech) work happens in complex organizations (cf. Boje 2001).

Conclusion

Using videographic elicitation interviews as a method of exploring technologies, practices and narratives – or socio-material practices (Orlikowski 2007) – in organizations is a fruitful extension of ethnographic fieldwork and videography. The elicitation of stories and anecdotes resonates well with the «narrative approach» in organization studies, the latter providing a rich corpus of detailed studies as well as the conceptual framework of narratives, work, and organizations. The elicitation of stories as accounts of organizational order provides a keyhole perspective of work in modern hospitals. Such stories convey a rich picture of organizational life which helps to explore the work of anesthetists beyond the observation of their day-to-day activities. We learn a lot more than just about the situation on video. We learn about hierarchies, informal alliances and about the difficulties and dilemmas of becoming a competent doctor after university training (Merton et al. 1957; Becker et al. 1961) is over.[2] Therefore, the stories not only bridge the gap between general biomedical knowledge and the individual treatment of a patient. They also bridge the gap between formal bureaucratic organization, professional autonomy, and informal control in hospitals. Furthermore, the interviews are an occasion for discussion and provide valuable accounts of the role of artefacts in medical practice. As has been shown, modern medical technologies may entail unforeseen and unforeseeable interrelations. They can obscure cause-effect relationships, too. Stories as accounts of technology deeply embed the use of technology in shared narratives, serving as a reservoir of indispensable knowledge for routine machine operation. Coping adequately with technical failures, false alarms, and dysfunctions in real time situations depends to a large extent on the availability of other people's experience in form of stories.

However, conducting videographic elicitation interviews is no one-way street. At the same time that the researcher validates her findings and further explores the organizational and technological aspects of work, the research subjects can benefit from the social scientist's conceptual approaches. This is even more so the case in complex, high-tech work settings where the «natives» are often university-trained professionals who have a strong interest in reflecting on their own work with the help of social scientists. The more remote such settings are from everyday life and the more organizationally and technologically complex they turn out to be, the more beneficial videographic elicitation interviews will be for both sides. In addition, the interviews can help to bring together the «narrative» with the «visual», two more or less distinct subjects which have gained attention in the social sciences after the so-called «postmodern turn» (cf. Clarke 2005: 181-260). As final remarks in this paper, I would like to put three aspects of videographic elicitation interviews in a broader context of empirical research.

First, one should be aware of some limitations of the method. As I pointed out, using video episodes as a focus for eliciting work practices is only one method among others. For high-tech work settings this includes the ethnographic fieldwork for generating the necessary knowledge of the domain and for establishing reliable access to the field as a prerequisite for video recordings. Also, the anecdotes and war stories elicited in the interviews should not be confused with larger narrative accounts studied in sociology or linguistics (cf. Polkinghorne 1988; Richardson 1990; Bamberg 1997). However, they are part of the knowledge circulation, storage, and structure of the workplace, and the establishment of so-called clinical incident reporting systems, such as the National Patient Safety Agency (2005) in the U.K, underscore the importance of individual stories for collective learning. Last not least, work, especially organizational

---

[2] We also believe that some dramatic depictions of organized medical practice, e.g. Samuel Shem's *House of God* or Lars von Trier's *The Kingdom*, may in some aspects not be too far off from the bizarreness of real world situations.

work and working with technologies, cannot be reduced to narratives. It entails material, spatial, temporal, embodied, and organizational qualities that have to be studied in their own right, e.g. the role of material agency (Pickering 1995) in the mutual tuning of anesthetists and medical technologies or the organizational effects of novel accounting technologies (Samuel et al. 2005).

Second, the video clips can serve as a «double focus» in the research process by a) focussing the ethnographic fieldwork on selected relevant situations for a more detailed study, and b) serving as a focus for the videographic elicitation interviews themselves. This way, many work situations can be quite easily compared and contrasted with each other, e.g. the similarities and differences in intubation procedures seen in expert-expert and expert-novice teams. The episodes help to ground the interview in the routine activities of day-to-day work, and the interview settings allow for a lengthy discussion and reflection on habits or rituals. The double focus therefore has two sides: one for narrowing down the analysis to certain issues and the other for broadening the scope of the analysis beyond the individual situations. The anecdotes and war stories described above are a good example of the latter.

Third, the benefits of conducting videographic elicitation interviews on top of ethnographic fieldwork and videographic analysis lies first of all in the communicative validation of the researcher's findings. Yet, eliciting the native's point of view delivers much more. It can provide rich accounts of personal experience and, equally important especially in organizations and concerning the work with machines, hearsay. Like keyhole surgery, this form of «keyhole ethnography» requires a certain level of competence and sufficient knowledge of the work, the technologies, and the organization for directing such an interview and making it a valuable source of information.

References

Atkinson, Paul, 1995: *Medical talk and medical work. The liturgy of the clinic.* London: Sage.
Bamberg, Michael G.W. (ed.), 1997: *Oral versions of personal experience. Three decades of narrative analysis.* A special issue of the Journal of Narrative and Life History. Mahwah: Lawrence Erlbaum Associates.
Barley, Stephen R., 1996: Technicians in the workplace. Ethnographic evidence for bringing work into organizational studies. In: *Administrative Science Quarterly*, 41, 3, 404-441.
Barley, Stephen R./Julian E. Orr (eds.), 1997: *Between craft and science. Technical work in U.S. settings.* Ithaca: IRL Press.
Bechky, Beth A., 2006: Talking about machines. Thick description, and knowledge work. In: *Organization Studies*, 27, 12, 1757-1768.
Becker, Howard S./Blanche Geer/Everett C. Hughes et al. (eds.), 1961: *Boys in white. Student culture in medical school.* Chicago: University of Chicago Press.

Boje, David M., 2001: *Narrative methods for organizational and communication research.* London: Sage.
Bowers, John M./Stephen D. Benford (eds.), 1991: *Studies in computer supported cooperative work. Theory, practice and design.* Amsterdam: North-Holland.
Chaiklin, Seth/Jean Lave (eds.), 1996: *Understanding practice. Perspectives on activity and context.* Cambridge: Cambridge University Press.
Cicourel, Aaron V., 1990: The integration of distributed knowledge in collaborative medical diagnosis. In: Jolene Galegher/Robert E. Kraut/Carmen Egido (eds.), *Intellectual teamwork. Social and technological foundations of cooperative work.* Hillsdale: Lawrende Erbaum Associates, 221-242.
Clarke, Adele E, 2005: *Situational analysis. Grounded theory after the postmodern turn.* Thousand Oaks: Sage.
Collier, John, 1967: *Visual anthropology. Photography as a research method.* New York: Holt, Rinehart & Winston.
Corsaro, William A., 1982: Something old and something new. The importance of prior ethnography in the collection and analysis of audiovisual data. In: *Sociological Methods & Research*, 11, 2, 145-166.
Czarniawska, Barbara, 1998: *A narrative approach to organization studies.* Thousand Oaks: Sage.
Denzin, Norman K., 1989 [1970]: *The research act in sociology.* Chicago: Aldine.
Dewey, John, 2002 [1922]: *Human nature and conduct.* Mineola: Dover.
Engeström, Yrjö/David Middleton (eds.), 1996: *Cognition and communication at work.* Cambridge: Cambridge University Press.
Fleck, Ludwik, 1980 [1935]: *Entstehung und Entwicklung einer wissenschaftlichen Tatsache.* Frankfurt a.M.: Suhrkamp.
Fox, Renée C., 1957: Training for uncertainty. In: Robert K. Merton/George G. Reader/Patricia L. Kendall (eds.), *The student-physician. Introductory studies in the sociology of medical education.* Cambridge: Harvard University Press, 207-241.
Garfinkel, Harold, 1967: *Studies in ethnomethodology.* Englewood Cliffs: Prentice-Hall.
Giddens, Anthony, 1984: *The constitution of society. Outline of the theory of structuration.* Berkeley: University of California Press.
Glaser, Barney G./Anselm L. Strauss, 1967: *The discovery of grounded theory.* Chicago: Aldine.
Goffman, Erving, 1966 [1963]: *Behaviour in public places. Notes on the social organization of gatherings.* New York: Free Press.
Goffman, Erving, 1983 [1959]: *Wir alle spielen Theater. Die Selbstdarstellung im Alltag.* München: Piper.
Goffman, Erving, 1999 [1967]: *Interaktionsrituale.* Frankfurt a.M.: Suhrkamp.

Goodwin, Charles/Majorie H. Goodwin, 1996: Seeing as situated activity. In: Yrjö Engeström/David Middleton (eds.), *Cognition and communication at work.* Cambridge: Cambridge University Press, 61-95.
Grant, David/Tom W. Keenoy/Clifford Oswick (eds.), 1998: *Discourse and organization.* London: Sage.
Harper, Douglas, 1984: Meaning and work. A study in photo elicitation. In: *International Journal of Visual Sociology*, 2, 1, 20-43.
Heath, Christian/Jon Hindmarsh, 2002: Analysing interaction. Video ethnography and situated conduct. In: Tim May (ed.), *Qualitative research in action.* London: Sage, 99-121.
Heath, Christian/Hubert Knoblauch/Paul Luff, 2000: Technology and social interaction: the emergence of «workplace studies». In: *British Journal of Sociology*, 51, 2, 299-320.
Heath, Christian/Paul Luff, 1992: Collaboration and control: Crisis management and multimedia technology in London underground line control rooms. In: *Journal of Computer Supported Cooperative Work*, 1, 1, 24-48.
Heath, Christian/Paul Luff (eds.), 2000: Technology in action. Cambridge: Cambridge University Press.
Heath, Christian/Paul Luff/Hubert Knoblauch, 2004: Tools, technologies and organizational interaction. The emergence of workplace studies. In: David Grant/Cynthia Hardy/Cliff Oswick/Linda L. Putnam (eds.), *The SAGE handbook of organizational discourse.* London: Sage, 337-358.
Heath, Christian/Paul Luff/Marcus Sanchez Svensson, 2003: Technology and medical practice. In: *Sociology of Health and Illness*, 25, 3, 75-96.
Heath, Christian/Marcus Sanchez Svensson/Jon Hindmarsh/Paul Luff/Dirk vom Lehn, 2002: Configuring awareness. In: *Computer Supported Cooperative Work*, 11, 317-347.
Hindmarsh, Jon/Alison Pilnick, 2002: The tacit order of teamwork. Collaboration and embodied conduct in anesthesia. In: *The Sociological Quarterly*, 43, 2, 139-164.
Hoc, Jean-Michel/Pietro C. Cacciabue/Erik Hollnagel (eds.), 1995: *Expertise and technology. Cognition & human-computer cooperation.* Hillsdale NJ: Lawrence Erlbaum.
Hughes, Everett C., 1971: *The sociological eye: Selected papers.* Chicago: Aldine.
Hutchins, Edwin, 1996: *Cognition in the wild.* Cambridge et al.: MIT Press.
Iedema, Rick, 2007: On the multi-modality, materiality and contingency of organization discourse. In: *Organization Studies*, 28, 6, 931-946.
Jordan, Brigitte/Austin Henderson, 1995: Interaction analysis. Foundations and practice. In: *The Journal of the Learning Sciences*, 4, 1, 39-103.
Knoblauch, Hubert, 1998: Pragmatische Ästhetik. Inszenierung, Performance und die Kunstfertigkeit alltäglichen kommunikativen Handelns. In: Herbert Willems/Martin Jurga (eds.), *Inszenierungsgesellschaft. Ein einführendes Handbuch.* Opladen et al.: Westdeutscher Verlag, 305-324.

Knoblauch, Hubert, 2001: Fokussierte Ethnographie. In: *Sozialer Sinn*, 2, 1, 123-141.
Knoblauch, Hubert, 2004: Die Video-Interaktions-Analyse. In: *Sozialer Sinn*, 1, 123-138.
Knoblauch, Hubert, 2006: Videography. Focused ethnography and Video Analysis. In: Hubert Knoblauch/Jürgen Raab/Hans-Georg Soeffner/Bernt Schnettler (eds.), *Video-Analysis, methodology and methods. Qualitative audiovisual data analysis in sociology*. Frankfurt a.M.: Peter Lang, 69-83.
Knorr Cetina, Karin, 1981: *The manufacture of knowledge. An essay on the constructivist and contextual nature of science*. Oxford: Pergamon Press.
Krebs, Stephanie, 1975: The film elicitation technique. In: Paul Hockings (ed.), *Principles of visual anthropology*. Berlin: Mouton, 283-302.
Labov, William/Joshua Waletsky, 1967: Narrative analysis. Oral versions of personal experience. In: June Helm (ed.), *Essays on the verbal and visual arts*. Seattle: University of Washington Press, 12-44.
LaPierre, Richard T., 1934: Attitude vs. actions. In: *Social Forces*, 13: 230-237.
Latour, Bruno, 1986: Visualization and cognition. Thinking with eyes and hands. In: Henrika Kuklick/Elizabeth Long (eds.), *Knowledge and society. Studies in the sociology of cultural past and present*. New York: Jai Press inc., 1-40.
Latour, Bruno/Steve Woolgar, 1979: *Laboratory life. The social construction of scientific facts*. London: Sage.
Lave, Jean, 1993: Situating learning in communities of practice. In: Lauren B. Resnick/John M. Levine/Stephanie D. Teasley (eds.), *Perspectives on socially shared cognition*. Washington D.C.: American Psychological Association, 63-82.
Lynch, Michael, 1985: *Art and artifact in laboratory science. A study of shop work and shop talk in a research laboratory*. London: Routledge.
Merton, Robert K./Patricia L. Kendall, 1946: The focused Interview. In: *American Journal of Sociology*, 51, 6, 541-557.
Merton, Robert K./George G. Reader/Patricia L. Kendall (eds.), 1957: *The student-physician. Introductory studies in the sociology of medical education*. Cambridge: Harvard University Press.
Montgomery Hunter, Kathryn, 1991: *Doctors' stories. The narrative structure of medical knowledge*. Princeton: Princeton University Press.
Moreira, Tiago E., 2004: Coordination and embodiment in the operating room. In: *Body and Society*, 10, 1, 109-129.
National Patient Safety Agency, 2005: *Building a memory: preventing harm, reducing risk and improving patient safety. The first report of the National Reporting and Learning System and the Patient Safety Observatory*. <www.npsa.nhs.uk/health/resources/pso.>
Orlikowski, Wanda J., 2007: Sociomaterial practices. Exploring technology at work. In: *Organization Studies*, 28, 9, 1435-1448.

Orr, Julian E., 1986: Narratives at work: story telling as cooperative diagnostic activity. Proceedings of the *Conference on Computer-Supported Cooperative Work (CSCW '86)*. December 3-5 1986. Austin: ACM Press, 62-72.
Orr, Julian E., 1996: *Talking about machines. An ethnography of a modern job.* Ithaca: ILR Press.
Parsons, Talcott, 1951: *The social system.* New York: The Free Press of Glencoe.
Pasveer, Bernike, 1989: Knowledge of shadows. The introduction of X-ray images in medicine. In: *Sociology of Health and Illness*, 11, 4, 360-381.
Pickering, Andrew, 1995: *The mangle of practice. Time, agency, and science.* Chicago: University of Chicago Press.
Polanyi, Michael, 1983 [1966]: *The tacit dimension.* Gloucester et al.: Smith.
Polkinghorne, Donald E., 1988: *Narrative knowing and the human sciences.* Albany: State University of New York Press.
Reiser, Stanley J., 1978: *Medicine and the reign of technology.* Cambridge: Cambridge University Press.
Richardson, Laurel, 1990: Narrative and sociology. In: *Journal of Contemporary Ethnography*, 19, 1, 116-135.
Rochlin, Gene I., 1999: The social construction of safety. In: Jyuji Misumi/Bernhard Wilpert/Rainer Miller (eds.), *Nuclear safety: A human factors perspective.* London: Taylor & Francis, 5-23.
Ruhleder, Karin/Brigitte Jordan, 1997: Capturing complex, distributed activities. Video based interaction analysis as a component of workplace ethnography. In: Allen S. Lee/Jonathan Liebenau/Janice I. de Gross (eds.), *Information systems and qualitative research.* London: Chapman and Hall.
Sacks, Harvey/Emanuel A. Schegloff/Gail Jefferson, 1974: A simplest systematics for the organization of turn-taking for conversation. In: *Language*, 50, 4, 696-735.
Samuel, Sajay/Mark W. Dirsmith/Barbara McElroy, 2005: Monetized medicine. From the physical to the fiscal. In: *Accounting, organizations and society*, 30, 3, 249-278.
Schensul, Jean J./Margaret D. LeCompte/Bonnie K. Nastasi/Stephen P. Borgati, 1999: *Enhanced ethnographic methods. Audovisual techniques, focused group interviews, and elicitation.* Walnut Creek: Alta Mira Press.
Schubert, Cornelius, 2006a: Video Analysis of practice and the practice of Video Analysis. Selecting field and focus in videography. In: Hubert Knoblauch/ Jürgen Raab/Hans-Georg Soeffner/Bernt Schnettler (eds.), *Video-Analysis, methodology and methods. Qualitative audiovisual data analysis in sociology.* Frankfurt a.M.: Peter Lang, 115-126.
Schubert, Cornelius, 2006b: Videografie im OP. Wie Videotechnik für technografische Studien genutzt werden kann. In: Werner Rammert/Cornelius Schubert (eds.), *Technografie. Zur Mikrosoziologie der Technik.* Frankfurt a.M.: Campus, 223-248.

Schubert, Cornelius, 2007a: Risk and safety in the operating theatre. An ethnographic study of socio-technical practices. In: Regula V. Burri/Joseph Dumit (eds.), *Biomedicine as culture. Instrumental practices, technoscientific knowledge, and new modes of life*. London: Routledge, 123-138.
Schubert, Cornelius, 2007b: (Un-)Sicherheiten der organisierten Apparatemedizin. Studien zur organisierten Krankenbehandlung. In: Irmhild Saake/Werner Vogd (eds.), *Moderne Mythen der Medizin*. Wiesbaden: VS-Verlag für Sozialwissenschaften, 139-159.
Spradley, James P., 1979: *The ethnographic interview*. New York: Holt, Rinehart & Winston.
Strauss, Anselm L./Shizuko Fagerhaugh/Barbara Suczek/Carolyn Wiener, 1997 [1985]: *Social organization of medical work*. New Brunswick: Transaction.
Suchman, Lucy A., 1987: *Plans and situated actions. The problem of human-machine communication*. London: Cambridge University Press.
Suchman, Lucy A., 1996: Constituting shared workspaces. In: Yrjö Engeström/David Middleton (eds.), *Cognition and communication at work*. Cambridge: Cambridge University Press, 35- 60.
Suchman, Lucy A., 2007: *Human-machine reconfigurations: Plans and situated actions*. Cambridge: Cambridge University Press.
Suchman, Lucy A./Randall H. Trigg, 1991: Understanding practice. Video as a medium for reflection and design. In: Joan Greenbaum/Morten Kyng (eds.): *Design at work: Cooperative design of computer systems*. Hillsdale et al.: Lawrence Erlbaum, 65-89.
Timmermans, Stefan/Marc Berg, 2003: The practice of medical technology. In: *Sociology of Health and Illness*, 25, 3, 97-114.
Wagner, Gerald, 1995: Die Modernisierung der modernen Medizin. Die «epistemologische Krise» der Intensivmedizin als ein Beispiel reflexiver Verwissenschaftlichung. In: *Soziale Welt*, 46, 3, 266-281.
Weick, Karl E., 1995: *Sensemaking in organizations*. Thousand Oaks: Sage.
Weick, Karl E., 2001: *Making sense of the organization*. Cambridge: Blackwell.
Weick, Karl E./Karlene H. Roberts, 1993: Collective mind in organizations. Heedful interrelating on flight decks. In: *Administrative Science Quarterly* 38, 357-381.
Wenger, Etienne, 1998: *Communities of practice*. Cambridge: Cambridge University Press.
Yoxen, Edward, 1989: Seeing with sound: A study of the development of medical images. In: Wiebe E. Bijker (ed.): *The social construction of technological systems*. Cambridge: MIT Press, 281-303.

About the contributors

About the contributors

Lars Frers
He is currently postdoctoral student at the post-graduate school «Topology of Technology» at the Technical University Darmstadt. His research interests are materiality and space, issues of social order, climate change in everyday life, and urban studies. He completed his doctoral thesis with a study on the phenomenology of perception-action at railway and ferry terminals.

Charles Goodwin
He is Professor of Applied Linguistics at the University of California, Los Angeles. Dr. Goodwin has been involved in numerous studies, including family interaction in the United States, the work of oceanographers in the mouth of the Amazon, archaeologists in the United States and Argentina, the organization of talk, vision and embodied action in the midst of surgery, and how a man with severe aphasia is able to function as a powerful speaker in conversation. As part of the Workplace Project at Xerox PARC, he investigated cognition and talk-in-interaction in complex work setting. His publications include «Conversational organization», «Rethinking context» (co-edited with Alessandro Duranti), and «Conversation and brain damage».

Marjorie Harness Goodwin
She is Professor of Anthropology at the University of California, Los Angeles. A long-standing concern of hers has been how people constitute their social organization through conversational practices. As a researcher with the Center for Everyday Lives of Families she is examining the interactive practices that are used to constitute the family. Her publications analyzing the social lives of children include «He-Said-She-Said: Talk as social organization among black Children» and «The hidden lives of girls: Games of stance, status and Exclusion».

Roger Haeussling
PD Dr. phil., sociologist, is an Assistant Professor at the Insititute of Sociology, U Karlsruhe. From October 2005 to March 2006 he was a Deputy Professor for Sociology at the U Koblenz/Landau. He received his academic education at U Mannheim, U Siegen and U Karlsruhe. He holds a M.A. (Magister Artium) in sociology and a Diploma in economics and engineering and worked as a lecturer and researcher at the U Karlsruhe, U Pforzheim and U Koblenz/Landau.

Ulrike Tikvah Kissmann
Dr. Phil. in sociology at the University of Kassel. She holds a Diploma (Dipl.-Phys.) in physics and a M.A. (Magistra Artium) in philosophy from the Technical University of Berlin, and a M.Sc. (Master of Science) in science and technology studies from the Research Centre for Social Sciences at the University of Edinburgh. She is currently the project director of the research project «The effect of computerized knowledge in the operating theatre from a gender perspective», which is funded by the German Research Association, at Humboldt-University Berlin.

Hubert Knoblauch
He is Professor of Sociology at the Technical University Berlin. His publications include the areas of sociology of knowledge and culture, language, interaction and communication, religion in present time societies, qualitative methods in the social sciences, and visual sociology. His edited volume «Video Analysis. Methodology and methods. Qualitative audiovisual data analysis in sociology» is of particular interest for video analysis.

Antonia L. Krummheuer
She is assistant at Klagenfurt University. She studied sociology at Bielefeld University and was a research fellow at the post-graduate school *Knowledge Societies* at Bielefeld University until 2005. Her doctoral thesis focuses on the empirical study of human-computer interchanges. Her research areas are qualitative methods and communication with and through media, and computer based technology.

Larissa Schindler
She holds a M.A. (Magistra) in social and economic sciences from the University of Vienna. From 2002 until 2006 she was a research fellow at the University of Munich. She is currently a research fellow for sociology at the University of Mainz.

Cornelius Schubert
Dr. Phil. in sociology at the Technical University Berlin. Since 2001, he has been a research fellow in different research projects that focused on the use of technology in hospitals and the innovation practices in the semiconductor industry. He completed his doctoral thesis with an ethnographic study of sociotechnical practices in operating rooms. He is currently a research fellow for science and technology studies at the Technical University Berlin.